Praise for *Harbingers*

"Timothy Heaphy had backstage passes to two of the most historic and troubling armed conflicts in recent America: Charlottesville and January 6. His blow-by-blow accounts are fascinating. His understanding of why these events happened is unmatched. His ideas about our country's future should be listened to by all."

— John Grisham

"Heaphy distills the common lessons of two stains on our history to tell us what happened and how we all can do better — governments, social media providers, and ordinary citizens. His deeply informed work is essential reading for all who hope to learn from the past so we don't repeat it."

— Former FBI director James Comey, author of
A Higher Loyalty: Truth, Lies, and Leadership

"Riveting. Heaphy analyzes dimensions of new threats to the American constitutional order that have not been seriously examined yet: the use of social media for purposes of spreading propaganda and planning political violence and the unpreparedness of law enforcement to reply to this virulent new peril. This is a soulful and significant contribution to defeating the authoritarian threat in America."

— Congressman Jamie Raskin, author of *Unthinkable:*
Trauma, Truth, and the Trials of American Democracy

"Whether January 6 marks the start of a new era of political violence or serves as an historic wake-up call will depend on how people of goodwill respond to the challenge. I urge you to read this book, then do your part."

— Adam Kinzinger, author of *Renegade: Defending*
Democracy and Liberty in Our Divided Country

"Heaphy offers an inside view on how violent extremism is endangering American democracy. His insights can help us reclaim a government that works for all Americans and restore faith in our democratic institutions."

— Barbara McQuade, author of *Attack from Within:*
How Disinformation Is Sabotaging America

"Heaphy takes us inside his search for the root causes of two violent alt-right-inspired attacks, and amid our nation's bitter political divisions, he offers a hopeful message of how to combat the misinformation and isolation that fomented both."

— Carol Leonnig, author of *Zero Fail: The Rise and Fall of the Secret Service*

"Heaphy's unique role as leader of investigations into both the 2017 violence in Charlottesville and the January 6 assault on the US Capitol has given him keen insights into the political divisions, collapse of public trust, and failures of government that bedevil America today. In this highly readable book, he shares his lessons learned and points constructive paths forward toward a healthier and more hopeful future."

— David Von Drehle, author of *The Book of Charlie: Wisdom from the Remarkable American Life of a 109-Year-Old Man*

"*Harbingers* is a must-read for anyone who wants to understand the toxic ideologies and violent threats lurking just beneath the surface of our fractured politics. Heaphy unflinchingly examines the forces that led to Charlottesville and presents the historic January 6 Select Committee's investigative work through the lens of disinformation, racism, and multiple failings among political and law enforcement leaders."

— Nicolle Wallace, host of MSNBC's *Deadline: White House*

"In his sobering re-telling of what he saw firsthand investigating the horrific events of January 6 and the Charlottesville white supremacist rally, Heaphy demonstrates the importance of democracy and why we all need to do our part to preserve it. This book is an essential read to come to terms with our past and build a path forward free from political violence, which sadly appears to be on the rise."

— Preet Bharara, author of *Doing Justice: A Prosecutor's Thoughts on Crime, Punishment, and the Rule of Law*

"*Harbingers* is a compelling mix of an authoritative historical record, investigative procedural, and true crime thriller. It is a searing look at some of the 'colossal failures' of law enforcement agencies and the race-based assumptions that may have fueled those failures, while also offering important lessons learned and suggestions about how we can all do better, both inside and outside government."

— **Glenn Kirschner**

"Heaphy does a great job detailing the cultural forces that seek to divide us and provides solutions to make sure our democracy stays intact. A must-read."

— **Senator Tim Kaine**

"Few Americans are as qualified as Heaphy to address the imminent danger of political violence in the contemporary United States. His prescriptions, born of experience, should be required reading for anyone interested in preserving — and improving — participatory democracy on these shores."

— **Robert Edwards, author of *Resisting the Right:**
How to Survive the Gathering Storm

"Two recent disturbing events have alerted us to the spreading poison of violence and hatred in our country — the racist, antisemitic march of white nationalists in Charlottesville, Virginia, in August 2017, and the shocking insurrection of January 6, 2021 that sought to stop the peaceful transfer of presidential power at the US Capitol. We must not forget them, and we need to understand them fully. Fortunately, Heaphy — who was deeply involved in investigating both — has penned this must-read book. If citizens are wise enough to follow his prescription for change, Americans will have a chance to cure what ails us before more damage is done."

— **Larry J. Sabato, director, UVA Center for Politics**

HARBINGERS

((•))

*What January 6 and
Charlottesville Reveal
About Rising Threats to
American Democracy*

TIMOTHY J. HEAPHY

STEERFORTH PRESS
LEBANON, NEW HAMPSHIRE

For information about permission to reproduce
selections from this book, write to:
Steerforth Press, 31 Hanover Street, Suite 1
Lebanon, New Hampshire 03766

Cataloging-in-Publication Data is available from the Library of Congress

ISBN 978-1-58642-401-5
Printed in the United States of America

1 3 5 7 9 10 8 6 4 2

CONTENTS

RELUCTANT EXPERT

It was a Washington, DC, day as dissimilar to January 6 as I could imagine. For one, it was sweltering, the kind of day when it's easy to remember the capital's swampy origins. It was also calm and quiet on this early Monday morning, with no line to pass through security at the O'Neill House Office Building on C Street SW. Despite the ordinariness of that morning, I was keenly aware of the importance of the day and the journey on which I was about to embark as I headed into my first day of work as the chief investigative counsel of the House of Representatives Select Committee to Investigate the January 6th Attack on the United States Capitol.

I was a new employee in Congress and pulled out my freshly made staff photo ID to show the Capitol Police officers at the gate that I belonged there. I made my way to the fourth floor and scanned into a cavernous, largely empty space that had been recently configured to house the investigative staff of the select committee. It looked like a newsroom, with rows of computers on empty desks separated into small workstations. No one yet occupied those carrels, as I had not yet approached my first task as chief investigative counsel: hiring investigators. There were five small offices along one wall, the last of which was mine. I walked into the sterile space wondering how I would fill it, and my time, over the coming months. While I was uncertain about what lay ahead, I knew that the work on which we were about to embark had the capacity to change American history.

Over the course of my career, I've learned that lawyers often become accidental specialists. The matters on which they work, the cases they try, and the endeavors they pursue inform their subsequent choices and opportunities. I did not set out to specialize in political violence. Nonetheless, I was standing in the empty House office building at the helm of a tremendously important investigation into the most searing episode of such violence this country has seen in many years. Through a series of unexpected challenges in the communities I call home, I have been fortunate enough to be part of the response, the understanding, and the healing. I am, in many ways, a reluctant expert in political violence and all it reveals about America.

A few years earlier, I led a team that conducted an independent review of the racist riot that occurred in my hometown of Charlottesville, Virginia, on August 12, 2017. Back then, I was a former United States attorney hired by the city government to conduct an after-action report detailing how the city prepared for and managed the Unite the Right rally that became a forum in which fascist white nationalists clashed with anti-racist counter-protesters in the small city in which I live. Our team issued a lengthy report that contained harsh criticism of law enforcement, city and state officials, and other decision makers for their failure to protect both public safety and free speech in Charlottesville. The Heaphy Report became the definitive account of that tragic day.

My experience in Charlottesville ultimately led to my role as chief investigative counsel for the January 6 committee. Over the course of my work on these investigations, I have spent considerable time looking closely at these two seminal events. Along with a team of experts, I spent untold hours reviewing footage and reading emails, text messages, and other documents generated before, during, and after by both people who perpetrated and those who tried to prevent them. This work has given me a keen understanding of political violence in America: where it comes from, how it manifests, and how to stop it. This book is an attempt to share that hard-gained knowledge in an effort to understand growing political violence in America as a continuous thread rather than discrete incidents. It's hard to look at and unsettling to see, but we must not look away.

Charlottesville and January 6 are inextricably linked in the consciousness of Americans. They have much in common, and examining both events informs broader lessons about the state of American democracy. As horrific as those days were, studying, considering, and talking about them can point us toward a way forward. A close look at the facts and circumstances reveals lessons that can help make spasms of political violence less likely in the years ahead.

This book will not rehash the results of our investigations. Readers interested in more detail about what happened in Charlottesville and at the Capitol can review the reports on which I worked, which tell those tragic stories in graphic detail. Instead, I intend to identify and derive meaning from commonalities between the events, beyond the simple fact that both turned lethally violent. And I will expose the dynamics that have escaped the notice and understanding of most Americans, even those who follow the news closely.

One central connection between Charlottesville and January 6 is that both events were planned online, in plain view, on social media. The organizers of the Unite the Right rally encouraged like-minded people to attend by actively promoting the event on Facebook, Twitter, Parler, Reddit, and other social media sites. A little more than three years later, the Proud Boys, Oath Keepers, and others who sincerely but misguidedly believed the 2020 presidential election had been stolen used these same platforms to draw attention to the January 6 certification proceeding at the Capitol.

The rapid and successful promotion of both events demonstrates the pervasive power of social media. Most Americans today receive news that is filtered through platforms on which false information proliferates. Social media companies are businesses that rely on keeping users engaged, actively clicking, reading, and reacting to content. Sophisticated algorithms track a user's interests and promote similar content, drawing and keeping their attention with material that is often increasingly provocative. Social media companies do very little to monitor, flag, or take down hate speech, far-out conspiracy theories, or other false and incendiary content, which makes these platforms unreliable sources of information. They also connect users to others with similar views in affinity groups, which become echo chambers for the spread of misinformation. This landscape is largely unregulated and misunderstood by consumers.

Despite the fact that both the Charlottesville rally and the January 6 attack on the Capitol were planned on open-source channels, law enforcement was woefully unprepared for them. In Charlottesville, the city was unable to protect either public safety or free speech despite the presence of ample numbers of officers and specialized units. At the Capitol, rioters were able to violently enter the seat of government during the joint session of Congress and came dangerously close to the vice president and other elected officials as they were forced to evacuate. These were not intelligence failures, as there was ample warning of potential violence before each event. They were not resource failures, as sufficient numbers of officers from different agencies were available and ultimately deployed to both locations. They were operational failures: Planning did not incorporate the intelligence.

There are many reasons for the law enforcement failures in Charlottesville and at the Capitol. Dozens of agencies collect information on domestic violent extremism. Those agencies do a poor job sharing that information and ensuring that it is available to planners in advance of mass demonstration events. Agencies like the Federal

Bureau of Investigation place unduly restrictive limits on their use of open-source information due to First Amendment concerns. And as is always the case in America, race matters. Police agencies routinely misperceive the threats of violence posed by different racial groups. They underestimate the potential for violence presented by white men like those who converged on Charlottesville on August 12, 2017, and the Capitol on January 6, 2021. This racial bias is also reflected in the overreaction to potential violence in the wake of the murder of George Floyd in the summer of 2020. We mistakenly expect violence from Black and brown protesters and fail to anticipate violence from angry white men. Our investigations found that this bias was implicit but persistent. Like the social media policy issues outlined above, these systemic law enforcement failures require attention and constructive solutions.

The most salient commonality between Charlottesville and January 6 was how they metastasized from one core issue to broader forums for the expression of anger at institutions. Charlottesville started as a protest about the removal of Civil War statues in public space. It became a protest at which a constellation of groups came together to express anger about how our increasingly diverse culture threatens their historic privilege. The unifying principle on January 6 was belief in the "Big Lie" that the 2020 election had been stolen from President Trump. Many participants in the attack on the Capitol were, however, drawn there by a broader cynicism about government and disbelief in what they routinely hear from politicians, the media, and educational institutions. As in Charlottesville, some January 6 rioters believed that the national government is run by self-interested elites determined to replace them with immigrants. Others were motivated by a belief that public health mandates during the pandemic were baseless and infringed their liberty. These groups came together under a common banner of resistance to a system that they regard as oppressive and believe does not work for them.

The core division in this country revealed by Charlottesville and January 6 prompts both anger and apathy among Americans. While some people express anger at mass demonstration events, others simply turn away. Many people in this country don't vote, pay attention to current events, or actively participate in their communities. Withdrawal is as dangerous as anger. A disengaged citizenry is a more insidious threat to democracy, and ultimately more destructive, than a large crowd of angry rioters.

Identifying effective solutions to this division in America will require grassroots involvement by a much wider spectrum of voices than those that currently participate in these discussions. Our future success will require everyone to care and contribute. The best way to restore faith in government is to make it more responsive to the core needs of the people governed. That requires participation and engagement, not apathy and withdrawal. When people of good faith fail to participate, extreme perspectives are amplified and get outsized attention. We need to run toward, not away from, the problems facing this country, those revealed by these episodes of political violence and many others.

"Truth and reconciliation are the only hope for nations that are bitterly divided," Nelson Mandela wrote in 1999.[1] I keep coming back to his words as I think through how we got here, and how to move forward. A clear-eyed view of what happened — and why — is essential to preventing similar events in the future. These awful days can help move us to a better place. This book strives to go beyond the core narratives that have emerged from commentators and among groups across the political spectrum to describe and better understand the underlying factors that allowed the violence to occur. Rather than offer politicized takes, I've tried to follow the evidence and provide an honest reckoning. It ends with some hopeful thoughts on ways to change the conditions that gave rise to the horrific events that continue to reverberate in Charlottesville, in Washington, and around the world.

"Those who cannot remember the past are condemned to repeat it," first wrote philosopher George Santayana in 1910.[2] Winston Churchill paraphrased Santayana when he told the House of Commons in 1948, "Those who fail to learn from history are condemned to repeat it."[3] My hope is that this book helps us understand Charlottesville and January 6 and becomes part of the light guiding us forward as we continue the great experiment in democracy that is America.

CHARLOTTESVILLE

I have lived in Charlottesville off and on since 1982, but it was not until the summer of 2017 that I began to understand my community in all its contradictions. I first came to town to attend the University of Virginia, and while I loved my time as an undergrad, I didn't venture much beyond the confines of the university grounds. After a couple of years working in Washington, DC, I returned to UVA in 1988 to pursue a law degree. As a graduate student, I explored more of Charlottesville, though my world was still limited by the academic and social calendar of the law school. Charlottesville was UVA to me, and I graduated without a full understanding or appreciation of the broader community.

I returned to Charlottesville many years later in 2003, when I began working as an assistant United States attorney in the Western District of Virginia. I had been a federal prosecutor in Washington, DC, for almost ten years, an intense professional experience that culminated in the thirteen-month trial of members of a violent street gang charged with racketeering offenses and thirty-one separate homicides. During that long trial, I received a call asking if I'd be interested in a similar position in Charlottesville. My wife and I had two young children and were drawn to the work/ life balance a move to Charlottesville offered. After the long trial concluded, we moved our family to a house less than a mile from the university grounds.

It quickly became apparent that we made the right choice. Our kids went to great schools. We formed really close friendships. We became the family we had always aspired to be, with my wife and I both working on issues that made a difference in the world while staying more engaged with each other and our children. As the years progressed, I changed jobs — leaving the Department of Justice for several years before returning to government service when President Obama appointed me to serve as United States attorney for the Western District of Virginia. Our kids grew up. Our circle of friends evolved. Over time, I joined the chorus of people who celebrated Charlottesville's uniqueness, its quality of life, its uncommon mix of big-city culture and small-town convenience.

It wasn't until the summer of 2017 that I realized I was seeing only half the picture. At the time, I didn't realize that "my" Charlottesville, the one I occupied as a privileged white male with professional opportunity and material success, was just one version of the story. There's another narrative about Charlottesville and its deep history of inequality, one that stretches all the way back to its founding and Thomas Jefferson.

Jefferson made his home at Monticello, a large estate in the mountains outside Charlottesville. To many, Jefferson was a visionary leader who helped forge American democracy. A gifted writer, Jefferson authored the Declaration of Independence, which included the foundational principle that "all men are created equal." After the Revolutionary War, he served the young nation in various capacities both at home and abroad, including his election as our third president. He founded the University of Virginia, which to this day celebrates its founder's legacy with statues and likenesses, inscribed words, and frequent references to Mr. Jefferson by university officials and faculty. To the vast majority of UVA alumni, the Jefferson legacy is a proud one, to be embraced and celebrated.

Thomas Jefferson was also a slave owner and, by admission in his own writings, believed in the inferiority of people of color. He held hundreds of people as enslaved laborers and used them to farm the land surrounding Monticello and to work in and around his home. Jefferson famously fathered multiple children with one of the enslaved laborers, Sally Hemings. Together, they had at least six children, four of whom survived past infancy. As historians at Monticello write today, "The nature of Sally Hemings's sexual encounters with Thomas Jefferson will never be known," but at the same time "enslaved women had no legal right to consent. Their masters owned their labor, their bodies, and their children."[1]

These facts demonstrate the complexity of Thomas Jefferson. He had many dimensions, ideals, and contradictions. He was both a visionary who helped forge the creation of America and a slave owner who subjugated the men and women among whom he lived. His life did not live up to the ideals of the founding documents he authored. The duality present in the life of Jefferson makes him a somewhat controversial figure in and around Charlottesville, and the nation. To many in this community he is a hero, while to others he is a symbol of oppression.

I came to fully appreciate during the summer of 2017 the wildly diverse perspectives and lived experiences of Charlottesville's residents. To some, Charlottesville is an idyllic southern small city that offers ample economic opportunity, incredible natural beauty, and the diverse culture one might associate with a world-class university. To others, Charlottesville is much less welcoming, particularly for people of color who point to the lack of affordable housing, a racially skewed achievement gap in public schools, and disproportionate minority involvement in the criminal justice system to support their view that Charlottesville is mired in a racially and economically segregated past.

In short, what you think about Charlottesville depends on where you live, worship, work, and socialize. For most Charlottesville residents, those communities are largely racially homogeneous. Despite its progressive reputation and voting history, Charlottesville remains a community with stark divides between white and Black, rich and poor, haves and have-nots. Like Jefferson's declaration of equality, our community fails to live up to its high-minded aspirations and rhetoric.

A series of events during the summer of 2017 blew the lid off my naïveté about Charlottesville and showed me that my positive views about our community were not shared by everyone. The first of those events occurred on May 13, 2017, a busy spring Saturday when a group of more than one hundred white nationalists marched unimpeded through downtown streets while chanting hateful slogans like "Jews will not replace us!" and "Blood and soil!" They gathered at a statue of Confederate general Thomas "Stonewall" Jackson that stood adjacent to the Albemarle County Courthouse and made speeches challenging the city's potential removal of the Jackson statue, claiming that attempts to do so were part of a broader war against white people and their heritage.

The same group marched again that Saturday night, this time carrying flaming torches. Their nighttime destination was the statue of Confederate general Robert E. Lee in another park just blocks away from the Jackson statue. As had happened earlier that day, several speakers delivered fierce warnings about a war against white people and expressed the desire to preserve the statues and the broader privilege they had historically enjoyed in this country. Their use of fire evoked a noxious history of racial intimidation, particularly alongside the Lee statue.

Both of these events were held without any advance notice or permits. The rallies, organized by Richard Spencer and Jason Kessler, surprised Charlottesville residents with the size of the turnouts they inspired and their racist messages. A very small group of counter-protesters gathered at the statues to confront the crowds well after they had begun to assemble. Law enforcement responded late as well, monitoring events but making no arrests.

The two marches were seen as a call to action requiring organized resistance to the racist ideology they promoted. Progressive activists hastily arranged a candlelight vigil on Sunday, May 14, which attracted a large crowd celebrating diversity and inclusion.

I don't remember where I was on Saturday, May 13, though I recall that the presence of white supremacists in our community came as a surprise to me and many others who were living in our idealized Charlottesville cocoon. I thought it had to be an anomaly, a one-off, a disturbing spasm of hate from a group of outsiders. As the Sunday-night protesters declared, I firmly believed that "this is not us." I didn't expect that the actions of the previous day and the attitudes of the marchers would presage subsequent, more emphatic confrontations in our city.

But less than two months later, on July 8, members of the Ku Klux Klan in North Carolina planned to hold a rally in Charlottesville. Unlike the May 13 marchers, the organizers of this event applied for a permit, and the City of Charlottesville granted it on First Amendment grounds. This advance notice meant that both city officials and citizens could prepare for what was to come. The KKK organizers worked with law enforcement on an arrival plan and entrance to the permitted area, allowing officials to create a barricaded space between the speakers and those who were expected to come to oppose the KKK's message. A loose coalition of counter-protesters included church leaders, community activists, students, and many other groups and individuals who planned to attend the event and shout down the KKK speeches.

The City of Charlottesville worked to actively discourage people from attending the July 8 KKK event. Counter-programming designed to highlight community included musical performances, interfaith ceremonies, and other events to be held that day. City officials intended these activities to stand in stark contrast with the hateful message of the Klan, and they hoped that their positive tone would encourage people to stay away from the Klan gathering altogether. "Our approach all the way through, from our police chief on down, has been to urge people not to take this totally discredited fringe organization's putrid bait at all," Mayor Michael Signer said at the time. "The only thing they seem to want is division and confrontation and a twisted kind of celebrity. The most successful defiance will be to refuse to take their bait and continue to tell our story. Then their memory of Charlottesville will be of a community that repudiated them by not getting drawn into their pathetic drama."[2]

Like many others in Charlottesville, I was frustrated at the Klan's attempt to use our community as a forum for racism and determined to stand in contrast with their hateful message. I was conflicted, however, as to the best way to express that opposition. I understood the encouragement to avoid the event so as not to give it credence or "oxygen." I also understood the strong views of others, particularly people of color, who believed that silence in the face of hate has historically given it tacit credibility. How best to respond was an intensely personal choice, one with which I struggled in the days leading up to July 8.

On that hot, summer day, I ended up attending a counter-programming event on Charlottesville's Downtown Mall, just a couple of blocks from the Jackson statue. I felt conflicted, though, as word circulated that tremendous crowds had gathered to resist the hateful message of what turned out to be only a handful of Klan members. While the Klan presence was about forty to sixty strong, the crowd opposing them numbered fifteen hundred to two thousand people.[3] Not only did the city's plan to prevent confrontation backfire, but it actually alienated a lot of people who believed the city's approach was paternalistic. Further inflaming the community was the perception that law enforcement was protecting the KKK.

With advance notice of the July 8 event, law enforcement devised a plan designed to accommodate the free speech rights and protect the safety of both Klan members and counter-protesters. They established a small area adjacent to the Jackson statue for the Klan to give speeches and conduct the rally for which they held a permit. They surrounded this area with bicycle racks and planned to limit access to members of the permitted group. They also created a small buffer area to enforce physical separation between the Klan and the counter-protesters.

The event itself was short-lived. Several members of the Klan group gave speeches as the others stood by holding Confederate flags, signs, and other symbols of their racist ideology. The large crowd outside the bicycle racks was extremely vocal, rendering the Klan speeches largely inaudible. There were some direct verbal exchanges between counter-protesters and Klan members, but no physical altercations. Some in the crowd hurled projectiles at the Klan, though there were no reported injuries during the event. While monitoring the crowd and trying to ensure that the confrontation did not descend into violence, the police made no arrests.

After about thirty-five minutes, the Klan members ended their rally and marched back through the crowd. But the departure of the Klan did not cause the larger throng of counter-protesters to disperse. Angered at the police protection of the Klan, many refused to depart the area and angrily confronted officers. At least one officer was assaulted in a scene described by another officer as a "mad house."[4] After more verbal and physical confrontations between protesters and police, a Virginia State Police (VSP) field force unit deployed tear gas. Charlottesville police chief Al Thomas was the overall commander of the police agencies at the event. He did not authorize the use of tear gas, which was a breach of the operational plan. Neither officers nor members of the crowd had much or any warning of the dispersal of gas, which caused injuries to both law enforcement and community members.

The use of gas did cause the majority of people to finally disperse, though it had a strong impact on public perception of law enforcement priorities. Many people who attended the event were struck by the lengths to which police went to protect the safety of the racist Klansmen juxtaposed with the aggression shown toward people expressing anti-racist sentiments. The Reverend Seth Wispelwey, the leader of Congregate C'ville, an interfaith group organized to oppose white supremacy, said, "It seemed like [the police] had no plan, other than protecting white supremacy."[5] Others remember hearing screams of pain in the crowd when the tear gas was released and street medics deployed to help flush people's eyes.

When concerns were raised in the community about the use of tear gas and the broader law enforcement approach on July 8, city leaders failed to respond constructively. A group of progressive legal organizations wrote to the governor, city council, and city manager, criticizing the "outsized and militaristic governmental response" to counter-protesters.[6] The letter alleged that the deployment of tear gas was unnecessary given the space between law enforcement and the crowd that remained. Rather than address these criticisms directly, Chief Thomas gave both false and incomplete explanations of the decision to deploy tear gas, and then turned down an invitation from the city council to appear and discuss the tear gas deployment and law enforcement response.

To many citizens of Charlottesville, the actions of police on July 8 were no surprise. The use of chemical agents and militarized equipment against people of color was consistent with their own lived experience of law enforcement bias. Many viewed police as hostile interlopers in their communities. Distrust in law enforcement goes back generations to Charlottesville's segregated past and, more recently, its aggressive prosecution of the "war on drugs." Like many other communities large and small, Charlottesville has impoverished neighborhoods that have been decimated by mass incarceration. Many people in these communities expect police hostility rather than protection.

But skepticism about police motivation was not a monolithic perspective in Charlottesville. Some people walked away from the July 8 event with praise for the police, giving them credit for managing a large, unruly crowd. Opinions about the performance of the police and city government varied, which exposed even more acutely the divisions that exist across the city's neighborhoods and communities.

While I thought the deployment of tear gas was heavy-handed, I was hesitant to criticize the action without more clarity on what specific conditions on the ground motivated the decision. I understood that July 8 created a difficult circumstance for law enforcement planners, who were constitutionally required to protect both the free speech rights of all people present as well as their safety. The intersection of those rights and the conflict that erupts from public declarations of hate create vexing challenges for police and city leaders. It was easy to criticize the city's lack of clarity in responding to community concerns, but I was hesitant to condemn the city's planning or execution without more specific information.

Residents of Charlottesville already knew that the much larger Unite the Right rally was planned for August 12, in a few short weeks. The UTR event was being planned in plain sight and promoted on social media, which gave community leaders ample opportunity to coordinate their response. The organizers planned to conduct a "free speech rally in support of the Lee Monument," according to the handwritten permit application filed by Jason Kessler, and forecast about four hundred participants.[7] The site of the rally would be a statue of Confederate general Robert E. Lee that had stood in the center of Charlottesville since the 1920s. City officials met with various stakeholders about preparations for an event at which hateful speech would be both uttered and protected, as required by the US Constitution.

The lack of clarity and controversy swirling around the police actions of July 8 had a direct effect on the city's ability to prepare. Progressive leaders were skeptical about both the motivation and the capacity of police leaders. To many residents, city leaders seemed inept and incapable of protecting public safety or providing truthful information. Many people were frustrated with the city's paternalistic directive that they avoid the Klan rally and became more determined to confront the UTR rally in person. Faith in government was shaken by the city's inconsistent explanations of what had occurred and why. July 8 created an atmosphere of distrust.

I followed the city's preparations for August 12 with trepidation, expecting that violence would be hard to avoid. I also had a decision to make: My daughter had a baseball game two hours away from Charlottesville in Washington, DC, at the exact same time as the rally. She was excited about the game and did not want to miss it. Baseball is something that she and I share, and I very much looked forward to our road trips for games. We were also planning to see my in-laws, who live just outside DC. Would I disappoint my daughter and my in-laws and stay behind in town that day to confront the hatred, in contrast with my more passive response to the KKK on July 8? In the end, I chose to go on the trip. My family has always come first, and I was determined not to let racists alter my life.

So, on the morning of August 12, 2017, I was in Washington, DC, watching my daughter play baseball. As she ran around the field with her middle-school teammates, my phone buzzed. My heart sank, anticipating what I'd see. There on my screen were the first searing images of violence. I watched footage of what looked like a war zone: highly armed combatants, some even in full head-to-toe fatigues, attacking civilians. Tinny screams of anguish and bellows of hate erupted from my phone's small speaker. I blinked at my phone as the building behind the crowd came into view: the quaint public library where I used to take my daughter to read as a little girl years ago.

Over the course of the morning, I watched news reports and fielded phone calls and texts from friends in Charlottesville. The streets of our university town turned into an arena in which neo-Nazis, fascists, and white nationalists brawled with anti-racist counter-protesters. The combatants assaulted one another with their fists, feet, makeshift weapons, and various projectiles while hundreds of uniformed police officers stood by and watched. By the time my daughter's game was finished and we were back at my in-laws' home, one activist in Charlottesville was dead and many others injured. Two Virginia state troopers died in a helicopter crash after a long afternoon of monitoring the violence from above. Was this really happening in Charlottesville? Little did I know at the moment that this event, which was then so hard to understand, would change the trajectory of my career and my life.

The next morning, I was still processing the events of the day while eating breakfast with my wife's family in their small kitchen in northern Virginia. My father-in-law sat beside me, curious about both the baseball game and the events in Charlottesville. He is a retired general and spent years moving up the ranks in the US Army, from a second lieutenant in Vietnam to army chief of staff. As we discussed what happened in Charlottesville, he explained that if an operational failure like the nation witnessed the day before in Charlottesville had occurred during his time in the army, it would prompt a thorough, objective review. He described the culture in which he was trained, which encouraged honest assessment and feedback in a process of continuous improvement. He suggested that effective organizations respond to mistakes with a fact-based clarity and incorporate lessons learned in future plans.

He asked me if Charlottesville would take a similar approach to evaluating the events of August 12. I recall him saying something like "Surely there will be an after-action," invoking the military term that he'd used throughout his career. His question prompted me to start thinking about an independent review of the Charlottesville events, and my own potential role in contributing to an after-action. I knew that many police departments and city governments had launched reviews after instances of mass demonstrations, police shootings, and other forms of violent unrest across the country. My father-in-law's logic made sense. Surely Charlottesville should follow the example of the US Army and municipal governments across the country and launch a credible effort to gather the facts surrounding August 12 in an effort to learn from that terrible day. But would they?

It was all I could think about on our two-hour drive back to Charlottesville. As we drove past fields and rolling hills approaching the mountains outside our hometown, I realized that I had the credentials, support, and unique relationships that made me a viable candidate to lead a potential investigation. At the time, I was a partner at the law firm of Hunton & Williams, a venerable Virginia institution with a tradition of public service. I was the chairman of the firm's white-collar investigations practice, which conducted internal investigations for clients across the country. The events in Charlottesville called for precisely the kind of investigation I offered clients, and I knew that the firm had the resources to support the substantial effort that this sort of engagement would require. I had come to Hunton & Williams about two years earlier, after serving as the Obama-appointed United States attorney for the Western District of Virginia. US attorneys work within the United States Department of Justice, serving as the chief federal law enforcement officers of their respective districts. My role as US attorney gave me supervisory responsibility over all federal prosecutions in the large, diverse district that encompassed fifty-five Virginia counties, including Charlottesville. During my five years as US attorney, I spent a lot of time engaging with law enforcement officials, from police chiefs and sheriffs to line officers. So I was familiar with the roles of the federal, state, and local officials involved in responding to the Unite the Right rally, including the Charlottesville Police Department, the Virginia State Police, the Federal Bureau of Investigation, and other agencies.

This experience gave me confidence that I had a unique ability to lead an after-action review and ensure that it was done with integrity. Beyond my résumé, I felt personally compelled to help. I wanted to be part of the solution, the healing, the appropriate reconciliation that would be required to repair the damage done to our community on that terrible day.

I expected that my partners at Hunton would support a pitch to conduct this investigation, despite the fact that we would likely earn well below our standard rates and occupy multiple lawyers in an intense, high-pressure endeavor. I also knew that there was reputational risk to the firm, as any facts found and recommendations made in the report of investigation would be controversial. This was the kind of undertaking destined to make some people angry, in Charlottesville and beyond, but pursuing it was consistent with our higher obligation as lawyers to pursue justice.

When I returned to Charlottesville, I immediately reached out to folks I knew in city government and on the city council, encouraging a comprehensive, independent review of preparations for and management of the UTR rally on August 12. I suggested that gathering the facts about what had occurred was an essential first step to restoring public confidence in government, confidence that was obviously quite shaken by the city's inability to protect public safety on August 12. I also offered to lead this review, with the caveat that it must be completely independent of the city's influence or control and explicitly free to reach any conclusion supported by facts. I was essentially arguing that the city should hire me to look closely at the facts and circumstances surrounding this awful day and issue a public report regardless of whose actions were criticized. At this point, I realized my decision to attend my daughter's baseball game turned out to be more impact-ful than I'd realized, as my absence from Charlottesville that day removed an arguable conflict of interest that could have prevented me from spearheading the review of the city's management of the event.

To their credit, the city hired me and my firm to lead an inde-pendent review, accepting the terms I'd set forth in my proposal. The city agreed to turn over all information our team thought potentially relevant and to make individual city employees avail-able for interviews. They promised we would have the freedom in our report to reach whatever factual conclusions we believed the evidence supported and make recommendations for change that we believed necessary. City manager Maurice Jones made this decision, though he first obtained the support of each member of the city council.

The "Charlottesville Independent Review" was announced on August 25, 2017, less than two weeks after the violence erupted. "As our City continues to recover from the rallies that brought great hate into our community, we must take time to reflect on our oper-ational response to these tragic events," city manager Jones said at the time. "Mr. Heaphy brings the right mix of legal experience and critical eye to conduct an impartial review of what we as a local government working with our state partners did well and where we can improve."[8]

I was proud to be a part of this work but felt the weight of its importance on my shoulders. This would be the most significant investigation I had ever been asked to do, and it had the potential to make a huge impact on the community in which I lived. The fact that the UTR rally brought the world's attention to Charlottes-ville raised the stakes even higher. I strongly believed that the way forward had to start with facts and a common understanding of what had occurred. With a report delivery deadline of Thanksgiv-ing, we got to work quickly.

The investigation we conducted would consume me and a small team of lawyers and other professionals in our firm's Charlottesville and Richmond offices for the next four months. We started by identifying sources of information, documents to gather and review, and people with whom we wanted to speak. Our investigation had no subpoena power, which meant that we could not compel anyone's cooperation, a markedly different situation from investigations I'd conducted at the Department of Justice.

The city pledged to make all information within its control available to us, without limitation. Much of that information would come from the Charlottesville Police Department, which had been primarily responsible for gathering intelligence about the UTR event in advance and managing the unrest on August 12. However, access to CPD documents became the first of many stumbling blocks we would face over the course of the investigation. After initially meeting with me and promising cooperation with our review, Police Chief Al Thomas subsequently asked to see and review all documents before they were released to our investigative team. He also wanted to speak to all officers both before and after their interviews with us. I expressed concern that this cumbersome process would slow down our inquiry, which was expected to conclude within months. The matter came to a head when we learned that Chief Thomas had directed the creation of some new documents regarding the department's preparation for the rally — falsely suggesting that they were created in August rather than later. Chief Thomas's attempt to impede our immediate access to everything ultimately backfired, as the city manager directed him to make all documents and people available to our team without filter or delay.

Resistance to our review from the Virginia State Police and other state agencies was perhaps even more surprising. VSP did not make any documents or individual officers available to our investigative team. They refused our requests for the VSP operations plan, intelligence reports, text and email communications, and video footage. They refused to allow individual troopers who were on the ground in Charlottesville to speak to us, offering the VSP superintendent — Colonel Steve Flaherty — as their sole interviewee. Despite their resistance to our work, we were able to obtain a great deal of important information from VSP sources. We received a copy of the VSP operations plan from a source who found it inside a building where a VSP field force was staged on August 12. We gained VSP emails, text messages, and footage from the VSP helicopter from CPD, which had obtained it separately from our review. Importantly, some troopers, troubled by what they had witnessed on August 12, spoke with us despite their command staff's direction not to do so. This information allowed us to piece together a detailed account of VSP's actions, and inaction, in the days before and on August 12.

Our approach with witnesses outside of government was to seek voluntary cooperation. We talked about the importance of an objective review and appealed to people's sense of obligation to help ensure clarity and truth in the community's efforts to recover. Many people sat with me and our investigators for hours, providing important details about their experience on August 12. Others we reached out to, though, were resistant and refused to cooperate.

Some of the event organizers sat with us for lengthy interviews. They described their actions in defensive terms, denying that their racist chants and militaristic tactics were designed to provoke a response. Other UTR organizers refused to talk with our investigators, citing the city's act of filing a lawsuit against various groups with an organized presence at UTR in the weeks after the event. Despite that resistance, we were able to interview a sufficient number of organizers to obtain an understanding of the UTR groups' objectives and tactics.

We also found it difficult to convince local and national anti-racist counter-protesters to cooperate with our investigation. Some of these individuals expressed skepticism about the independence of our review. Given that the city had hired us, they believed our findings would ultimately justify the city's actions. Others were concerned about my history as a prosecutor and believed I would be an apologist for the police. The National Lawyers Guild represented a number of these individuals and declined to make them available without two main assurances from our team: one, that we not share information they gave us with city officials and, two, that we modify our engagement with the city to compel public release of all information gathered. Compliance with these conditions would have constituted violations of the ethical rules governing the practice of law, so we had to decline.

Fortunately for our review, many ant-racist counter-protesters did cooperate with our investigation and provided extremely valuable information. Emily Gorcenski was centrally involved in the resistance to UTR and had a large and very active social media presence in the days before the event. She sat with us for a lengthy interview and helped us understand the organized resistance to the rally. Several members of Congregate C'ville, a group of progressive clergy who helped organize the counter-protest, also cooperated, including the group's co-founder, the Reverend Seth Wispelwey, who hosted nonviolent resistance training sessions and was part of an interfaith group that physically blocked the entrance to the park where the rally was to be held on the morning of August 12.

One important decision early during our process was to solicit community input to our review. We established a 1-800 telephone line and website to receive information from anyone who wanted to contribute. We received hundreds of submissions, including photographs, video footage, and narrative accounts of events. We ended up using many of them in our final report. Additionally, the tipline and website provided an important outlet for people who wanted to tell their story and contribute to community understanding. Many told us that their experience of sharing what they knew and felt was cathartic, which I came to believe was an important collateral benefit that flowed from the city's commitment to the independent review.

The investigative team pored over hours and hours of video taken on August 12. Many participants in the UTR rally recorded their activities; some even livestreamed them. Video was both given to us by witnesses and pulled from open sources. So much footage can be a blessing and a curse for investigators. Even though video provides direct evidence of events, it can also be superfluous, redundant, and ultimately unhelpful. The only way to separate the wheat from the chaff is to review all of the footage, looking for salient moments that reveal important facts or require follow-up. Our team included a number of paralegals and researchers who closely watched this video, looking for those critical moments. In the end, some of the video evidence was central to our findings.

As I conducted interviews, reviewed document and video evidence, and began putting together the final, 207-page report, an image of what really happened that summer came into focus. I learned so much that I hadn't known as a casual observer, as a civilian. And I knew that it was important to share my new clearer picture with the community.

In short, our investigation found that, as its name implied, the Unite the Right rally intended to bring together a coalition of far-right groups unified in their opposition to the removal of the Lee and Jackson statues and who were more broadly united in their belief in white supremacy and modern-day fascism. They promoted the event online, on both public and encrypted platforms. They were successful in recruiting members of various organizations to come to Charlottesville, including Identity Evropa, the National Socialist Workers Party, the Proud Boys, the League of the South, Fraternal Order of Alt-Knights, East Coast Knights of the Ku Klux Klan, and the Traditionalist Worker Party.

While it was not possible to ascribe common expectations and intent to everyone from the alt-right who came to Charlottesville, it seemed clear that the UTR organizers and attendees expected confrontation. They wanted to be seen as victims rather than perpetrators of violence. They knew that their hateful message would provoke extreme anger in response. They expected Antifa, Black Lives Matter, and other groups to organize a large presence in opposition to them, as had occurred at similar events in Portland, Oregon, Berkeley, California, and Pikeville, Kentucky. Rather than avoid stoking the ire of the anti-racist crowds that they knew would be in Charlottesville, they intentionally provoked violence as a justification for their own violent response. They knew that chanting slogans like "Jews shall not replace us" while marching through a liberal college town would incite the crowd to lash out at them, justifying a violent response in "self-defense." The UTR attendees armed themselves for this expected climate of confrontation, many carrying shields, clubs, and poles and wearing helmets and other protective gear.

The advance warning about the UTR rally gave people opposed to the organizers' extreme, far-right views time to organize a confrontation. Through the investigation, I learned that just as the organizers of the rally solicited participation and assembled the coalition of alt-right groups that came together on August 12, anti-racist counter-protesters similarly organized and recruited others to come to Charlottesville. For some, the goal was to resist, confront, or shout down the speech that was expected at the rally. For others, it was to counter hate with a contrary message of unity and inclusion and to demonstrate in numbers that there were many more people opposed to the racism that motivated UTR than those prepared to stand for that ideology.

As with the alt-right rally-goers, we did not find a monolithic approach among the crowd of anti-racists who came to oppose the UTR hate speech. There were some within the crowd who were willing to use violence to prevent that speech from happening. These individuals came to the event well organized and outfitted, wearing gas masks, padded clothing, body armor, walkie-talkies, and shields.[9] At least one had a firearm. Others, including members of Congregate C'ville, prepared to resist the event without violence. They formed a human shield in front of the entrance to the park, risking arrest to prevent the attendees from entering the permitted area.

The individuals in Charlottesville who organized the resistance to the UTR event did not share information with police or other local officials in advance. Our investigation found that their refusal to cooperate with public safety planning stemmed from the law enforcement response to the July 8 event. Their skepticism created a climate of distrust that made effective communication and planning much more difficult. Law enforcement leaders reached out to members of the Clergy Collective and Congregate C'ville, representatives of Showing Up for Racial Justice (SURJ), a local anti-racist group, and other progressive leaders who had been involved in organized resistance to the Klan. Many of these individuals pointed to the tear gas deployment and to their perception of the overall law enforcement approach on July 8 as reasons for refusing to cooperate with police or share their plans for August 12. A lawyer representing the anti-racist groups characterized police outreach to them as "aggressive inquiries" being used as "an intimidation tactic intended to curtail leftist speech and expressive conduct."[10] The tenuous relationship between progressive groups and police made it difficult for city officials to anticipate and understand plans to confront the UTR event as August 12 approached.

Our investigation found that rather than rely on the City of Charlottesville, those who organized resistance to the UTR rally established parallel support systems — transportation, medical assistance, and security — designed to facilitate their plans and protect the people who came to confront the rally organizers and participants. They obtained permits for two other parks downtown near the Lee statue to facilitate these services and provide a safe space for resisters to gather and recover. Progressive clergy in Congregate C'ville conducted training sessions on nonviolent resistance and prepared for mass arrests. This degree of preparation was inclusive and transparent, open to anyone interested in joining the organized resistance to the rally.

Law enforcement began preparing for August 12 immediately after the July 8 Klan event, but both the expected size of the UTR turnout and the relatively uncooperative attitude of event organizers in comparison with the Klan made their job more difficult. We found that the first critical error police officials made in the run-up to the UTR rally was the failure to appreciate crucial differences between UTR and the Klan rally. Planners saw UTR much the same way that they'd viewed July 8 — a free speech rally in a confined area next to a statue surrounded by a larger group of counter-protesters. This informed an operational plan that was designed to fortify the small area surrounding the Lee statue rather than more broadly protect public safety. Law enforcement decided to surround the park with two rows of bicycle rack barriers, with a small buffer zone between. They created ways to get into the park area, at the southwest and southeast corners. They separated the park into two sections of roughly equal sizes and designated one side for the rally organizers and another for the crowd of opponents. Officers were assigned to five zones surrounding the park, with a mix of CPD officers and VSP troopers in each zone. The officers were wearing regular summer uniforms, as planners believed tactical gear was more likely to generate a hostile response from the crowd and escalate the potential for violence. The officers were positioned behind the bicycle racks, not among the crowds of people streaming to the event.

The operational plan devised by CPD did not include groups of officers stationed away from the park along likely routes of ingress and egress, nor at parking garages or along streets leading to the event. There were hundreds of officers from different agencies massed near the statue but almost no police presence around the city where people were assembling. This was a critical mistake, as the plan provided no police protection where and when violence was most likely — the morning hours before the scheduled event, when people were moving toward the park.

The second critical law enforcement error our investigation uncovered was the complete lack of coordination between the Virginia State Police and the Charlottesville Police Department. VSP sent hundreds of officers to Charlottesville, from troopers in regular uniforms who stood in the zones surrounding the park to tactical units trained in crowd control; a VSP helicopter circled the event and relayed information to command staff. The field force units were not pre-positioned at the event but rather were staged some distance away, awaiting activation in case of an unlawful assembly. VSP devised its own operational plan for troopers in Charlottesville, though they did not share that plan with CPD. The troopers who were positioned behind the bike racks were told by VSP supervisors not to intervene in violent disorders outside the barriers, though this was not conveyed to CPD leadership.[11] Perhaps most problematical, the VSP and CPD officers could not speak to each other or coordinate because their radios operated on separate channels that did not facilitate interagency communication. This lack of coordination undercut the effectiveness of the large police presence, as line officers did not have a clear understanding of the direction or actions of their counterparts.

Our investigation also highlighted another major failure exacerbating the events of August 12: an attempt by the city to move the planned rally location. As they had prior to July 8, city officials met with community members to gather and provide information about UTR planning. Predictably, many individuals and organizations urged city leaders to deny the UTR permit, given the hateful message that was expected and the potential for violence. Downtown business owners were particularly active in encouraging city councilors to prevent the rally from taking place. City officials felt enormous political pressure to prevent or deny the permit for the UTR rally and received almost no encouragement to allow it. In the face of this public pressure, city officials discussed alternatives to accommodating the permit, consulting with police leadership and lawyers about possible options.

Just days before the rally, the city announced in a press conference that they were moving the permitted event to an area outside of downtown Charlottesville where it could more easily be controlled.[12] "There is no doubt that Mr. Kessler has a First Amendment right to hold a demonstration and to express his views," city manager Maurice Jones said at the press conference. "Nor is there any doubt that we, as a City, have an obligation to protect those rights, the people who seek to exercise them, and the broader community in which they do. We have determined that we cannot do all of these things effectively if the demonstration is held in Emancipation Park."

This satisfied downtown merchants who were worried about property damage but angered the UTR organizers, who claimed that proximity to the Lee statue was essential to their speech. The American Civil Liberties Union of Virginia filed a lawsuit on behalf of the UTR organizers in federal court, arguing that the city's attempt to move the rally away from the statue violated the organizers' First Amendment rights. Their motion for an injunction was considered on an expedited basis. On Friday night, August 11, the night before the event was to take place, Judge Glen Conrad granted the ACLU motion to enjoin the city's transfer of the location of the event. The judge specifically found that the city's proposed move violated the First Amendment rights of the permit holders, as the city had not denied other permits obtained by counter-protesters for areas downtown close to the Lee statue. The judge also found that the intelligence presented by the city did not suggest that the UTR speakers intended to directly incite violence.

The attempt to move the rally away from downtown Charlottesville was misguided and prevented the city from ensuring clear community expectations. The success of the ACLU lawsuit was predictable, given clear First Amendment case law making prior restraint of protected speech extremely difficult. The intelligence that the city presented in the litigation suggested that the UTR speakers intended to defend themselves from the violence they understood their words and actions would likely provoke, rather than to initiate violence. That made it difficult for the city to meet the high evidentiary standard required for the prior restraint of speech and to avoid the "heckler's veto" represented by their cancellation of the event.[13]

The heart of our report was a factual summary of the events surrounding the UTR rally. We sketched out details of the planning for and participation in the event from multiple perspectives: police and city officials, UTR and anti-racist participants, and numerous citizens who were present for various relevant events. As we intended from the beginning, our main job was to create a credible account of what occurred, supported by testimony, documents, images, and other information gathered over the course of the investigation. We were there to tell the true story of the UTR rally and dispel myths and misconceptions as to what happened. Those facts would lay the foundation for evaluations of accountability and recommendations as to how to prevent similar outcomes in the future.

Our report's detailed story of the UTR event itself begins the night before August 12, on the grounds of the University of Virginia. The UTR organizers and many attendees arrived in Charlottesville on Friday, August 11, and immediately began to execute their strategy of provocation. On Friday night, a large group of alt-right protesters gathered at a field on the UVA grounds. Our investigation found that Jason Kessler informed a lieutenant on the university police force of the group's plans on Friday afternoon, though he did not provide specificity as to timing. After dark on Friday night, the protesters gathered at Nameless Fields, an open recreation area adjacent to a gymnasium. There, they distributed and lit torches and carried them along university streets, chanting "Jews will not replace us" and "Blood and soil," a common neo-Nazi refrain. They moved up the historic lawn in the center of UVA's campus and surged around the Rotunda building toward a statue of Thomas Jefferson. A small group of students and community members caught wind of this march and quickly assembled to form a small human chain around the base of the statue. The anti-racist group was soon overrun by the large torch-wielding crowd, who surrounded the students and attacked them.

Our investigation found that the university's response to the torch march on August 11 was tardy and inadequate. Despite being made aware of the plans for a march on the grounds earlier that day, university leadership failed to deploy sufficient police resources to prevent the predictable violence. And despite repeated offers of mutual aid, they did not pre-position police resources from other departments or take any steps to separate the conflicting groups. Instead, the university police stood by as the angry marchers approached the small group of students who had encircled the statue. University police officials did not request assistance from city police until after the brawl had started, and by the time reinforcements arrived, the fighting was mostly over and folks were leaving. Several people were injured in the violence, though no one was arrested. The UTR group dispersed, celebrating their ability to move through UVA relatively unimpeded.

Our investigation found that the Friday-night event set an important but dangerous precedent for the next day and motivated people on both sides. The UTR organizers were encouraged by the large crowd they had assembled and the unified message of hate they had summoned. They were also surprised at the lack of police presence at their event, particularly given their explicit communication with police officials before it took place. The passive response to their presence emboldened them and strengthened their resolve for similar provocation the next day. Many residents of Charlottesville were surprised at the size and vehemence of the UTR group and disappointed at the law enforcement response. This motivated some to attend the rally the next day, to confront the racism on display on Friday night. The UVA event therefore served as a catalyst to further confrontation and disruption on August 12.

Saturday morning dawned hot and humid in Charlottesville, a typical summer day. Our investigation included a description of an interfaith prayer service at sunrise, reaffirming the commitment of clergy and other faith leaders to resist hate in the coming hours. The group encouraged people at the service to join a march to the Lee statue, which was just a few blocks from the church. They reiterated their intent to resist the UTR event with nonviolence and encouraged people to join them only if they were prepared for potential arrest. The Reverend Cornel West and anti-racist leader Traci Blackmon led a march of approximately fifty people from the church to the Lee statue, where they stood in a line in front of the park awaiting the arrival of the UTR protesters.

We detailed that the clergy group was met by a makeshift group of armed militia members standing in front of the park in military gear. These men said that they came to Charlottesville to protect the safety and speech rights of all attendees. Their possession of long guns and communications equipment confused many in the crowd that morning, who believed they were a military unit. Our investigation found that prior to August 12, the militia group attempted to coordinate with CPD officials, who refused to share information or operational plans. The militia group stood immediately in front of the clergy, forming an odd double line along the southern perimeter of the park.

Many of the UTR attendees met outside of town in McIntire Park, preparing to travel together in cars and vans toward the Lee statue downtown. They moved to various parking lots and garages and began marching toward the park. UTR organizers refused to share information with CPD and did not agree to arrive at the park through a designated point of entry. Instead, they began marching toward the park from all directions in small clusters, clad in protective gear and chanting various racist slogans. Well before the scheduled start of the event, they began their confrontational path toward the statue.

Law enforcement got a similarly early start on the morning of August 12. VSP troopers received an all-hands briefing that was exclusive to their agency and included no one from CPD or other agencies. The troopers moved to their designated zones around the park, and the field force units staged in pre-assigned locations some distance away. CPD officers also moved toward their assigned zones. They did not wear their riot gear but rather staged it in an area inside the park. Some CPD officers received this specialized equipment for the first time that morning, having never previously put on the helmet and other equipment. Officers staffed their positions behind the bicycle rack barricades that had been placed by public works officials and watched the crowd swell over the course of that morning.

As we described in great detail in our report, violence erupted quickly as people with a wide array of views streamed into downtown Charlottesville. As expected, the noxious chants of the angry alt-right marchers provoked a violent response. Fights erupted around the city well before the scheduled start of the UTR rally. Clergy formed a human chain at the southeast corner of the park, attempting to block entry. Led by the League of the South, UTR protesters easily pushed through the line as they began to fill the area adjacent to the Lee statue. Immediately outside the park, alt-right rally-goers violently clashed with anti-racist opponents. While the park itself was relatively secure due to a heavy law enforcement presence, the streets immediately in front of and around the park were lawless zones, with open fighting, throwing of projectiles, and angry exchanges erupting at multiple locations.

This violence occurred in plain view of the police officers standing behind the bicycle barriers yet provoked no arrests or other law enforcement response. Officers we interviewed followed their instructions to stand back and allow some measure of violence to occur without intervention. CPD officer Lisa Best, who was stationed in the zone commanded by Lieutenant Brian O'Donnell, told me that they were told officers "were not going to go in and break up fights" or enter the crowd to make arrests "unless it was something so serious that someone will get killed."[14] VSP officers similarly were told that they were not going to "wade into the mess on Market Street" in front of the park, according to interviews we conducted.[15] Participants in this violence on both sides noted the lack of police response, which only encouraged them to engage in further violence.

Charlottesville police chief Al Thomas had a bird's-eye view of the scene from his comfortable perch in the command center in the Wells Fargo building overlooking the park. According to two eyewitnesses we spoke to in the course of our investigation, Chief Thomas's instructions were to "let them fight"; this would create grounds for the declaration of an unlawful assembly and subsequent dispersal of the crowd.[16] Thomas did ultimately declare an unlawful assembly, based largely on the frequent skirmishes that were occurring at the rally site and elsewhere. That declaration led CPD officers to withdraw from their stations at the barricades to retrieve their riot gear and prepare to clear the park.

Our investigation found the clearance of the park was similarly disastrous. VSP and CPD field force units assembled inside the park near the Lee statue. As several officers used bullhorns to order people to disperse, the field force units pushed the UTR protesters directly south, out of the park. This forced movement thrust them right into the crowd of anti-racist counter-protesters with whom they had been fighting earlier. Predictably, more fights occurred as the park was cleared. Bands of white nationalists began roving the city, engaging in fights with smaller groups of anti-racist opponents. A group of UTR rally-goers assaulted a young, Black school worker, DeAndre Harris, hitting his head with wooden sticks and stomping him in the Market Street parking garage. Law enforcement was unable to keep pace with assaults like that of Mr. Harris, as they were largely assembled in the park and arrived at reported scenes of assault well after the violence had occurred.

The most tragic episode of violence occurred in the early afternoon at 1:41 PM. The nerve center of Charlottesville is the Downtown Mall, a roughly ten-block stretch of Main Street in the center of town that has been converted from a regular city street to a pedestrian mall. Lined with restaurants, cafés, art galleries, and boutiques, it draws thousands of locals and tourists on a summer weekend like August 12. The mall is closed to vehicular traffic but for two crossovers where cars can move across the pedestrian surface. The two crossovers were blocked off as part of the CPD operations plan. The Fourth Street crossing was overseen by a single officer, school resource officer Tammy Shifflett. After Chief Thomas's declaration of an unlawful assembly, Officer Shifflett expressed concern for her safety and asked to be relieved of her post guarding the crossing. With command staff permission, she left her post, which resulted in the automobile crossing being blocked by only a single sawhorse.

James Fields was a UTR rally-goer who came to Charlottesville from his native Ohio. Clad in khaki pants and a white polo shirt, he appears in photographs joining a group of Vanguard America members at the Lee statue while carrying a shield.[17] According to the Department of Justice, he "engaged in chants promoting or expressing white supremacist and other racist and anti-Semitic views."[18] Sometime after he left the park, Fields exploited the security vulnerability at the Fourth Street crossing to drive his

Dodge Charger onto the Downtown Mall. He saw a large crowd of anti-racist counter-protesters who were moving from Water Street up Fourth Street, in the direction of the two parks that had served as staging areas for those resisting the UTR event. Fields sped into the crowd, killing a young paralegal named Heather Heyer and seriously injuring at least thirty-five others. He sped away but was soon apprehended, with tracking help from the VSP helicopter.

Fields's murder of Heather Heyer served as a sort of tragic exclamation point on the day. UTR attendees largely dispersed after the car attack, as did the larger crowd gathered to resist their hate speech. National Guard soldiers arrived to protect the Downtown Mall from property damage, and the violence subsided. Late in the afternoon, the VSP helicopter that had been circling the city and had assisted the apprehension of James Fields crashed due to mechanical failure. Berke Bates and Jay Cullen, the two troopers inside, both died at the scene. Their deaths were a sad denouement to an awful day in which the city failed to protect public safety or accommodate free speech.

It's hard to imagine a more derelict response than the actions of CPD and VSP on August 12. They first allowed the initiation of violence without intervention, stood by as it continued, then retreated from their positions to begin to clear the park. Their actions in clearing the park caused additional violence around the city after the unlawful assembly was declared. Numerous officers with whom I spoke expressed frustration with the passive operational plan that had them stationed behind barricades rather than engaging with the crowd and de-escalating conflict. They were prevented from protecting their community, which caused frustration during the event and cynicism after the fact. In the words of CPD captain Jim Mooney, officers "had [their] thumbs up [their] ass."[19] I shared that frustration and was unsparing in my criticism of the command staff decisions in the report. This was a failure of leadership and a tremendous disappointment to me, given my prior work in law enforcement and respect for police. Its substantial long-term consequences included spreading a loss of trust in law enforcement across the entire community, well beyond the heavily policed communities of color that had already lost that trust.

((•))

Throughout our investigation, our clients in city government and the Greater Charlottesville community were anxious for completion. We pulled together a report within ninety days of launching our review. In every investigation, there are things left undone — additional witnesses with whom we could have spoken, sources of information we could not reach. This investigation was no different. While there were certainly holes we could not fill in the limited time we were given, our independent review was able to access sufficient information to capture the core story of August 12 in great detail.

On December 1, 2017, we delivered our report to the city and the community. It was a scathing indictment of our client and roundly criticized law enforcement planners, city and state officials, and numerous individuals whose actions contributed to the violence. The report included a thorough factual summary of what occurred at each of the three summer protest events. It proceeded to make specific findings as to what went right and what went wrong with respect to the handling of these events, with a much longer list of mistakes than of successes. The report concluded with some specific recommendations: changes in law, policy, and procedure that we hoped would guide Charlottesville and other small cities in their preparation for and response to future mass demonstration events.

Throughout the investigation, our team adhered to the fundamental principle that a concise narrative of facts has to guide any credible after-action report. We had to start with facts, wherever they may have led. The facts must be verifiable, corroborated, and based on reliable evidence, not speculative, hypothetical, or informed by unreliable narrators. We resisted the temptation to include information in the report that, while salacious and provocative, was not sufficiently documented to meet our high standard of reliability. We took a careful approach in drafting the factual narrative to ensure that our conclusions were well founded and would withstand the scrutiny we knew would follow. A clear-eyed, honest assessment of what happened on those terrible days in Charlottesville is the foundation that informed our conclusions and recommendations.

It was not difficult to assign blame for the mistakes made in the days before and on August 12. We were extremely critical of law enforcement leadership across the agencies that responded to the event. The failures we noted were operational, as police agencies had ample intelligence about the UTR rally that forecast potential violence, and there were adequate police units and personnel present in Charlottesville to protect public safety. Nonetheless, the flawed and disconnected operational plans of the CPD and VSP failed miserably to achieve that goal. The plans they devised protected the park but left city streets unguarded and resulted in the persistent violence and death that followed. The officers' passive response to that violence encouraged further violence and severely eroded public confidence in law enforcement and government. The unlawful assembly declaration was horribly executed and further facilitated violence, as the UTR protesters were pushed directly toward their antagonists, which led to skirmishes across the downtown area. The lack of coordinated planning and communications between CPD and VSP undercut the effectiveness of both agencies, depriving line officers and troopers of vital information about overall response to the event. The report made clear that these line officers were frustrated with their leaders' poor planning and failure to protect the community. This was a command staff failure, not a lack of will, valor, or desire by the men and women in uniform.

The independent investigation led to personnel changes in law enforcement. Soon after the report was issued, Charlottesville police chief Al Thomas resigned and VSP superintendent Steven Flaherty retired. While neither tied their departure to the Charlottesville events, the report led to public pressure for personnel change that made their continued leadership more tenuous.

The Charlottesville City Council fared no better in our critical report. We specifically found that the misguided attempt to move the UTR rally away from downtown was based on a flawed understanding of the law and created a tremendous, unnecessary distraction in the week before August 12. The lawsuit was doomed to fail, as the intelligence did not suggest affirmative incitement or threats sufficient to satisfy the stringent legal standard of prior restraint. Moreover, the city's act of singling out the UTR permit for the enforced change in location while granting other permits to anti-racist counter-protesters informed the court's view that the city's action was content based rather than content neutral. Because the location of the rally was uncertain, little information was available to the public about what to expect on August 12, which left many city residents in the dark about plans and expectations. Rather than educate their constituents about the preparations they were putting in place to protect the odious but constitutionally protected speech, city officials capitulated to voices encouraging them to prevent the rally. They also consistently meddled in operational details typically delegated to the city manager and chief of police. Again, public pressure drove their actions much more than a consideration of constitutional rights or informed expertise.[20]

The report named organizations and individuals who hampered the city's response and made violence more possible. The refusal of Christ Episcopal Church and the Jefferson-Madison Regional Library to make the buildings they owned adjacent to the park available as staging areas for tactical field forces slowed down the police response to the unlawful assembly declaration. The militia members who came to "protect free speech" played no role in maintaining order but rather caused confusion, uncertainty, and fear among attendees. The University of Virginia's failure to adequately protect students despite clear warnings of violence on the school's grounds set a dangerous precedent for the following day. Governor McAuliffe's suggestion that the city ban guns in advance of the event was advice that contradicted Virginia law, and the state government's refusal to cooperate with our review reflected a disappointing lack of constructive effort to learn from the clear mistakes of August 12.

After I announced the core findings of the report at the press conference on December 1, 2017, I also gave a lengthy presentation regarding our independent investigation to the city council in a public meeting on December 4, 2017. City leaders had not redacted the report or influenced its findings or conclusions in any way. To their credit, city councilors received the information about their own conduct without a defensive response or justification. This was an important step in the city's recovery from August 12 and, in my view, was an example of enlightened leadership. In any relationship, the ability to hear and respond constructively to criticism is a sign of strength and confidence. The council was true to city manager Jones's initial intention to gather the facts wherever they led and reveal them plainly to the community.

At council meetings and other forums that took place after the issuance of the report, some city residents criticized it for its lack of explicit criticism of the ideology that motivated all three summer events and our inclusion of the perspective of alt-right organizers and participants. Rick Turner, the former head of the Charlottesville branch of the NAACP, told a local radio station that the report should have examined the role of race more specifically. "If the author of the report was a conscious Black person, he couldn't miss the relevance of race in this context," he told the local news. "Instead, this report never mentioned it. We live in a state of steadfast denial." This surprised me, as I did not believe the report needed to make the obvious point that the alt-right speech that was delivered or intended was odious, hateful, and morally wrong. My response to this criticism was also an explanation of the scope of our work. My firm was hired to conduct an independent review of the city's handling of the events, which required an effort to solicit information about the events from participants of all types, regardless of their level of moral culpability.

The critics of our report who voiced those objections were vastly outnumbered by others who saw it as a necessary step in recovering from August 12 and helping the city move forward. Despite our criticism of CPD and VSP, many men and women from those agencies have thanked me for telling the truth about the law enforcement failures. They expressed the view that the criticism was both warranted and necessary for their agencies to improve. Many of the people who contributed their testimony, personal history, photographs, and video from the event appreciated the opportunity to contribute to our work. Any number of citizens whom I'd never met before have approached me in Charlottesville to say thank you, which to this day is welcome and appreciated.

In the years since, I've been invited to several small cities around the country to present to law enforcement and civic groups about the Charlottesville events and consulted with individual officers and city leaders about specific events in their communities. As we hoped when we drafted the report, it has helped inform a broader discussion of the effective management of mass demonstrations and ideally helped other departments learn from the systemic failures we identified. Since that awful day in 2017, the name of our city, Charlottesville, has become a buzzword, shorthand for that time and place where a crowd of fascists were able to organize and perpetuate violence without law enforcement resistance.

Our community has become a symbol of the potential for racial violence that simmers beneath the surface in this country. Unite the Right is what comes to mind for many at the mention of Charlottesville. It is a stain that has not faded and may never entirely disappear.

JANUARY 6

About three and a half years later, on January 6, 2021, I was back in Charlottesville working as the University of Virginia's chief legal officer, or university counsel. It was the middle of the pandemic. I was at my desk in Madison Hall, the building largely empty. Just like on August 12, 2017, I was two hours away from the violence, so my first inkling of what was occurring came via alerts on my phone. I watched on CNN as the horrific violence unfolded at the US Capitol. An immediate thought occurred to me: It looked like Charlottesville on August 12. I was less surprised this time, seeing these scenes play out again on a national stage.

Over the course of the 2020 presidential campaign, I had been focused more on COVID-19 than on the ins and outs of the race. As the general counsel of a large public research university, my focus was on advising my clients how to safely operate during a global pandemic. While the nation evaluated the candidates and decided whether to rehire the incumbent or move in a new direction, I was immersed in running a small law office grappling with the uncertainty of the virus and how best to manage risk.

The pandemic presented vexing legal challenges to higher education. Most days, I felt like I was back in law school, taking an exam with no clear answers, precedent, or guidelines. We struggled to get the best medical information we could about this insidious new virus, knowing that so much of that information was provisional and uncertain. We talked about social distancing requirements, limits on gatherings, and mask mandates. The task before us was nearly impossible — trying to convince college students not to do what they come to college to do. We relied heavily on the epidemiologists at our academic medical center, who provided their best medical advice. We looked at what peer institutions were doing with respect to distance learning, student activities, athletics, and communications. But we just didn't know much about the properties and seriousness of the virus. It felt like we were feeling our way around a dark room, hoping not to bump into a large piece of furniture.

The distance I felt from Washington suddenly shrank as the searing images from the Capitol gripped the nation's attention. I knew that what was unfolding was unlike anything that had happened before. The world would be watching and wondering what this would mean for American democracy. The similarities with August 12, 2017, were immediately clear, but to an even greater degree my thoughts and feelings turned to September 11, 2001, certain that this day would change America.

On September 11, 2001, I was an assistant US attorney in Washington, DC. I watched the planes fly into the World Trade Center towers from a television in my supervisor's office. I was working with a group of FBI agents on a long-running gang investigation. After the towers fell, I also felt the urge to help, to do something in response. All my colleagues felt the same. Our office immediately started organizing for the prospect of mass arrests and a potential rush of cases that might ensue in what was obviously a large-scale, coordinated act of terrorism. Of course, mass domestic arrests never happened, but we all felt compelled to help in some way, even if we weren't sure exactly what form that help would take.

I felt that same urge to help on January 6, from the very onset of the violence. As on 9/11, I wanted to make sense from chaos, be a part of the response, and offer solutions. In contrast with September 11, I had a specific skill set that might actually help — the experience honed by the independent review in Charlottesville. As I watched the violence at the Capitol, I immediately began to think about whether there would be a similar kind of after-action and how I might contribute to that effort. Even before the attack was repelled and order restored, I knew I wanted to help pick up the pieces and enhance the nation's understanding of what had occurred.

It would be months before I saw a path to get involved, though. From my distant perch in Charlottesville, I watched as Congress debated various ways to structure an after-action review. The first option was an independent, non-partisan commission, modeled on the successful 9/11 Commission. I thought it was a good idea, and as Congress debated it, I even went back to read the final report of the 9/11 Commission, hoping it would serve as a template for whatever came next in the January 6 investigation.

Respective party leaders in Congress chose Democratic representative Bennie Thompson of Mississippi and Republican representative John Katko of New York to hammer out the details of such an independent commission. On May 14, 2021, the two struck a deal that would have led to the creation of a ten-member panel of independent experts, with half appointed by Democratic members and half by Republicans.[1] The commission would have subpoena power, with approval of both the chair and vice chair required for issuance, and it would perform its work quickly, with a deadline for issuance of a final report by the end of 2021.

The Thompson/Katko agreement was hailed as a bipartisan achievement as the proposal moved toward consideration on the House floor. But eventually, politics dashed any hopes of such a bipartisan effort. Minority leader Kevin McCarthy ultimately opposed it. The compromise proposal did pass the House on a largely partisan vote but was defeated in the Senate due to a Republican filibuster. Despite the seriousness of the attack on the Capitol and the successful model of the 9/11 Commission, Congress failed to pursue a similarly apolitical process with respect to January 6. And on a personal level, my hopes were dashed of ever getting involved in an after-action investigation.

Once the independent commission was defeated, Speaker Nancy Pelosi pivoted to a backup plan — a select committee of the House of Representatives tasked with evaluating the January 6 attack on the Capitol. Select committees are created to evaluate discrete issues by majority vote of the House. They are limited in duration to the Congress in which they are enacted. Through the years, the House has formed select committees to investigate a number of issues, including the famous Select Committee on Presidential Campaign Activities, known as the Watergate Committee, whose actions led to President Nixon's resignation. In just the 117th Congress alone, there were also select committees on the climate crisis, on economic disparity and fairness in growth, and on the modernization of congress.[2]

On July 1, 2021, the House of Representatives approved House Resolution 503, which created the Select Committee to Investigate the January 6th Attack on the United States Capitol. The vote was largely along party lines, with only two Republican members voting to create the committee (Representatives Elizabeth Cheney and Adam Kinzinger). H. Res. 503 called for the appointment of thirteen members of the committee, eight appointed by Speaker Pelosi and five by Leader McCarthy. Speaker Pelosi promptly named seven Democrats to the panel: Representatives Bennie Thompson, Jamie Raskin, Pete Aguilar, Zoe Lofgren, Adam Schiff, Elaine Luria, and Stephanie Murphy. To the surprise of many, she also named Republican representative Cheney to the panel. She named Representative Thompson the committee's chair.

Despite his opposition to the creation of a select committee, Leader McCarthy named Representative Jim Banks as the Republican leader of the panel and Representatives Jim Jordan, Rodney Davis, Troy Nehls, and Kelly Armstrong to serve as the Republican members. Just two days later, Speaker Pelosi informed Leader McCarthy that she would not accept Representatives Jordan and Banks to the panel, given their personal involvement in some of the central events surrounding the January 6 attack. She agreed to accept the recommendations of Representatives Nehls, Davis, and Armstrong.

Rather than replacing the two members that the Speaker had rejected, McCarthy withdrew all five Republican members. "Unless Speaker Pelosi reverses course and seats all five Republican nominees, Republicans will not be party to their sham process and will instead pursue our own investigation of the facts," McCarthy said. He refused any further Republican participation with the panel. Soon after, Speaker Pelosi appointed another Republican, Representative Adam Kinzinger, to the panel. She would later name Representative Cheney the vice chair.

Watching this process from Charlottesville, I wasn't sure at first that the committee would be as influential as a truly independent commission. I worried that this investigation had the potential to be unserious, given the heightened political context in which it would occur. I wasn't sure how it would be viewed by others in the short or long term. But at the same time, I saw an opportunity to help make it a truly independent, credible investigation, as nonpartisan and independent as possible given the structure, just as I had in Charlottesville. Maybe this was actually the perfect role, and challenge, for me to take on. If I was in the room, I could work to ensure that such a historically and politically significant investigation would be credible and influential. I decided to do everything in my power to get involved.

I knew the committee would have to assemble a professional staff to guide its investigative effort. I reached out to a friend and law school classmate who was serving in Congress, Representative Sean Patrick Maloney from New York. Sean chaired the Democratic Congressional Campaign Committee, which earned him a seat in Speaker Pelosi's leadership team. I knew Sean had the ear of the Speaker, and I asked him for advice about how to get involved with the select committee. I specifically talked with Sean about my desire to lead the investigative effort. Sean understood that my experience in conducting the independent review in Charlottesville as well as my long years as a federal prosecutor gave me a unique set of credentials for this important assignment. He became my ally with the Speaker and other House leaders, ensuring that I would be considered to lead the investigation.

Speaker Pelosi's team led the initial round of staff hiring for the committee. They assembled names, conducted interviews, and ultimately recommended specific people for staff leadership. This process resulted first in the designation of David Buckley as staff director of the committee and Kristin Amerling as its chief counsel. The process moved quickly, as the committee held its first hearing on July 27, approximately one month after it was formed.

Sometime after the first hearing, I received a call from Speaker Pelosi's chief of staff, Terri McCullough, asking me to come to DC for an interview for the job of chief investigative counsel, the lawyer who would supervise the investigative work of the select committee. I would be in charge of the daily work of the investigative staff and manage the fact-gathering process. I would also stay in close touch with the members of the select committee, briefing them on investigative developments and ensuring that they were abreast of our work. I would work closely with David, Kristin, and other staff leaders to supervise the lawyers and others hired to work for the committee, and I would have primary responsibility for identifying lawyers and other professionals to work on the investigative team. The job sounded very much like what I'd done in Charlottesville, with the important distinction of having nine members of Congress as clients to whom I would report.

I knew I could accomplish this task, if assigned, but I still had a major concern: I did not want to contribute to an effort that was politically motivated and designed to affirm a predetermined outcome. I was only interested in signing on to a credible, fact-bound investigation. I feared that the narrative coming from Leader McCarthy and other Republicans — that the committee's work was destined to be "impeachment three" and a "witch hunt" against the former president — would influence public opinion, diminish the select committee's credibility, and dilute its ultimate effect. I also worried that no one would pay attention to the work done by the committee, other than those who had already determined that the attack on the Capitol was caused by the former president and his desire to prevent the transfer of power. I wrestled with these questions and compared them with my ongoing desire to be part of the way forward in the wake of the attack on the Capitol.

As I considered these questions and mulled the opportunity to lead the committee's investigation, I had an introductory call with Chairman Thompson. He began the conversation by thanking me for my interest and willingness to serve on the committee and complimenting my work in Charlottesville. I told Chairman Thompson that I was drawn to do this investigation primarily because of what I'd seen in Charlottesville, as there were clear parallels between the two events. I expressed my view that facts and a clear-eyed assessment of events must be the baseline condition for learning from January 6. I shared with Chairman Thompson my concerns about the political environment in which the committee would operate and the potential for its work to be criticized as an effort to assign blame to former president Trump.

Chairman Thompson responded to my concerns by articulating his vision for the committee and its priorities. He wanted the investigation to "follow the facts, wherever they lead." He said he wanted an investigation with integrity. He talked about history and the legacy of the committee and explained that its work must proceed with unimpeachable integrity given the scrutiny it would draw. He said he wanted me to apply the lessons I'd learned in Charlottesville and during my time at the DOJ to run an investigation that would tell the truth about January 6, as developed by a careful, thorough investigation. He rebuffed the criticism that the committee was politically motivated by reassuring me that he would not allow it to be undercut by politics or any other improper factor. By the end of the conversation, Chairman Thompson had reassured me of his intention that this would be a credible, objective investigation, not the partisan exercise that others had already claimed it would become.

In addition to my concerns about the integrity of the investigative process, I had other questions about the practicalities of taking on the committee's chief investigative counsel role. I was enjoying my time as university counsel and concerned about how my departure would affect my small office of lawyers and the school. I spoke to UVA president Jim Ryan, who reassured me that I could take a leave of absence to work for the select committee and that he and other university leaders would support my temporary departure. In Virginia, chief legal officers for public universities are employees of the state attorney general. I had a similar conversation with Virginia attorney general Mark Herring, who agreed to allow me to take a leave of absence to facilitate my important work on the select committee. I learned that many university deans, faculty, and other leaders take similar leaves to perform public service work. I felt confident that I could do my work in DC and return to my job when the committee's work was done.

The last and most important consideration before I agreed to take on the select committee role was my family. It was clear that the work of the committee would be intense and all-consuming.

This was not a job that could be done remotely. Leading the investigation required physical presence in Washington, DC, working closely with the investigative team. While the world had become used to teleworking during the pandemic, the nature of investigations requires personal contact and building relationships. In the summer of 2021, two of my three children were in college and no longer living in our family home. My daughter was a sophomore in high school, entrenched within our community (and still playing baseball!). If I took the job in DC, it would mean being away from home Monday through Thursday. My wife, Lori, would become a single parent in Charlottesville during the weeks. A leave of absence from UVA would also require a significant pay cut, which meant we'd have to navigate these challenges on a tighter budget.

As she has done so many times over the course of our lives together, Lori said yes and supported my desire to serve. While she knew that working in Washington would require sacrifice, she never hesitated in encouraging me to accept the chief investigative counsel role. She could see my desire to contribute and had faith in my ability to perform this important work. "Go. You have to do this," she said. With that encouragement, I took the job.

I began as chief investigative counsel to the select committee on August 16, 2021, and started drafting a proposed investigative plan. Our immediate priority was defining scope, and we didn't have a lot on which to base that crucial definition.

H. Res. 503 was quite broad. It directed the select committee to "conduct an investigation of the relevant facts and circumstances relating to the attack on the Capitol" and to "identify, review, and evaluate the causes of and the lessons learned from this attack," as well as "write and publish a report to this effect." That broad formulation of the committee's mandate wasn't terribly helpful as we devised an investigative plan. What were the areas of inquiry most likely to identify relevant facts and circumstances? How far beyond the riot itself should we extend? Should we attempt to plug January 6 into a broader historical perspective, or stick to the events at the Capitol? What about systemic issues of race and inequality — were they within the committee's scope? I struggled with these issues at the outset, mindful that how we structured the whole investigation would also dictate how we structured the investigative team, and we had to start hiring fast.

I had an idea to split the investigative staff into a few color-coded teams to keep things organized and clear. I proposed five subgroups, each of which had a specific area of focus. We assigned each investigative team a color that loosely correlated to their work. We started with the events at the Capitol and created two teams — one to focus on each side of the barricades along the security perimeter. The Blue Team would, appropriately for its color, look into the law enforcement and military preparations for and response to the attack. They would evaluate intelligence gathering and dissemination and how that intelligence did (or did not) inform preparations for January 6. They would also gather facts about how various agencies responded to the violence that occurred at the Capitol in real time.

Focusing on the other side of the barricade, the Red Team would develop evidence about the planning and organization of the riot. Named for the red MAGA caps that were ubiquitous in the crowd at the Capitol, Red Team investigators would speak to dozens of rioters and others present in an attempt to piece together how much coordination took place. They would study the Proud Boys, the Oath Keepers, and other organized groups present at the Capitol. Finally, they would obtain information about the permitting process and communications inside the White House that informed expectations for the joint session of Congress at which the 2020 election results were to be certified.

Next, we zoomed out to create two teams that would evaluate the broader issues that motivated the riot. The Gold Team would investigate issues surrounding the election and efforts by the former president and others to prevent the certification of the election for President Biden. Over the course of their work, they would find evidence of the generation and submission of fake elector certificates in various states and the role of those certificates in a legal strategy to prevent certification. They would also find evidence of pressure on state officials, the leadership of the Department of Justice, members of Congress, and ultimately the vice president to take actions that had no basis in fact or law. The Gold Team's work would eventually lead it to consider the "Big Lie" of election fraud, the persistent assertion that the outcome was infected by systemic fraud.

I was mindful of the danger of assessing the attack on the Capitol in a vacuum, ignoring how it connected to other similar events that had gone before. That's where the Purple Team came in. That team would evaluate the broad ascent of domestic violent extremism and how January 6 fit within that development. Members would focus on social media's role in providing a forum for the dissemination of misinformation and its use as a mechanism to recruit support and participation. The Purple Team would also examine allegations of systemic racism in law enforcement and how race may have affected preparations for the riot.

The final team was focused on funding streams, evaluating who paid for various aspects of the event. The appropriately named Green Team would follow the money and do forensic accounting. They would obtain thousands of pages of financial records and would be able to identify the primary financial patrons of the January 6 events. They would also develop important information about campaign fundraising and how the Trump campaign continued to raise money by propagating false theories of election fraud well after the election was over.

While each of these teams was distinct, their areas of focus overlapped. The Purple Team's focus on domestic violent extremism required looking into the Proud Boys, the Oath Keepers, and other organizations that had an organized presence at the Capitol, the very issue the Red Team was investigating. The Green Team's focus on campaign fundraising entailed interviewing a number of witnesses also involved in efforts to discredit the results of the election, which required collaboration with the Gold Team. The teams did not operate in silos but rather leapfrogged one another as they pursued their unique areas of interest.

My proposed color-coded teams differed slightly from what the other staff leaders had in mind at first. Given my role as the chief investigative counsel and my experience organizing teams of lawyers engaged in complicated investigations, they quickly deferred to my judgment. The chairman and other committee members also blessed the structure, with the explicit caveat that we remain flexible and open to adjustment as we went along.

With the team structure in place, it was time to hire people to fill these teams. I knew that the people best suited for this undertaking would have the same concerns that I had when evaluating this potential opportunity. They would have to temporarily leave law firms, United States attorney offices, other congressional committees, and other established roles. Would the investigation be fair and objective? Would anyone pay attention? Would working on this investigation be a professional step forward or a career killer? I prepared to answer those questions as I made a list of lawyers to approach.

Given the committee's aggressive timeline, we needed experienced investigators who could immediately begin the important work of gathering and assessing information. I needed to identify and hire a senior investigative counsel to lead each of the five teams as well as filling several investigative counsel positions for each team. The lawyers hired as investigative counsel to the committee would have to quickly review documents, conduct interviews both formal and informal, assess the relevance of that information, and incorporate it into an evolving investigative plan. Investigations are dynamic, and they require the ability to quickly identify facts that are most important and worthy of further development. This was not a role that could accommodate on-the-job training. It required experienced hands who had worked on investigations in other contexts.

The lawyers I knew with these skills came largely from the Department of Justice. I learned how to conduct a thorough investigation as an assistant US attorney (AUSA), so I knew how those jobs provided a sound foundation of experience that would translate to the work of the select committee. We ended up hiring more than a dozen former federal or state prosecutors, more than half the lawyers on the investigative team. This approach to hiring reflected not a desire to find evidence of crimes but rather the skills demanded by the nature of our work.

Most of the former prosecutors hired as investigative counsel had not previously worked in Congress. As a result, the culture of our staff was quite different from that of other congressional committees, and not just in the sense that they came from positions and backgrounds that required a scrupulous disregard for political concerns. AUSAs are used to a great deal of autonomy, working on small teams with agents to pursue evidence and make case decisions. Conversely, the Hill is much more hierarchical, with the members of Congress dictating committee priorities and directing the work of staff counsel. AUSAs are used to robust internal discussion and constructive disagreement with supervisors. Congressional staff do not typically function with that same culture, particularly when it comes to interaction with members. The staff we assembled at the select committee was consequently different in both style and substance from the normal congressional committee staff. I believe it worked to our benefit and laid the foundation for our ultimate success.

The select committee staff was also starkly different from most congressional staff because of its diversity. From my first conversation with Chairman Thompson, to conversations with other members of the committee, it was a priority for us to hire lawyers who brought varied experience to our team. I have always believed that diverse teams are stronger than those that are homogeneous, as they incorporate varied perspectives and are better prepared to avoid groupthink and tunnel vision. I wanted lawyers to challenge my own decisions and theories, to help make me aware of my own blind spots. I wanted to find lawyers with deep investigative experience who would ultimately make up a team marked by diversity and camaraderie. This was important at all levels of the committee, from team leadership on down to the most junior staffers.

Our investigative staff was ultimately made up of about 40 percent lawyers of color, well beyond the typical roster in almost any law office. We had several Black lawyers who brought experience honed at the DOJ and in other congressional offices. Several Latino lawyers were recruited from a list compiled by Representative Aguilar with the help of the Congressional Hispanic Caucus. Beyond race, our staff was diverse with respect to gender and sexual orientation, with several LGBTQ+ lawyers and women in significant leadership roles. We also sought and achieved ideological diversity, with lawyers who had been appointed to jobs in Republican administrations or otherwise been involved in Republican politics. The investigative staff reflected the diversity of America.

It was essential for the investigators on every team to collaborate. We would need to share information and ensure we prevented duplication of effort. Investigators on each team would need to jointly conduct interviews, flag pertinent information in important documents, and coordinate schedules. The importance of collaboration was made even more acute by our time-limited schedule. We simply could not afford to waste any effort given that the committee would almost assuredly expire at the end of the Congress.

We worked toward this collaboration in a few ways. As a starting point, each team drafted a proposed investigative plan outlining the issues and sources of information they intended to pursue. Once committee members approved these plans, we shared them across the staff to ensure that each team knew the directions proposed by their counterparts on other teams. These plans formed the foundation of the investigation and helped ensure clarity about who was responsible for what specific issues going forward.

As we worked, the committee obtained hundreds of thousands of documents related to the investigation, and we needed a way to organize them all. We ended up creating a shared database that allowed lawyers to review documents from various locations, categorize documents, and leave feedback for other investigators. We could also monitor access to the system and restrict access to particular categories of sensitive information to a more limited universe of people. Without a document control system such as this, we would have had a far more difficult time coordinating the work of the investigative teams.

The most important manifestation of our team collaboration was old-fashioned — talking to one another in a robust, regular information-sharing process. Every Monday morning at 10:00 AM, the senior investigative counsel who led each team gathered with me and other staff leaders in our large conference room in the O'Neill House Office Building on C Street SW. We would literally go around the room and get updates regarding the activity of each team. The team leads described what they'd learned the previous week and told us what they had scheduled for the week ahead. These meetings often became free-flowing exchanges during which ideas were floated, theories articulated, and new directions charted. I ran these weekly meetings and tried very hard to create a culture in which every participant felt comfortable contributing and expressing their perspective. I encouraged thorough reporting and asked people to share thoughts that were not yet fully formed.

I allowed conversations to take detours beyond our agenda, which inevitably led to long discussions that lasted beyond our allotted time. I knew that these meetings were our best opportunity to ensure common ground for our evolving understanding of key facts. I also believed the meetings provided a forum in which we could take full advantage of the investigative experience and talent we had worked hard to assemble on our staff.

Our collaboration was made easier by Representative McCarthy's decision to withdraw his nominees to the select committee, allowing its members and staff to operate as a unified entity rather than under the traditional congressional model with majority and minority members and staff. But this also meant that the Republican leadership would have no representation on the select committee or involvement in its operations. While the participation of Vice Chair Cheney and Representative Kinzinger ensured that the committee's work was bipartisan, there would be no members or staff with contrary views about our philosophical and practical approach to the investigation or its direction.

Even before we were fully staffed, I started conducting some key interviews of important witnesses, including chairman of the Joint Chiefs of Staff general Mark Milley, Acting Attorney General Jeffrey Rosen, and Acting Deputy Attorney General Richard Donoghue. We just couldn't wait for these interviews, given the enormous amount of information we needed to gather and the deadline we faced. Given this urgency of our work, I was determined to be both a supervisor and an active participant in the investigation. I maintained that approach even as we hired full teams of lawyers.

For the next sixteen months, I was thinking about January 6 and the investigation wherever I was. I was living in an odd back-and-forth between DC and Charlottesville, long days and nights in DC during the week and most weekends back home in Charlottesville. I was on calls, on Zooms, and reading and preparing through the weekends, even when I was home. This was an all-consuming job, and I had a hard time escaping from it. My family was great — supportive but willing to pull me away periodically. I also ran a marathon in the fall of 2021, as I'd been training through the pandemic. I ran a lot during the investigation, as it was a way to productively process the stress I felt leading this effort. Many nights over the course of our work, I would change in a small locker room in O'Neill House Office Building and go for a run around the Capitol and down the National Mall. I'd look up at the Capitol on these runs — the very place where the events in which I was immersed had taken place on January 6. I'd then go back to my office upstairs and spend hours getting ready for what was coming next.

Our team structure proved sufficiently flexible to accommodate new facts and directions. The best investigations are dynamic, presenting new information and areas of inquiry as they proceed. It is important in every investigation not to become wedded to a theory, a suspect, or a narrative, as doing so may make the investigators fail to appreciate the significance of a particular fact. They start with a hypothesis that provides direction, though they remain flexible enough to pursue new directions, alternate theories, and issues not originally contemplated. For this reason, it was important over the course of our work regarding January 6 that we not allow ourselves to rigidly adhere to our original structure. Each team ended up taking on issues that were not part of their original investigative plans. The Green Team, for example, began with issuing subpoenas to charter bus companies that brought people to DC on January 6 but ended up spending a lot of time evaluating the fundraising activities of Trump-controlled leadership PACs. The term *fake electors* did not appear in the initial investigative plan of the Gold Team, though it ended up being one of its most important areas of inquiry. While the color-coded teams did not change over the course of our investigation, our hypotheses evolved as new facts emerged.

In addition to trying to ensure efficiency in the daily work of the investigation, I spent a lot of time briefing members of the committee regarding our progress. The select committee was unlike other congressional committees in the involvement of the members. The work of the typical congressional committee is largely done by staff. Members of these committees are much like television anchors, reading questions drafted for them by staff who have gathered information and prepared the members for hearings. In contrast, the members of the select committee participated directly in the fact-gathering process, guiding and augmenting the work of the investigative staff. The committee met frequently, sometimes more than once per week during particularly busy stretches. I would typically give the members investigative updates during these meetings. Those reports would often stretch well beyond their scheduled time, given the members' interest in and familiarity with the daily work of the investigation. They asked detailed questions and made concrete suggestions. They were not passive observers in our work but rather active participants.

Members of the committee also frequently participated in interviews themselves. Rather than defer that work to staff, they would join interviews and ask specific questions. We facilitated their participation by establishing a link that allowed them to join electronically, sometimes popping in and out of an interview around the congressional schedule. If a member wanted to ask a question, they would simply turn on their camera, which we understood as a signal that they wanted to participate directly. Vice Chair Cheney was the most frequent participant. She often stayed for entire interviews and actively participated during the questioning. All of the members asked good questions and added value to the process.

The work of the committee was both grueling and satisfying. We worked at a rapid pace, given our tight time frame. During our busiest periods, we would conduct multiple interviews per day. I recall moving between conference rooms where various interviews were being conducted simultaneously and joining interviews via the members' electronic link while conducting other business. The team worked long hours, preparing late into the nights for interviews. We had very few administrative staff, which meant that lawyers and other investigators were standing at the copy machines preparing binders of exhibits right before their interviews began.

In addition to supervising the work of the investigative staff, I continued to directly participate in the fact-gathering process throughout the investigation. I conducted the interviews of many of the central witnesses and pored over documents in our database, particularly those marked as pertinent by other investigators. I spent hours negotiating with various witness' attorneys, discussing potential privilege claims, scope of proposed interviews, and document production issues. All of this allowed me to perform my reporting obligation to the members and other senior staff and maintain clarity on the overall themes and scope of our investigation. My work required constant back-and-forth from focusing on a specific witness and set of facts to a broader view of how all investigative information affected our overall understanding of the facts. It was challenging but important to maintain both a deep and a broad understanding of the most important issues we were developing.

When I began working on the investigation, I believed the 9/11 Commission report was the gold standard that we should attempt to emulate with our own final report. The work of the 9/11 Commission has been hailed by historians as credible, balanced, and impactful. It told the core story of what happened on that fateful day and traced both its causation and its aftermath. The commission's report led to specific changes designed to remedy the factors that informed our vulnerability to the terrorist attack, including enhanced coordination between national security and criminal investigators, the creation of the Department of Homeland Security to coordinate our national terrorism prevention strategy, and the provision of new authorities to allow investigators to monitor nefarious actors and gather intelligence regarding their activity. These reforms have fundamentally changed our approach to terrorism and are widely viewed as positive steps forward.

I came to realize, however, that had we approached the disclosure of our investigative findings like the 9/11 Commission and waited to announce our conclusions at the end of our investigation, we would not have been as successful in educating the American public as we aspired to be. America is different now from what it was when the 9/11 Commission issued its report. We are used to receiving information in shorter bursts, often visually. Our members understood this evolution and believed that we should begin announcing our core findings in hearings before we completed the investigation. They knew that we needed to convey our central findings sequentially over time in televised hearings, rather than in a single lengthy written volume issued at the end.

To prepare for the hearings, we began videotaping all of our interviews soon after we began the investigation. We insisted on videotape for every interview regardless of whether it was voluntary or compulsory, short or long, relatively significant or not. While we made a few exceptions to this rule as an accommodation to secure cooperation, we were able to capture not only information from witnesses but also facial expressions, gestures, and nonverbal communication. Clips from the videotaped interviews became staples of our subsequent hearings, as they allowed the viewing public to see the witnesses describe relevant events. Rather than a member of Congress quoting from an interview transcript, America could hear the witness herself describe a conversation or event, convey an opinion, or provide important context that was not evident from the written record.

The videotaped interviews became essential building blocks of the hearings presented by the select committee in the summer and fall of 2022. We ultimately held ten hearings, nine of which occurred with the assistance of a team of television producers hired to help prepare them. James Goldston, the former president of ABC News, led the production team. James brought a wry sense of humor, a knack for persuasion, and meticulous perfectionism to the select committee staff. He and the producers he hired worked with the lawyers and other professionals on the investigative team to script each hearing. The collaboration was quite successful. The lawyers would take a particular witness interview and identify the specific parts that provided the facts on which we relied in our ultimate findings. The producers would watch the videotaped interviews and evaluate that witness's demeanor, expressions, and manner of presenting those important facts. The clips played in each hearing emerged from this collaborative process.

The hearings were carefully scripted, with each word subject to factual review to ensure scrupulous accuracy. I pored over each script, ensuring that the draft language fairly characterized our evidence and would stand up to the scrutiny that would follow. The hearings were timed to the minute to accommodate the schedule dictated by television networks that showed them live. Before each one, the members held several practice sessions, homing in on the specific clips, visuals, and factual narratives that would be presented.

In contrast with typical congressional hearings, the members of the committee agreed to defer their speaking time and create more streamlined presentations. Rather than every member speaking for a designated period of time, only the chair, vice chair, and one or two designated members would speak at each meeting. Each member of the select committee was assigned a "chapter" of our findings to feature in a single hearing he or she would lead. Beyond the hearings for which they had assigned speaking roles, the members of Congress agreed to sit silently and observe, much like the rest of the audience. This allowed the hearings to be much more focused and predictable than the normal congressional proceeding.

It also enabled the members and staff to stage the hearings in ways that would be more interesting, engaging, and informative for the American public.

Hearing days were exciting. They felt much like days when I gave closing arguments in criminal cases as an AUSA. They took place in a room that felt majestic — the large, ornate Caucus Room in the Cannon House Office Building.[3] Each hearing represented the culmination of hours and hours of hard work and gave us a public stage on which to share the significant information we were developing. I sat behind the dais for each hearing and, for one of our final proceedings, at the dais next to Chairman Thompson. I watched the teleprompter scroll through the scripts we had crafted and our investigative interviews come to life on the screens set up in the hearing room. From my vantage point, I could monitor the audience's reaction to the facts we had developed. It felt much like we were letting everyone in on secrets we possessed, stories about which only we were aware.

We were encouraged by the attention the hearings got and the favorable reviews they received. The realization that millions of Americans watched our presentation of evidence was humbling. We were uncertain, though, as to whether the hearings and our findings were reaching audiences beyond those previously sympathetic to the story that the evidence we were discovering further developed regarding the president's responsibility for the attack. From our cocoon in Washington, it was hard to tell how the hearings were landing in various parts of the country, and what effect, if any, they were having on public opinion. When I returned home to Charlottesville on the weekends, I heard from friends that they were paying close attention to our work. But what about other parts of America, particularly in places that largely voted for the former president?

The hearings were reminders that the effort in which we were engaged was one of historical significance. We knew the whole country, if not the world, was watching. The integrity of the investigation was of utmost importance. Our investigation would create the definitive account of this seminal event in American history. That realization motivated me and the other investigators on a daily basis. It also reminded me of the need to keep our work focused on Chairman Thompson's direction in our first conversation — that we must proceed with integrity as we "follow[ed] the facts wherever they lead." Even as hard evidence of the former president's culpability in efforts to subvert democracy and the violence that ensued continued to mount, our focus remained on using our limited window of opportunity to determine and memorialize the truth.

We knew from the outset that we would produce a detailed report at the end of our investigation — a document that would include many more facts than those that could be presented during our scripted hearings. We ultimately issued an 845-page report detailing our core findings, describing our process, and making specific recommendations for change.

The report's main conclusion is rather straightforward — former president Trump and a group of co-conspirators engaged in an intentional, multipart plan to disrupt the joint session of Congress and prevent the transfer of authority. This plan was dependent on questionable legal theories regarding the power of various state and federal officials, which judges have now rejected. The president and others acting on his behalf used those theories to exert pressure on state officials, federal agencies, and Vice President Pence to take actions that they believed would violate their oaths of office. When those officials refused to yield to this pressure, the president turned to his loyal followers. He encouraged them to travel to Washington on January 6 and invited them to "fight like hell" to prevent the election from being "stolen" from him. He spoke to an angry crowd that morning and directed them to march on the Capitol, where he would join them during the joint session of Congress. They took his words seriously and stormed the Capitol on that day, briefly interrupting the joint session.

The report starts with a thorough description of what the committee found to be the primary impetus for the attack on the Capitol — the "Big Lie" that the 2020 election was infected with voter fraud and therefore "stolen" from President Trump. We detailed the exhaustive efforts undertaken shortly after the election by the FBI, the Department of Justice, and various state officials to investigate allegations of fraud, and the fact that none of those efforts produced any evidence of systemic fraud sufficient to undermine the result of the election in any state. We explained that the Trump campaign and Republican National Committee filed sixty-two lawsuits in state and federal courts around the country, all of which were dismissed but for a single procedural matter in Pennsylvania that did not affect the results in that state. We described how President Trump's campaign staff, his appointed attorney general and other DOJ officials, and numerous state elected officials patiently and persistently explained to him that they had found no evidence of voter fraud sufficient to undermine the outcome. In one particularly noteworthy exchange outlined in the report, the president told Acting Deputy Attorney General Richard Donoghue that he didn't care about actual fraud but rather wanted the DOJ to simply declare that it exists and "leave the rest to [the President] and Republicans in Congress."[4] The report juxtaposes the specific times when various officials told the president that various theories were not supported by evidence and the times he subsequently repeated them nonetheless. This "Big Lie" of election fraud motivated much of the subsequent conduct we identified in the report, including the attack on the Capitol itself.

The committee report describes how various individuals involved in President Trump's campaign and government were fired or marginalized when they told him that he had lost the election. Campaign manager Bill Stepien poignantly described the group of campaign professionals he led as "Team Normal" and contrasted them with a group of lawyers that took over after the election had been declared for President-elect Biden. This team of lawyers was led by Rudolph Giuliani, the former mayor of New York, who enlisted a number of other lawyers to assist in his effort to uncover fraud and prevent the transfer of power to President Biden. Attorney General William Barr, another self-declared member of Team Normal, repeatedly told President Trump that the claims he was making publicly about the election being stolen were "bullshit."[5] Barr described the Guiliani team that took over the president's legal strategy as a "clown car" and soon thereafter resigned.[6]

The report also details the pressure the president and his team of lawyers brought to bear upon Republican officeholders at all levels of government. President Trump called Republican local election officials in Michigan to suggest that they refuse to certify the results of the election in their jurisdiction. He contacted Republican state legislators in Arizona, including the Speaker of the Arizona House of Representatives, Rusty Bowers. As Bowers told the committee in a public hearing, President Trump asked him to "violate his oath of office" by calling a special session to investigate alleged voter fraud of which he had seen no evidence. Bowers testified that Mr. Giuliani actually admitted that the "clown car" of Trump lawyers had "a lot of theories, but not a lot of evidence."[7] In a taped conversation with President Trump, Georgia secretary of state Brad Raffensperger calmly rebutted each of the specific claims of election fraud raised by the president. Nonetheless, President Trump encouraged him to "find 11,380 votes," which was "all [he] need[ed]" to overturn the Georgia result. President Trump brought Pennsylvania officials to the White House to encourage them to pursue baseless allegations of fraud. These persistent efforts to pressure state officials did not work, as Bowers, Raffensperger, and others refused to yield to his demands.

The legal strategy that informed this pressure on state officials also led to the creation of "fake elector" certificates. State law in all fifty states provides that the certified electors must meet on December 14 and cast their votes for the winner of the popular vote, after which an official certificate is prepared, marked with an official seal of each state, and sent to Washington for opening on January 6. Despite this clear, consistent approach, the Trump campaign solicited Republicans in various contested states to meet on December 14 and cast their votes for President Trump despite the state's official declaration that President-elect Biden had won the election in those states. These fake elector certificates were then sent to Washington, where the campaign hoped they would be considered by the vice president and members of Congress at the certification session.

The architects of this legal strategy were Ken Chesebro and John Eastman, two conservative lawyers who became involved in the president's post-campaign legal efforts. Chesebro authored several memos regarding the fake elector plan, suggesting that these certificates were necessary to facilitate congressional consideration of what would be a "contested" election. Eastman similarly wrote about this strategy, specifically focusing on the power of the vice president to unilaterally reject certified slates of electors and either accept the fake elector certificates or send them back to the states to evaluate alleged voter fraud. When the select committee subpoenaed documents from Eastman's email account at Chapman University, Eastman asserted an attorney–client privilege objection to the production. We litigated this privilege issue, which led to a finding by US district judge David Carter that Eastman's proposal was "a coup in search of a legal theory."[8] He specifically found probable cause that there was evidence that Eastman, Trump, and others were engaged in criminal activity in the execution of this plan, which overcame the attorney–client privilege. We subsequently obtained important information regarding Eastman's communications about the vice president's authority, including communications in which Eastman admitted that his theory would likely lose 9–0 in the Supreme Court if litigated.

The report details the repeated instances in which President Trump pressured Vice President Pence to execute the strategy devised by Chesebro and Eastman and reject the certified results of the election in various states. Pence and his counsel consulted many others in his evaluation of this prospect, including former vice president Dan Quayle and conservative former court of appeals judge Michael Luttig. All of this advice and the consistent precedent of prior joint sessions led him to the conclusion that his authority at the joint session was fairly limited. He was duty-bound by the Constitution to accept only the elector certificates submitted by the official authority in each state. He could not, as the president urged, unilaterally reject those certificates and either accept the fake electors or send the issue back to the states for further review. Our report details how this pressure reached a crescendo on the morning of January 6, when the president called the vice president a "pussy" in a heated phone conversation from the Oval Office. The vice president repeatedly explained his reasoning to the president and ultimately stood firm in the face of the tremendous pressure exerted by Trump. Like Bowers, Barr, and Raffensperger, Pence elevated his oath to the Constitution over his political self-interest — an important theme of our report.

After Attorney General Barr resigned in late December 2020, the president encouraged the acting leadership at the DOJ to continue to investigate alleged voter fraud. When they reaffirmed Attorney General Barr's conclusions and rebutted the various theories of fraud that the president presented, President Trump contemplated personnel change at the DOJ that would have produced official conduct without basis in fact or law. The report sets forth the efforts of Jeffrey Clark, a lower-level DOJ official who was introduced to the president by Congressman Scott Perry. Mr. Clark drafted a letter to legislatures in various contested states, falsely suggesting that the department was engaged in the investigation of "credible allegations of voter fraud." The letter further suggested that the legislatures convene special sessions to investigate these baseless claims. The report describes a dramatic Oval Office meeting on January 3, 2021, at which the acting leadership of the Department of Justice and White House lawyers discouraged the president from appointing Mr. Clark, criticizing his credentials and suggesting that the entire appointed leadership of the department would resign in protest if he took the actions he proposed. The president ultimately relented, though his willingness to consider the misuse of the Department of Justice is indicative of a broad disregard for the evidence showing that he had been defeated in the election.

The president considered other, more radical proposals to disrupt the transfer of power, none of which had a basis in fact or law. Our report details a confrontational meeting that took place at the White House on Friday night, December 18, 2020, at which members of Team Normal pushed back a number of possible efforts to pursue unfounded allegations of voter fraud. At that meeting, Sidney Powell, Michael Flynn, and Patrick Byrne urged the president to invoke a national security provision designed to prevent foreign influence as authority to seize voting machines. Doing so would have been illegal, as there was no evidence of foreign interference in the 2020 election. The group also urged President Trump to appoint Ms. Powell as a special counsel to investigate alleged voter fraud. Again, there was no basis for such an appointment; the Department of Justice had thoroughly investigated and would continue to pursue any credible allegations of election fraud. The Team Normal voices in the room persuaded the president not to take these steps, which meant that the certification of his electoral defeat was closer than ever.

After this meeting concluded, the president turned to his final audience — his loyal followers who were listening to his repeated declarations of a stolen election. Early in the morning of December 19, 2020, the president issued a tweet that served as an emphatic invitation to come to Washington on the day on which the election was to be certified — January 6, 2021. "Big protest in DC on January 6th. Be there, will be wild!"[9] Our investigators spoke to many people who viewed this tweet as a rallying cry and began organizing to travel to Washington on January 6. Members of the Oath Keepers and the Proud Boys specifically identified the president's tweet as the instigation of their efforts to converge on the Capitol. Others similarly planned to come to Washington to oppose what they believed to be the certification of a "stolen" election.

Many of the people who viewed the December 19 tweet as the president's request that they come to Washington were sincerely convinced that the election had been stolen from him. They believed that the election was infected by widespread voter fraud that skewed the result toward President-elect Biden. They adopted the post-election rhetoric coming from President Trump and Mr. Giuliani as they repeated various allegations of fraud. Despite the lack of evidence that these theories were valid and the consistent efforts by the Department of Justice and others to rebut them, the president's persistent repetition of these false claims led to many of the protesters at the Capitol sincerely but falsely believing that the joint session would certify a fraudulent election.

Our investigation revealed substantial evidence that extremist groups and other specific individuals planned to resist the certification of the election with violence on January 6. We uncovered operational plans regarding the infiltration of congressional office buildings, maps of the tunnels surrounding the Capitol, and plans to stash weapons for potential use in an armed conflict at the Capitol. Law enforcement officials monitored this intelligence showing the risk of violence on January 6, though they did not sufficiently prepare to protect the Capitol complex.

Everyone in America witnessed the culmination of these methodical steps to prevent the certification of the election. On January 6, the president gave a speech at the Ellipse in which he repeated yet again many of the claims of voter fraud that his own administration and campaign had rebutted. He encouraged his followers to march to the Capitol and suggested that he would join them there. The crowd streamed toward the Capitol as the joint session began, and many surged past the bicycle rack barriers that had been established by the Capitol Police. As detailed in our hearings, the Proud Boys were the first to breach the perimeter, on a sidewalk surrounding the Peace Circle. They used the bicycle racks as weapons, pushing Officer Caroline Edwards and her fellow officers backward and rushed forward toward the Capitol.[10] The Proud Boys were the tip of the spear, creating an opening through which other rioters moved toward the Capitol.

For several hours, a large crowd of rioters rampaged through the Capitol. They broke into locked offices, destroyed property, and stole documents and other items. They chanted "Hang Mike Pence" and "Where's Nancy?," making clear their violent intent. One rioter was shot as she climbed through a broken window leading to the Speaker's Lobby immediately outside the House chamber. Others penetrated the Senate chamber, rifling through desks and sitting at the desk on the dais. The mob moved through the building relatively unimpeded for hours as law enforcement scrambled to assemble a reinforced response.

As the rioters overran the Capitol building, members of Congress were quickly evacuated, first the Senate, and then the House. But as the horde gathered at the door of the House chamber, some members were still inside; they donned gas masks and hid beneath desks and chairs. Capitol Police officers moved them out of the chamber into secure locations, bringing them dangerously close to the rioters who were moving through the building. The United States Secret Service evacuated Vice President Pence just minutes before the Senate chamber, where he had been presiding, was breached. As our hearings showed, a group of rioters came within approximately forty feet of the vice president during his movement to a secure location in a parking area beneath the building.

The select committee report includes a detailed account of the president's action and inaction during the attack on the Capitol. We developed evidence that, during the riot, President Trump ignored the advice of his close advisers, his daughter Ivanka, and numerous outside parties who encouraged him to take steps to quell the violence that he was aware was ongoing at the Capitol. As rioters surged toward the Senate chamber where Pence was presiding, the president issued a tweet alleging that his vice president "didn't have the courage to do what should have been done to protect our Country." This amplified the anger of the crowd and placed the vice president in greater danger. He subsequently issued two tweets that urged the crowd to "stay peaceful" and "remain peaceful." The committee developed evidence that the president "doesn't want to do anything" to discourage violence and that he "thinks [Vice President Pence] deserves it."[11] For more than three hours, the president watched the violence unfold on television and failed to act — a stunning dereliction of duty.

At 4:07 PM, the president finally and begrudgingly issued a video statement via Twitter in which he urged his followers to "go home in peace." He also told them he loved them and justified their actions as a reaction to the election that was "stolen from us." This tweet led many of his followers to leave the Capitol. A large number of law enforcement resources also arrived, which allowed authorities to clear the building. Congressional leaders of both parties were determined to resume the joint session, and they were able to safely reconvene at approximately 8:00 PM. President Trump, Mr. Giuliani, and others continued to encourage members of Congress to object to the certification. Those efforts were ultimately unsuccessful, as Congress resolved the objections and certified President-elect Biden as the winner of the 2020 election in the early-morning hours of January 7.

In its final report, the select committee made several criminal referrals to the Department of Justice. The committee believed that it had developed evidence that the president and others had violated several federal criminal statutes, including obstruction of an official proceeding in violation of 18 US Code §1512, conspiracy to defraud the United States in violation of 18 US Code §371, conspiracy to make a false statement in violation of §§ 1001 and 371, and incitement of insurrection in violation of 18 US Code §2383. To facilitate the department's review of these potential crimes, the committee delivered all of its evidence to the special counsel appointed to investigate the January 6 attack on the Capitol.

Like any summary of findings, the committee's final report does not include all the information we pursued or develop all the issues we explored. It consolidated the core narrative of January 6, though there is additional context that merits further exploration. To facilitate additional consideration of those issues, the committee made all of its interview transcripts (but for a handful of national security witnesses) publicly available at the conclusion of our investigation. We also published all documents cited in the report. The members of the committee wanted to ensure that the raw material that informed our findings was transparent, both to allow others to follow up on specific issues and to rebut allegations that we mischaracterized facts. This book is intended to be a step in that direction: the exploration of some of those broader contexts of January 6 that merit further evaluation.

The select committee expired at the end of the 117th Congress. On New Year's Eve, I left for a two-week trip to New Zealand, where my son was studying for a quarter during his junior year in college. Far from the daily grind of the investigation and the attention paid to the attack on the Capitol, I had a feeling of pride in the work we achieved. I believed we'd been true to Chairman Thompson's direction and conducted an investigation with integrity that would stand up to the scrutiny of history. I was also exhausted and had trouble adjusting to the sudden lack of any commitment. Over the course of the investigation, I was never able to fully detach from the work. I woke up to unread emails and text messages and was always thinking of what needed to be done. In New Zealand, I had nothing to do but explore — a weird and sudden change of pace.

I expected that the completion of the select committee investigation would lead me back to UVA. Unfortunately, I was not able to return to the university because the newly elected attorney general of Virginia, a fervent supporter of the former president, had replaced me as university counsel during my leave of absence. He gave me no reason for his termination of my at-will employment and refused the university's request that I be maintained in my role upon the completion of my leave. It seemed like pure politics, as my clients at the university were very supportive of my work and attempted to reverse the termination decision. The only plausible explanation for the decision was that as a fervent supporter of the former president he could not allow one of his subordinates to investigate the attack on the Capitol. I viewed my termination as unfair, particularly given the lack of any explanation or due process. I have come to accept it as an unfortunate manifestation of the polarized times in which we live.

SOCIAL MEDIA

I n the fall of 2020, Stephen Ayres was a thirty-nine-year-old carpenter living in southeastern Ohio, about midway between Pittsburgh and Cleveland. He was a supervisor at a cabinet company where he had worked for more than twenty years. In his own words, Ayres was "a family man, working man" at the time of the 2020 presidential election.[1] He was a supporter of President Trump, as he "just liked the way . . . [Trump] presented himself with . . . his views and beliefs."[2]

Ayres was surprised when President Trump lost to Joe Biden, so he started reading posts about the vote count on Facebook, Twitter, and other social media sites. He quickly found himself devouring content that falsely claimed the election had been infected with widespread fraud and was "stolen" from President Trump. His immersion in narratives online led him to Washington, DC, on January 6. As Ayres testified before the select committee, "I was on social media a lot back then, you know, I'm talking hours a day. I think it just got into my head and eventually, you know, got into my head and being in my head, oh, you know, it's not good, you know. The President is calling on us to come. You know, we need to get down there and, you know, show up basically."[3]

Ayres provides a good example of how social media is the primary source of information for an increasing number of Americans and how these platforms are used to organize large gatherings like the UTR and January 6 events. Most participants in both were motivated by information they obtained online. Their understanding of the issues that inspired the rallies and their expectations for them were forged through their social media feeds. Both investigations I led make clear that social media has become a powerful organizing vehicle for domestic violent extremists. I suspect that neither UTR nor the attack on the Capitol would have occurred but for the increasing popularity of this relatively new, largely unregulated channel of communication.

I was surprised by this revelation, first in Charlottesville and again in my investigation into January 6. I'm not a big consumer of social media in my personal life; far from it. I've had a Facebook account for many years but have never posted. My usage consists essentially of just keeping up with friends' lives now and then. I don't rely on social media at all for news curation. Similarly, I only begrudgingly created a Twitter account after release of the January 6 report to refute mischaracterizations of its conclusions about the role of law enforcement that day. So in 2017, and even still in 2021, while I had an intellectual understanding of the importance of social media in people's lives and its ability to radicalize them, I didn't appreciate just how persuasive and influential it can be for many. I lacked the information necessary to fully comprehend how it is designed to influence these users. To borrow a phrase from the tech world, social media's tendency to hook users, warp their perceptions, and manipulate their emotions is a feature, not a bug.

Social media platforms are businesses, run like any other private company. Their goal is to maximize profit by motivating users to join and use the service. They do this by using sophisticated algorithms that monitor user engagement and promote content that is more likely to draw and hold a user's interest. They also connect users to others with similar views through the creation of affinity groups or other vehicles that, like the algorithms, make it more likely that users will remain on the platforms. The social media companies do little to moderate content. They rarely remove or restrict posts, label false information, or prevent problematic material from being promoted via the algorithms. The companies have little incentive to do any of this because they enjoy immunity from defamation suits or other legal proceedings based on content created by users. Because of this, extremist organizations often use social media to coordinate, plan, recruit, and otherwise communicate. According to a 2018 study sponsored by the Department of Homeland Security, "social media played a role in the radicalization processes of nearly 90% of the extremists" in their dataset.[4] Or as terrorism expert Juliette Kayeem put it in a 2019 *Washington Post* op-ed, "White-supremacist terrorism has what amounts to a dating app online, putting like-minded individuals together both through mainstream social media platforms and more remote venues, such as 8chan, that exist to foster rage."[5]

Understanding this landscape is essential to a thorough accounting of the events of Charlottesville and January 6, and failing to appreciate social media's role will make future spasms of political violence more likely. In this chapter, I will explore the ways that people use social media to spread misinformation and ideology and to encourage individual participation on a tactical level. I'll delve into how social media platforms were used to promote and organize the events and disseminate information about the underlying issues that inspired them. I'll share what I've learned about the methods and technologies that social media platforms use to lure and maintain users. Finally, I'll consider the policy implications of these facts and evaluate possible regulatory responses.

(•)

Since its advent, white supremacists and other hate groups have used the internet as a medium for spreading their inaccurate and misguided views about history, including false theories of Holocaust denial and Jewish control of American institutions. KKK leaders Don Black and David Duke created the first racist hate website, Stormfront, in 1999. Over time, and as the internet has grown in complexity and social media platforms have proliferated, white supremacists have continued to promote online their noxious manifestos about racial superiority and belief that white people are somehow threatened by the advancement of people of color. This technology has allowed fringe perspectives to come out of the shadows, and their unfettered dissemination and snowballing attraction have provided a sense of legitimacy to those inclined to buy in to them. People who would be too timid to express certain views in public conversation were empowered by the anonymity of social media and encouraged by their linkage to others with similar views or did not even realize they were being insidiously exposed to increasingly radicalized material. As media scholar Aniko Bodroghkozy writes in *Making #Charlottesville: Media from Civil Rights to Unite the Right*, the alt-right around 2017 "displayed remarkable facility with new media tools," especially "mastering the art of creating and circulating edgy internet memes to lure disaffected young males into a sense of affinity with white supremacy through seemingly innocuous cartoon characters like Pepe the Frog." These groups also often use Greco-Roman culture and European history as a dog whistle to attract new followers, such as phrases like "Protect your Heritage" accompanying images like Michelangelo's *David*. As Bodroghkozy writes, "These signifiers of white European masculinity and heritage could seem almost benign to young web-surfers. But . . . [they] are about recruiting and about linking to other, often increasingly virulent, sites."[6]

In addition to spreading hateful ideology, white nationalist leaders used social media platforms in 2017 to organize the Unite the Right rally in Charlottesville. Jason Kessler and Richard Spencer solicited participation from groups and individuals via social media channels, promoting the UTR event and billing it as an opportunity for a constellation of organizations to come together in Charlottesville in the name of preserving the Civil War statues and, more broadly, white supremacy. White supremacist groups including the organizers and members of Vanguard America, Identity Evropa, the Traditionalist Worker Party, League of the South, and Anticom all used a social media platform called Discord to promote and organize the rally. The contents of the Discord forum were later leaked to anti-fascist news site Unicorn Riot and eventually introduced as evidence in a federal civil rights case against Kessler that found him and others liable for the UTR violence.

"Chat topics in the logs range from mundane topics such as food, water and restrooms to bloodthirsty calls for genocide and preparations for violence against antifascist counter-protesters," Unicorn Riot reported. "Audio recordings of meetings held over Discord voice chat reveal organizers' planning discussion leading up to Unite The Right. They discuss an operational document drafted by white supremacist organizer Elliott Kline (alias Eli Mosley) for the event . . ."[7] The Center for Investigative Reporting also analyzed ten weeks of social media communications among participants in the UTR rally, writing that it "paints the picture of a gradually coalescing movement well aware its actions would almost certainly trigger fierce and violent clashes with counter protesters." Messages show attendees noting that Ku Klux Klan members were welcome, but only if they did not "show up in full regalia," according to a user named "Kurt." The social media communications also included advice about how to build defensive shields and body armor that could also be used as weapons. Kessler himself wrote, "I recommend you bring picket signs, posts, shields and other self-defense implements which can be turned from a free speech tool to a self-defense weapon should things turn ugly."[8]

White supremacist groups also used more public platforms like Twitter, Facebook, and YouTube to recruit members. For example, members of the Rise Above Movement (RAM) used social media to attract people who might be drawn to their ideology and confrontational tactics. After a March 2017 rally in Huntington Beach, California, a few months before the UTR rally, RAM members posted news coverage and other videos and pictures of their members assaulting protesters in an effort "to recruit members to engage in violent confrontations at future events," in the words of the Department of Justice.[9] Between then and April, RAM members continued to post pictures and videos of their preparation for violence, including training in MMA street-fighting techniques, as well as white nationalist propaganda.

As a citizen living in Charlottesville, I had no idea that these posts were out there, or that people were coordinating and planning the event that would come to define my community. While I knew that a permit had been submitted that would lead to the convening of a Unite the Right rally, I expected something much the same as the July 8 KKK event — a small group of racists pathetically preaching their outdated and hateful views, surrounded by a much larger group of anti-racist counter-protesters. I was not following the amplification of these groups' ideology and the organizational activity that was unfolding on Discord and other platforms.

Thankfully, law enforcement leaders were monitoring the recruiting and organizing activity that took place on social media in the days before August 12. The report summarizing the findings of our team's independent review specifically cited this intelligence gathering as one of the few successes local authorities had achieved: "In the weeks before August 12, law enforcement received accurate information about possible attendance and the potential for violence at the Unite the Right rally from multiple sources. CPD investigators monitored social media and obtained useful information about the Unite the Right event from both its promoters and opponents."[10] We also noted that the use of open-source platforms to organize events like UTR provides a valuable opportunity for law enforcement agencies and facilitates more informed preparation: "The fact that we live in an electronically interconnected world creates real benefits for law enforcement decision makers. Both before and during the event, technology provided important information to those tasked with protecting public safety. We found no evidence of a 'fog of war' effect — the uncertainty of conditions that leads to uninformed decisions. To the contrary, we believe officers who planned for and reacted to these events were armed with reliable, accurate, and timely information," but didn't use that intelligence to properly plan for the event (a failure that will be discussed further in chapter 4).[11]

The January 6 attack on the US Capitol followed a similar pattern, with social media playing a central role in spreading misinformation about the 2020 election as well as organizing specific activities that took place on that day. Social media's outsized reach and influence began with the "Big Lie" of election fraud. On election night, President Trump claimed that the process had been tainted by fraud and declared victory, despite the fact that many states had more than enough outstanding votes to swing the outcome.[12] I remember watching the speech from my home in Charlottesville, surprised at the hubris of his premature declaration of victory.

Throughout the period between the election and January 6, the president repeated false claims of fraud over social media despite being told repeatedly that they were untrue. He tweeted these claims, which amplified the message and encouraged others to repeat them. He was aided and abetted by Rudolph Giuliani, Sidney Powell, and a number of lawyers and others who helped spread the lie despite the lack of evidence to support it. Other users posted this false information on Gab, Parler, Telegram, and TheDonald.win, as well as web forums like 4chan and 8kun, all of which explicitly allow content that is not permitted on mainstream platforms. These sites also don't require any kind of fact checking or labeling of false information, whereas the mainstream media I watched and read would report on the allegations with caveats, such as "meritless" or "without foundation."

Followers of President Trump were repeatedly served these incendiary and false posts. Stephen Ayres is a good example of how this pattern of disinformation led individuals to become radicalized, then manipulated by tactical planners to show up on January 6 and ultimately engage in violent behavior, even if they were not part of organized groups. Ayres was a voracious consumer of social media, as he testified during two transcribed interviews before the select committee. "I wasn't very political until I got on — well, social media I feel that's what really got me more political, more following politics and whatnot," he said. "Facebook, Instagram, Twitter . . . that whole outlook on there, you know, it's very easy. Everyone's expressing their views and opinions, and it gets very, you know, fired up . . . [U]p until the social media and stuff, I really didn't follow politics . . . all that well."[13] He was a follower of the president's own messages on Twitter as well as other conservative voices like Candace Owens, Charlie Kirk, and Ben Shapiro.[14] He trusted these sources much more than traditional media, such as television networks and newspapers. "I always strayed from the mainstream media because in my opinion they're going too far left, too far right," he said.[15]

Mr. Ayres was surprised when the mainstream media declared that President Trump had lost the 2020 election. He turned to social media and the voices he trusted and began reading about allegations of election fraud. These sources claimed that the election was infected with illegitimate ballots and manipulated voting machines, which led to a fraudulent outcome supervised by corrupt election officials and a "rigged" system. As Mr. Ayres testified, "My entire social media [was] covered with this stuff . . . you know — you start believing it more . . . If you say it enough, it becomes the truth kind of thing."[16] I was honestly surprised by his testimony and had a deeper understanding afterward of just how someone could get turned around and be radicalized by social media.

President Trump and others used social media for much more than misinformation and radicalization. They used it for organization and to generate turnout for specific events on January 6. His December 19 tweet that read, in part, "Big protest in D.C. on January 6. Be there, will be wild!"[17] was just the beginning, but it "set in motion a chain of events that led directly to the attack on the U.S. Capitol," according to the select committee's final report.[18] As mentioned in the previous chapter, many people who had been following President Trump and his "Big Lie," including violent white nationalist and alt-right organizations, saw that tweet as a call to action.

Much like Richard Spencer and Jason Kessler in Charlottesville, leaders of alt-right groups used both encrypted and unencrypted social media channels to begin recruiting participation. Some of these folks had even been at the UTR protest in Charlottesville, including Nick Fuentes, a member of America First / the Groypers, who responded to Trump's tweet on December 19 by announcing, "I will return to Washington DC to rally for President Trump on January 6th!"[19] The Proud Boys and the Oath Keepers, two groups with significant differences, worked together via social media and Facebook Messenger to coordinate their approaches to January 6.[20]

Lucas Denney, a member of the militant group the Three Percenters, who later pleaded guilty and was sentenced to fifty-two months in prison, "repeatedly cited President Trump's tweet," in answer to why he rioted on January 6. "Trump himself is calling for a good protest in DC on January 6th. I'm not going to miss this one," he told a colleague, according to court documents. He was further excited by the news he heard spreading on social media about the president's involvement: "Rumour has it that he may march with us," he wrote on Facebook.[21] Russell Taylor, another

Three Percenter, sent the link to Trump's "will be wild" tweet to a group chat and wrote, "Who is going?"[22] Doug Jensen, a QAnon believer who was arrested for chasing a US Capitol Police officer on January 6, told FBI agents after his arrest that he'd only gone to DC because "Trump posted make sure you're there."[23] There are numerous other examples cited in the January 6 committee's report of other rioters who specifically came to Washington because of what they saw on social media, mainstream sites including Twitter and Facebook as well as Trump-supporting sites including Parler and TheDonald.win.

Tactical plans were also openly discussed on social media platforms. Users planned openly on TheDonald.win to construct a gallows on the grounds of the Capitol. On that and other platforms, people shared maps of the tunnels beneath the Capitol, discussed bringing zip ties to aid in capturing members of Congress, and debated various ways to conceal weapons.[24]

Many of these individuals were ultimately prosecuted for seditious conspiracy based on their communications regarding weapons, forced entry of the Capitol, and calls for violence.[25] "More people were convicted of seditious conspiracy in connection with the siege of the Capitol on January 6, 2021, than any other criminal event since the statute was enacted during the Civil War," wrote the Department of Justice.[26] One of them was Stewart Rhodes, the leader of the Oath Keepers, a loose affiliation of individuals who claimed to be protecting constitutional order by resisting "tyranny." Since 2009, Rhodes had been using social media and the internet to recruit members to his group, including through a blog he started for that purpose, according to the Southern Poverty Law Center.[27] On January 6, Rhodes organized a paramilitary response to the joint session of Congress, including gathering weapons across the river from the Capitol that could be deployed by the president if he invoked the Insurrection Act. Rhodes used both public and private social media to coordinate and recruit participants, according to the DOJ. That included Signal group chats, GoToMeeting (an online meeting site), the Oath Keepers' own website, and Zello. One of Rhodes's accomplices used Facebook messages to coordinate participants as well, writing, "You guys Gonna carry?" and "Ok we aren't either, we have a heavy QRF 10 Min out though," referring to a quick-reaction force. Rhodes and other Oath Keepers were convicted of seditious conspiracy on November 29, 2022, after a high-profile eight-week trial and later sentenced to eighteen years in prison, the longest sentence at the time for any January 6 rioter.[28]

Another key figure convicted of seditious conspiracy is Enrique Tarrio, the leader of white nationalist organization the "Proud Boys." After the 2020 election, Tarrio posted public messages on social media casting doubt on the results of the election and calling for violence. "The media constantly accuses us of wanting to start a civil war," he wrote, according to court documents from the case that would eventually find him guilty of seditious conspiracy. "Careful what the fuck you ask for we don't want to start one . . . but we sure as fuck finish one." Tarrio similarly called for an armed resistance to the transfer of power on January 6. "If Biden steals this election . . . we won't go quietly . . . I promise," he wrote. In internal messages, Tarrio was even put in charge of a "Marketing" team to promote the January 6 rally, a job he took seriously. On January 1, 2021, he posted on social media: "Let's bring this new year with one word in mind . . . Revolt." He continued to post up until the 6th.[29] He used social media to recruit about two hundred participants to march on the Capitol and then instead of marching on the Capitol himself, supervised them from afar, sending messages including "don't fucking leave" once marchers were inside.[30]

On May 4, 2023, a jury found Tarrio and three other co-defendants guilty of multiple felonies, including seditious conspiracy. "Today's sentencing demonstrates that those who attempted to undermine the workings of American democracy will be held criminally accountable," said FBI director Christopher Wray in a DOJ release in September 2023. "The FBI will always protect those who peacefully exercise their First Amendment rights. But we will never condone the actions of those who break our laws, and we will continue to work with federal prosecutors to ensure those perpetrators are held responsible."[31]

But while some people who were planning to march on the Capitol were affiliated with specific hate groups and alt-right organizations and were coordinating an attack, other Trump supporters simply wanted to back their candidate publicly. That included Stephen Ayres. In the days prior to January 6, Mr. Ayres heard about a "wild protest" that was scheduled to take place in Washington, DC. "I basically was just coming for the rally because, you know, the President was 'Hey, come down to D.C. Stop the Steal rally."[32] Fueled by a sincere but misguided belief that the election had been stolen and motivated by the invitation from his president, Ayers joined friends from Ohio for the trip.

Once he was in DC, social media informed Mr. Ayres's movements there as well. He attended the president's speech on the Ellipse and heard him encourage the audience to march to the Capitol. He followed the crowd as it moved along Pennsylvania Avenue. Along the way, he learned that Vice President Pence had distributed a statement that he was not going to reject the certified electors, as President Trump had suggested he had the power to do. Ayres was upset upon hearing this news, as it made the injustice of the "stolen" election more likely. He continued toward the Capitol with the crowd and ultimately entered the building. Mr. Ayres left when he heard that President Trump had asked the crowd to disperse by issuing a video statement on Twitter. As he explained to the select committee, "That's basically your President, you know, asking you, you know . . . Hey, chill out . . . I wish he would have done it, you know, 10 minutes after he seen what started and what was going on. But kind of following that . . . let's get out of here, which I wish it would have been done a little earlier, honestly."[33]

Ayres was later arrested for his actions on January 6. He pleaded guilty to a misdemeanor charge of disorderly or disruptive conduct in a restricted building or grounds, in violation of 18 US Code §1752(a)(2).[34] He received a sentence of two years of probation and one hundred hours of community service.[35] He has also changed his perspective on the 2020 election and no longer believes it was stolen from President Trump. He has stopped consuming information via social media, as he believes he was used as a pawn on January 6: "I just felt like, with the whole January 6th thing, the Capitol thing, I kind of felt like we were kind of — basically were kind of played on, you know, from — from the President telling us we need to march down there, we should march down there and, you know, show our support or disdain or whatever his words were, you know, that is one of the things that bothers me the most. Because I kind of feel like personally he used us as kind of — a pawn or chess piece."[36] As he testified at a select committee public hearing, "I felt like I had horse blinders on. I was locked in the whole time. Biggest thing for me is take the blinders off. Make sure you take the blinders off, before it's too late."[37]

It wasn't just Ayres. There were many others in the crowd on January 6 whose perspective and conduct were shaped by their social media feeds. In early 2020, Eric Barber was a city councilman in Parkersburg, the fourth largest city in West Virginia. A former Democrat, Barber says he was "radicalized" primarily by Facebook. "It really damaged me. And this is where I blame all of the problems we have as America," he told the select committee in a transcribed deposition.

"With social media, a lot of it was, like, hard right . . . I didn't follow politicians on social media before I got into office. So, eventually . . . I started following these different things on social media.

And within 12 to 18 months, I'm convinced we're in a cultural war for the soul of our country. And I just fed into what I was already kind of predisposed to believe. And the more I consumed it, the more I engaged it, the more I was involved with it, as far as the more conservative component. The more I became angry and bitter and concerned and thinking that we're in a cultural fight. And if we don't — if our side don't win, it's going to be over for America. It was all born on social media."

In the lead-up to January 6, Barber was fed a steady diet of January 6 advertising. He pointed to one Facebook post in particular, showing Trump's back to the camera with a huge crowd, "and at the bottom it was kind of like a meme . . . and it said 'it would be wild.'" Based on his social media radicalization, he decided to attend and contribute to his social media community by livestreaming part of the event. "I expected . . . to go seek out a voting pack of White moderate conservatives like me," he said. "But that's not what happened. Somehow when I showed up to the Capitol, there was a full-blown riot. I didn't realize it was a riot until later. I mean, I had to get really close before I discovered like, oh this isn't normal." Once he was inside the Capitol building, his phone died, so he pocketed a phone charger from an abandoned C-SPAN station and took selfies. Then he went home.

Almost immediately, Barber said he regretted participating. "My immediate judgment was we were wrong, and we shouldn't have done it," he told the committee. "It shouldn't have happened, and it was wrong . . . It's not something I'm proud of. I'm concerned about how my family is going to judge me and my young daughters in the future when . . . they read about it in history books." Barber later pleaded guilty to charges of theft and unlawful demonstration in the Capitol.

Barber told the committee that by the time of his interview, in March 2022, he was "in recovery" from his social media radicalization, which was actually helped by the fact that Facebook deleted his profile after his participation in the riot. "Well they did me a favor, even though it bothered me. But when I opened up a new Facebook, I don't follow any type of conservative craziness," he told the committee. "I'm trying to revert back to where I was before I got into politics. So I can't say I completely don't care anymore, but my level of engagement has drastically been reduced."[38]

A similar story is found in the case of forty-four-year-old Daniel Herendeen, who was a construction worker with his own epoxy floor business before January 6. He told the committee that he was not interested in politics until Trump ran for the presidency ahead of 2016, at which point he mostly got his news from Facebook. "I was engaged the whole time through Facebook basically. And it seemed like all the same people on Facebook were engaged in the same thing around the same time," he said. He relied on the posts that Facebook's algorithm chose for him on his news feed, which he now points to as part of how he was radicalized. "Now that I look back at it, it was just — I was getting one-sided feeds the whole time, you know." That continued through the November 2020 reelection campaign, at which point he became convinced that the election was stolen from President Trump, "and all these coincidences happened at all these main cities at the same time, water main breaks, postal deliveries all around the same time. They just put stuff out there, make it — I don't know if it's true or not, but it made it very convincible that the election was stolen." He didn't use Twitter, but saw Trump's "will be wild" tweet reposted on Facebook and, with some friends, decided to attend the January 6 protest. Worried about violence between protesters and Antifa, a common subject of his Facebook feed, he packed bear spray and a bulletproof vest for DC. He also bought knives but then learned they were illegal in DC and left them behind.

Herendeen ended up marching to the Capitol and as part of the surge of protesters, entering the building for about fifteen minutes. He told the committee he left so quickly because there were too many people and he heard folks were being violent and damaging property, which he said he didn't want to be a part of, but he ended up facing charges anyway. "I feel a little betrayed, a little abandoned, a little frustrated" toward President Trump and the US government, he told the committee. "It was a ride I didn't like when I got off it."[39]

The Capitol rioter who was shot and killed, Ashli Babbitt, also seemed to be radicalized on social media. She was a fourteen-year veteran of the US Air Force and had voted for Barack Obama. But in October 2016, she posted "#Love" next to Trump's name "in the first of more than 8,000 tweets," Jeff Sharlet writes in *The Undertow: Scenes from a Slow Civil War*.[40] She came to believe that the 2020 election was stolen and that she should fight for him. She did, and ended up dead.

((•))

These cases reveal a pattern of access to often false information that is an essential context of UTR and January 6. Social media outlets allow users to distribute and amplify misinformation, identify others who share their views, and organize activity that erupts into violence. The way these platforms operate and the lack of content moderation create real danger.

An increasingly large share of the population only accesses mainstream media through links in their feeds on social media. Rather than reading their hometown newspaper or watching the evening news, more and more Americans only see those sources of information if items produced by them appear on their curated social media feeds. According to a Pew Research Center report published in 2023, "Today, half of U.S. adults get news at least sometimes from social media."[41] That includes Facebook, Twitter, and other social media sites. If those platforms promote a link to an article in the *Washington Post* or a story on NBC News, they will receive that information. But if not, those traditional sources of news are invisible to them. The social media platforms are screeners of information, filtering the news that reaches users based on their own viewing histories so they are most likely to see items that bolster their passionate engagement, usually in negative ways, eliciting anger, disgust, fear, and outrage.

The effect of this narrowing and amplification of interests is supercharged by the fact that social media companies cannot be held accountable under current laws for information that is transmitted through their platforms. Traditional media outlets are governed by a set of legal standards and traditions designed to promote accuracy. The common law tort of libel, for example, provides a remedy to individuals who are damaged by false statements about them that are published. Newspapers are exposed to civil liability for libel if they intentionally or negligently publish false information about a named individual or organization. If the false information involves a matter of public concern or involves a public figure, the plaintiff must show "actual malice" to recover damages for libel.

The term *actual malice* comes from the landmark Supreme Court case *New York Times Company v. Sullivan* in which Justice William J. Brennan Jr. wrote in a unanimous opinion for the court that the target of the allegedly libelous statements must prove the person making them either knew they were false or had a reckless disregard for the truth. *Malice* in this context doesn't actually refer to malicious intent but rather knowledge or gross recklessness.[42] As explained by Cornell Law School's Legal Information Institute, "The Court reasoned that speech related to matters of public concern is at the heart of the protections guaranteed by the First Amendment and outweighs the State's interest in compensating individuals for damage to their reputations. This 'actual malice' test created a national judicial standard for whether speech qualifies as libel."[43] These common-law standards are well established, honed by courts around the country for many years in other cases.[44]

Given their legal exposure, news outlets pay close attention to libel and have created large institutional mechanisms to ensure the accuracy of the information they publish. Lawyers for these organizations pore over specific language in news content to ensure that it is legally defensible. Watchdog organizations like FactCheck.org, Opensource, and PolitiFact monitor the veracity of news content and flag information that is unverified or inaccurate.

Failure to adhere to the *New York Times v. Sullivan* standard has tremendous legal and reputational consequences. Dominion Voting Systems sued Fox News when some network commentators promoted the baseless theory that Dominion machines had been manipulated during the 2020 election. Evidence produced in discovery during that case demonstrated that Fox hosts repeated false allegations that Dominion voting machines were penetrated by foreign adversaries and skewed election results. Text messages revealed that Fox hosts knew this information was false and repeated it nonetheless. The case settled with Fox agreeing to pay $787 million in damages to Dominion — an outcome that demonstrates the consequences of failing to police content.[45]

In addition to legal exposure, news organizations suffer reputational damage when they recklessly publish false content. Consumer trust in their adherence to standards of journalistic integrity is essential to maintaining their influence and market share. Fox News's reputation was damaged by the Dominion settlement, resulting in a decline in viewership. "A survey conducted by Maru Group for Variety Intelligence Platform found that 21 percent of Fox News viewers over 18 trust Fox News less after the revelations . . ." reported the Hill.[46] When outlets discover that they've erred in a specific story, they often publish a correction or retraction to ensure accuracy. Given the competition in the media marketplace, an outlet's reputation for accuracy is crucial.

Social media sites are not governed by these legal or reputational standards. It's established in 47 US Code §230 that "no provider or user of an interactive computer service shall be treated as the publisher or speaker of any information provided by another information content provider." This clause of the Communications Decency Act of 1996 affords social media platforms legal protection from libel suits based on information posted by users. "Courts have interpreted Section 230 to foreclose a wide variety of lawsuits and to preempt laws that would make providers and users liable for third-party content."[47] Section 230 reflects a congressional determination that, unlike content generators such as traditional newspapers or television networks, social media platforms are not publishers; their users generate the content and publish it on the platforms. Section 230 itself provides that "the Internet and other interactive computer services offer a forum for a true diversity of political discourse, unique opportunities for cultural development, and myriad avenues for intellectual activity . . . The Internet and other interactive computer services have flourished, to the benefit of all Americans, with a minimum of government regulation."[48]

Without a legal or reputational requirement to ensure accuracy, social media platforms are free to highlight and promote false information in their incessant efforts to heighten user engagement. The primary goal of Facebook is to lure users to the platform and keep them there for as long as possible. Ensuring the accuracy of information, ensuring balance in the perspectives expressed, and moderating content in any way are not part of the equation. Facebook founder Mark Zuckerberg has often called for his platform to be considered a free speech zone where users are able to post content regardless of accuracy. In an oft-cited 2019 speech at Georgetown University, Zuckerberg oversimplified the issues at play: "Will we continue fighting to give more people a voice to be heard, or will we pull back from free expression?" His comments suggest that a determination of permissible content on Facebook is a binary decision — free speech versus censorship. In reality, Facebook's own community standards show that content moderation is much more nuanced, requiring the consideration of context. Furthermore, Zuckerberg demonstrated a misunderstanding of the *New York Times v. Sullivan* decision when he said, "We didn't get the broad free speech protections we have now until the 1960s, when the Supreme Court ruled in opinions like *New York Times vs Sullivan* that you can criticize public figures as long as you're not doing so with actual malice, even if what you're saying is false."

The primary way in which Facebook and other platforms pursue user engagement is through the use of sophisticated algorithms. The platforms use artificial intelligence programs to closely monitor how users engage with particular content. These programs keep track of what users read, open, retweet, like, or disseminate to others. That data is used to construct a user's feed: content that is prioritized, highlighted, or otherwise flagged for that user's attention. The result is a curated trail of content that reflects a user's tastes, based on their historical use of the platform. If a user has consumed information about a particular sports team or a vacation destination, they will begin seeing more and more information about that team or that location when they return to the social media site.[49] The connection between their historical use and the information sent to them by the platform is more likely to keep them on the platform. The more time people spend on these platforms, the more they can entice subscribers, sell advertising, attract commercial users, and make money.

The algorithms that monitor user engagement and promote content do not just mirror that user's interests. They actually promote content that is increasingly provocative over time. The algorithms take the core interest of users and build upon it with content that is incendiary, outlandish, and more and more likely to grab and hold a user's attention. The use of increasingly provocative content is necessary to hold user interest, as data suggests we are more inclined to engage with content that enhances rather than maintains our understanding of an issue. A user's interest in a sports team, for example, must do more than restate basic facts about that team's competitive success. To hold their interest, the algorithm brings them content about dramatic highlights from years past; predictions about future drafts, trades, and competitions; and information about past, current, and future players and coaches. In other words, the content must be dynamic and aspirational to hold an interest, not simply a repetition of known facts.

The business model imperative of using provocative content to promote user engagement has grave consequences for the accuracy of information shared on these platforms. Misinformation proliferates, in part because it's stickier. In 2019, Facebook conducted an internal study that demonstrated how quickly its algorithm disseminates misinformation. The study created a fake profile of a housewife in North Carolina, given a fake name of Carol, who was a Trump supporter and interested in content about politics. This hypothetical user began receiving information about QAnon, election fraud, and other plainly false content within just a week of joining Facebook.[50] Within three weeks, the researcher in charge of the project wrote that Carol's feed "became a constant flow of misleading, polarizing, and low-quality content."[51] This research was meant to stay internal, but in late 2021 a thirty-seven-year-old product manager named Frances Haugen leaked the documents along with a cache of tens of thousands of pages as a whistleblower.

"The thing I saw at Facebook over and over again was there were conflicts of interest between what was good for the public and what was good for Facebook. And Facebook, over and over again, chose to optimize for its own interests, like making more money," Haugen said on *60 Minutes* after she revealed her identity.[52] She pointed specifically to the algorithm that decides what content to show users as an enormous part of the problem. "And one of the consequences of how Facebook is picking out that content today is it is — optimizing for content that gets engagement, or reaction. But its own research is showing that content that is hateful, that is divisive, that is polarizing, it's easier to inspire people to anger than it is to other emotions," she said. Or, put even more simply, "Facebook has realized that if they change the algorithm to be safer, people will spend less time on the site, they'll click on less ads, they'll make less money."

The use of these algorithms is what led Stephen Ayres to misinformation about the "stolen" 2020 election. What began with support for President Trump manifested into a consistent stream of false information about voting machines that had been tampered with, dead people voting, and ballots being counted multiple times in particular Democratic-led jurisdictions. The more he read about election fraud, the more content on that subject was pushed to him via the algorithms of the platforms that were his exclusive sources of information. Ayres credited this information, particularly when he heard it repeated by President Trump.

In contrast with Fox News and other old-guard media outlets, Facebook, Twitter, and other social media companies have no legal or reputational impediment to the proliferation of misinformation. The protection of Section 230 allows these platforms to promote misinformation within their algorithms without risk of libel or other litigation. They do not lose users or suffer any business consequences by promoting false information. To the contrary, the promotion of false information via algorithms actually maintains the interest of users and increases popularity of the platforms.

Another key way that social media platforms promote user engagement is through the use of affinity groups to link people with similar interests. Stephen Ayres is, again, an instructive example. Because of Ayres's interest in election fraud, he was invited to join various groups of other users on Facebook who shared that interest. Within this election fraud affinity group, users promoted additional content falsely suggesting that the election had been stolen. Ayres reviewed and shared this false information, which both reinforced his belief in election fraud and strengthened his loyalty to Facebook. Daniel Herendeen similarly became indoctrinated by Facebook content posted by these groups without even officially joining any Facebook groups. He'd still see the public group posts on his news feed, and as he told us, "I was getting one-sided feeds the whole time."[53]

Affinity groups were also at play in the run-up to the Charlottesville riot in 2017, recruiting new members to come and march. As previously discussed, the Rise Above Movement (RAM) was one such group. They frequently posted videos of previous assaults, like those at Berkeley, to attract new members who would find them on social media, which became their forum of choice to present outlandish, racist perspectives. Readers drawn to this content connected with RAM members online and in person, creating an affinity group of fighters motivated by racism. A ProPublica investigation into RAM found that members consistently "espouse blatantly anti-Semitic and racist views" on their social media accounts, especially Facebook. Records show members posting anti-Black rhetoric, including suggestions that "African Americans are 'shit' and that former President Obama is a leech; and to cheer the fatal shooting of a black man," according to ProPublica, and extensive anti-Semitic postings as well. ProPublica found that "skillful use of social media and the broader internet has allowed some of these organizations to metastasize quickly into formidable operations." The report found specifically that many of the marchers in Charlottesville in 2017 were "fresh converts to white supremacist organizing, young people attracted to nativist and anti-Muslim ideas circulated on social media by leaders of the so-called alt-right, the newest branch of the white power movement."[54]

Many of these ad hoc groups became more formalized on Facebook through the site's Groups and Events function — namely, there was an official Facebook "Event" for the Unite the Right rally. This public group allowed users to invite their friends and spread logistical and organizational information. According to an investigation from the Tech Transparency Project (TTP), Facebook allowed this official group to remain on their platform, despite specifically adding "organized hate groups" to the "Dangerous Organizations" section of its community standards in July of that year.[55] The Southern Poverty Law Center told the *Guardian* that months before Unite the Right, they provided a spreadsheet with links to more than two hundred Facebook pages and groups tied to American hate organizations, but when they checked back with Facebook in July 2017, the "vast majority" of the pages and groups "remained live."[56] The official UTR event page was only finally removed one day before the rally, much too late.[57] And despite this failure, and promises from Facebook that clamping down on such Groups and Events was a priority, these groups still proliferate. According to a 2020 investigation from TTP, "Dozens of white supremacist groups are [still] operating freely on Facebook, allowing them to spread their message and recruit new members."[58]

Affinity groups such as these operate as echo chambers, reinforcing the beliefs of members. The algorithms continue to push provocative content to the individuals within these groups, which is then reinforced through dissemination to other members. These electronic assemblies of like-minded individuals are like rocket fuel to the AI-driven algorithms, enhancing the ultimate influence of the misinformation that proliferates.

The final piece of the social media landscape that allows misinformation to proliferate is the lack of content moderation by the platforms. Some social media sites used by rioters at the Capitol explicitly disclaim any content moderation. Platforms like Discord, Gab, and TheDonald.win make clear that they allow information to be posted without limitation. Parler similarly claimed to be a "free speech site" and did not restrict content, though the platform did share information suggesting the potential for violence at the Capitol with the FBI.[59]

Mainstream social platforms like Facebook, X, Instagram, and YouTube do have content moderation policies, though they are inconsistently applied and enforced. The Facebook community standards set forth the rules that govern the platform's policing of particular content. They provide that Facebook content moderators will remove user posts that contain "nudity or other sexually suggestive content, hate speech, credible threats or direct attacks on an individual or group, content that contains self-harm or excessive violence, fake or impostor profiles, or spam."[60] However, the content moderation process at Facebook, and other companies, is conducted by people, often foreign contract workers. Unlike AI-powered features that push content as if through a firehose, there are only so many posts humans can look at, and the work is dispiriting, even dangerous to mental health. Some of the individuals who moderate content and enforce the Facebook community standards report extreme mental anguish, with some describing thoughts of suicide.[61] As one contractor put it, "The despair and darkness of people will get to you."[62]

Furthermore, each website applies the content moderation process on a case-by-case or post-by-post basis, which can lead to contradictory decisions and a vast amount of content simply falling through the cracks. The Carnegie Endowment for International Peace and their Partnership for Countering Influence Operations recently studied the community standards of thirteen social media and messaging platforms including Facebook, Instagram, Gab, Reddit, and others. Their analysis found that "platform community standards largely avoid the umbrella terms most familiar to experts and the public, like 'disinformation,'" and instead focus on specific prohibitions like "coordinated inauthentic behavior" and "civic integrity," each based on their own definition of those terms. This report suggested that "start-up platforms may need help developing such standards," and "perhaps a consortium of companies and experts could develop a model document that anyone could use (or modify) for their own platforms, similar to the American Law Institute's Model Penal Code and Uniform Commercial Code."

Notably, the list of content specifically banned by these platforms does not include false information about election fraud, posts advocating white nationalism and the alleged inferiority of other races, or other content that fueled participation in the Unite the Right rally and the attack on the US Capitol on January 6. As Mark Zuckerberg said, Facebook is a free speech zone and is not legally responsible for restricting the speech of its users absent certain extreme examples as outlined in the community standards. Other platforms similarly allow the promulgation of false information by users and even promote inaccurate content through the algorithms designed to maintain user engagement. Incentives operate in precisely the opposite fashion to how they do for mainstream news organizations. Rather than discourage the publication of false information, they actively encourage it.

The select committee received direct testimony from former employees at Facebook and Twitter who explained the platforms' lack of content moderation. As the *Washington Post* put it, transcripts from these interviews "show the companies used relatively primitive technologies and amateurish techniques to watch for dangers and enforce their platforms' rules. They also show company officials quibbling among themselves over how to apply the rules to possible incitements to violence, even as the riot turned violent."[63] Anika Collier Navaroli was a senior member of Twitter's safety policy team. In a transcribed interview with the committee, Navaroli explained that she and others raised concerns about user content using words like "locked and loaded" and "1776" in advance of January 6, only to be told that such chatter was not clearly restricted by Twitter's policies. She pushed for a "coded incitement to violence" policy, though one was not finalized prior to January 6. Navaroli described how violent rhetoric overwhelmed Twitter's understaffed content moderators on January 6, resulting in users posting real-time information about violence on the platform with almost no intervention from Twitter. She also explained how Twitter applied a different standard to President Trump than to other users, given his substantial following on the platform and the company's desire to avoid criticism for political favoritism.[64] These inside accounts demonstrate the futility of the large social media platforms' efforts to enforce their own standards or otherwise prevent their use as a forum to plan and encourage violence.

((•))

While assessing the information landscape that motivated the violence in Charlottesville and at the Capitol is relatively straight-forward, consideration of possible remedies is much more complex. The obvious place to start is the possible repeal of Section 230. There are several bills pending before Congress that would repeal Section 230 and remove the protection it provides to "interactive computer services." Slate.com maintains a Section 230 Reform Hub to track the enormous number of legislative efforts to repeal and remove the provision. Bills are separated into categories, ranging from repealing Section 230 altogether to a focus on repealing or restricting Section 230 for a variety of specific topics, including child abuse, foreign interference, and generative AI.[65] These bills all have as their central feature the removal of immunity for social media platforms for the publication of user-generated content. The repeal of Section 230 would allow those harmed by misinformation posted on social media to sue Facebook, X, Instagram, TikTok, and other social media companies just as they can now sue the *New York Times*, NBC News, or other mainstream media outlets.

Without the protection of Section 230, the social media platforms would be forced to operate much like news outlets and more aggressively police content on their sites. They would likely remove or label content that has been determined to be false or inaccurate. While this would remove some of the incendiary hate speech and election misinformation that fueled the violence in Charlottesville and at the Capitol, it would likely also result in the platforms' restriction of other forms of speech otherwise protected by the First Amendment. Determinations of truth or falsity, fact or opinion, threats or advocacy are very subjective in many instances. Platforms would likely err on the side of restriction in making these judgment calls, which would result in the removal of a great deal of speech that the government could not restrain without violating the First Amendment.

Some examples illustrate the dangers of the potentially over-inclusive restriction of speech. If a user posts an invitation to a Defund the Police rally and expresses the view that the frequent shootings of unarmed Black men by police officers show that police officers are motivated by racism, some would argue that such content is threatening to police officers or incites violence at the noticed event. While such an interpretation would be inconsistent with the fact that the overwhelming number of Defund the Police and Black Lives Matter protests have been peaceful, it nonetheless could be viewed as incendiary and therefore restricted. Social media platforms on which this content is posted would be forced to navigate these difficult issues and make decisions fraught with danger regardless of outcome. To protect themselves from liability, the platforms may choose to restrict any content that could conceivably lead to violence or threaten individual users. Their screening of content containing controversial views would arguably deprive users of information that could constructively help shape their discussion and understanding of contentious issues.

Proponents of Section 230 cite concern for an overinclusive response in their support of maintaining the protection provided by the statute. The ACLU is a strong supporter of Section 230 and writes that "the internet as we know it would be a very different place . . . without this protection." In other words, "Section 230 promotes free speech by removing strong incentives for platforms to limit what we can say and do online."[66] The conflicting views on this issue have stalled reform efforts in Congress, where there is no current consensus on measures that would require platforms to more aggressively moderate content.

Short of repealing the legal protections the platforms enjoy today, Congress could require more transparency as a means of informing users how the information that reaches them is generated. For example, the FCC could require the public disclosure of the algorithms that are employed by social media platforms in exchange for their licensure. Since 2019, Senator John Thune has repeatedly proposed a bill called the Filter Bubble Transparency Act, which "would require large-scale internet platforms that collect data from more than 1 million users and gross more than $50 million per year to disclose algorithm use to consumers and allow users to view content that has not been curated as a result of a secret algorithm."[67] If users had access to the formula that is used to populate what they see on Facebook, X, or other platforms, they would be better informed about the sources of information they receive and could use that knowledge to make decisions about what to consume and/or credit. Of course, not every social media consumer has the requisite background to assess newly transparent and ever-changing algorithms — and realistically, even those that do, won't. Most consumers likely appreciate the promotion of content that reflects their interests and are not all that concerned with its veracity. It is difficult to determine how the range of possible responses to increased transparency would shake out. But greater public access to the currently opaque inner workings of content promotion algorithms would likely be beneficial in at least a couple of ways. Social media companies would likely up their game with respect to the technology they produce to monitor their own community standards if they knew savvy watchdogs would be reviewing and commenting on it. And the mere practice of casting sunlight on the toxic nature of the content pushed most aggressively and the echo chamber patterns of its dispersion could only be helpful. The surgeon general's warnings on cigarette packages and calorie counts on restaurant menus and food packaging have not eliminated smoking or obesity, but they have played positive roles.

To thwart the rapid promulgation of misinformation via the algorithms used by social media companies, some have proposed the elimination of "bots" or accounts not tied to identifiable users. Foreign governments have used bot accounts to amplify disinformation, including false theories of election fraud.[68] For example, "Russia widely spread contentious and often false narratives by using over 50,000 bots on Twitter alone to create profiles appearing to belong to everyday Americans," reports federally funded research organization CNA.[69] If platforms would more robustly screen accounts by requiring identifying information, they would reduce the ability of nefarious actors to disseminate manipulative information through false-front accounts. While there are no federal regulations about bots, a state-level law in California "makes it illegal to use a bot to knowingly mislead a person in California about an account's artificial identity in order to influence their vote or persuade them to participate in a commercial transaction," according to CNA. This could be a framework for federal legislation.

As with many pressing social problems, addressing the demand for a dangerous product is as important as restricting its supply. The demand for social media is voracious and not likely to diminish in the foreseeable future. Given how popular these platforms are, we should teach children and other users how to think critically about the information they receive. Transparency about the algorithms and affinity groups should be part of that education, to inform users about the contents of their feeds. We should go beyond simply explaining algorithms and more broadly teach and promote critical thinking. The diversity of options for the receipt of information creates a challenge to users that will only get more complex in years ahead. To meet that challenge, we should teach children to seek contrasting views and challenge their own perspectives. We should model constructive engagement in our discourse and encourage young people to disagree without moral judgment. Content in today's social media landscape will always include misinformation, increasingly so with rapid advancements in AI. As a result, we should arm our social media consumers to identify suspect information and sift what they read and credit. Demand-side solutions like this are both more realistic and ultimately more effective than repeal of Section 230 or other supply-side reforms.

CHAPTER FOUR

LAW ENFORCEMENT

L ike the use of social media to promote and organize the events, the law enforcement response to the Unite the Right rally in Charlottesville and the attack on the US Capitol on January 6 were strikingly similar. In both instances, law enforcement gathered ample intelligence that accurately predicted violence. Planners had a large array of interagency resources at their disposal, suffi- cient to prevent the violence suggested by the intelligence. None- theless, police agencies in Charlottesville and Washington, DC, failed to protect public safety. These events represent two examples of a dangerous pattern of law enforcement failures to adequately understand the threat of violence presented by largely white domestic violent extremist groups. Unless we accurately assess and learn from this phenomenon, we are doomed to repeat it.

I've worked with police officers for much of my career and have immense respect for what they do. When I was a child, my father was director of training and personnel for the New Haven Police Department in New Haven, Connecticut. I remember sitting in the back seat of our family car next to his binders of training mate- rials, including a summary of the Connecticut Penal Code. He left that position to serve as special assistant to the police commissioner in New York City, working closely with Chief Patrick Murphy. He followed Chief Murphy to Washington, DC, when he was named director of the Police Foundation, a nonprofit agency that provides grants to police organizations. My father served as an assistant director of the Police Foundation for several years, traveling to various cities to evaluate police departments and help them use their grant funds wisely. I recently discovered that my father authored a chapter of a 1978 book titled *The Future of Policing*. The chapter he contributed was called "The Future of Police Improvement." In it he wrote about the necessity of police agencies soliciting feedback from and responding to the communities in which they work.[1] While we never discussed these ideas, it is uncanny how much they mirror my own appreciation of the necessity of police–community communication as a condition of law enforcement effectiveness.

As I've mentioned before, I've spent much of my career as a federal prosecutor. The evidence I presented in court when I was an assistant US attorney in both DC and, later, Charlottesville was largely generated by police officers. Their investigations provided the raw material I used to build criminal cases. I've always believed that the most effective cases are the product of close coordination between prosecutors and investigators. My general rule as a prosecutor was that officers were primarily responsible for investigative steps (search warrants, controlled transactions, wiretaps, and other means of gathering evidence) while I was responsible for charging decisions, plea offers, and sentencing allocutions. I liked to have a voice in those investigative steps, but police officers executed them and it was their domain.

In 2009, I was fortunate enough to be nominated to serve as United States attorney for the Western District of Virginia by President Obama. I was confirmed by the US Senate and served in that position for more than five years. As US attorney, a large part of my job was establishing or maintaining relationships with state and local law enforcement. I traveled our large and diverse district, meeting with police chiefs, sheriffs, and commonwealths' attorneys. In each community I visited, I learned about the unique criminal justice challenges there and asked how federal resources could provide assistance in meeting those challenges. I also worked closely with the leaders of the FBI, ATF, DEA, and other federal law enforcement agencies in our district, setting priorities and building criminal cases.

All of this experience working with law enforcement professionals has reinforced my respect for the important work they do. I believe the vast majority of men and women drawn to police work are motivated by a sincere desire to serve their communities. In the context of their core function enforcing the law, we ask police officers to manage a wide array of social problems — domestic violence, substance abuse, mental health challenges, homelessness, and a range of systemic social problems. Officers generally follow the rules set forth by law and policy and strive to do the right thing in all situations. They work in stressful environments and often face skepticism or scorn from many people they encounter. Even in these fraught circumstances, most police officers exercise their vast discretion wisely and demonstrate good judgment.

Of course, not all police officers meet this standard. We've seen too many occasions when officers have used excessive force or otherwise abused their power. Repeated instances of police violence against unarmed Black men have contributed to a climate of distrust in many communities, distrust that affects both officers and heavily policed communities. In too many neighborhoods, police are seen as hostile interlopers rather than protectors. Officers too often adopt a warrior mentality rather than a guardian approach, which increases community resistance to their authority. As researchers wrote in a DOJ-funded exploration of the topic for the National Institute of Justice, "The guardian operates as part of the community, demonstrating empathy and employing procedural justice principles during interactions. The behavior of the warrior cop, on the other hand, leads to the perception of an occupying force, detached and separated from the community, missing opportunities to build trust and confidence based on positive interactions."[2] Community skepticism makes the job of the police officer more difficult and leads to more mistakes, only reinforcing the dynamic of distrust.

While I am critical of high-profile incidents of police abuse, I believe they are anomalous. The vast majority of police–citizen interactions do not lead to violence or other deprivations of civil rights. To the contrary, the vast majority of officers exercise their immense discretion with responsibility and integrity. When officers fall short of the high standard of professionalism required by their job, they negatively affect the reputation of all other officers. Individual mistakes tarnish the badge and make it harder for the majority of responsible officers to do their important work of protecting public safety. The biggest critics of officers who break the law are other officers, as they know that these incidents directly affect their own safety and ability to function. Responsible officers harshly, and in my view deservedly, judge the clear mistakes of their fellow officers.

I brought this level of respect for members of the law enforcement community and their challenging jobs to my work investigating the events in Charlottesville and at the Capitol. I approached each assignment with the expectation that police officers acted responsibly and worked in good faith to manage the difficult circumstances with which they were presented. Nonetheless, my confidence and trust in police were undermined by the consistent demonstrations of poor judgment, inadequate preparation, and faulty execution we identified in both Charlottesville and Washington, DC. I came away from the investigations harshly critical of the decisions of police leaders at both events who horribly mishandled admittedly challenging situations. The law enforcement planners who were tasked with protecting public safety failed to achieve that goal. They gathered ample intelligence about each event but did not operationalize that intelligence. They did not take advantage of the ample resources available to protect community safety. Their performance fell short of the high standard demanded of police agencies in mass demonstration events.

The mistakes we identified during our investigations of UTR and January 6 were made largely by command staff — the leaders tasked with preparing for the demonstration events and managing the police response in real time. Those mistakes did not extend to the line officers, who demonstrated the bravery and fortitude required to overcome the failures of their leadership. In Charlottesville, officers were frustrated by orders to remain behind bike racks as violence erupted and by their withdrawal from the barricades when the unlawful assembly was declared. At the Capitol, officers surged to areas where they witnessed violence and worked together to repel the advances of the rioters. Even without clear direction from an operations plan or on-scene command staff, they did what they believed needed to be done to protect the Capitol building and those inside.

There is perhaps no better illustration of the valor demonstrated by line officers in these events than US Capitol Police Officer Caroline Edwards, who was part of the USCP Civil Disturbance Unit. As she later testified in a public hearing of the select committee, Officer Edwards was initially stationed at the Peace Circle — a small traffic area at the end of Pennsylvania Avenue and the edge of the Capitol complex. She and four other officers were posted behind a row of bicycle racks at the Peace Circle when a group of Proud Boys breached the perimeter and rushed onto the Capitol grounds. The crowd surged forward, and "we started grappling over the bike racks," she testified. "I felt the bike rack come on top of my head and I was pushed backwards and my foot caught the stair behind me and I — my chin hit the handrail. And then I — at that point I had blacked out. But my — the back of my head clipped the concrete stairs behind me."[3]

Even after her serious head injury, Officer Edwards moved up to the west front of the Capitol to protect the building from rioters. She stood near fellow officer Brian Sicknick and a group of other officers holding back the growing surge of rioters pushing toward the building. Officer Edwards was then hit in the face with pepper spray, which forced her reluctant withdrawal inside the Capitol building, where she continued to try to repel the rioters' advance. She was eventually taken off the front line to receive medical attention for injuries that would keep her on desk duty for years after the riot.[4] Officer Edwards's bravery was not isolated. Many other officers similarly defended the Capitol in the face of violent assaults that directly threatened their safety. These line officers were put in horrible positions by their command staff, who bear the responsibility of the law enforcement failures common to Charlottesville and January 6.

((•))

While the police responses to the Unite the Right rally in Charlottesville and the January 6 attack on the Capitol had much in common, the agencies involved faced some distinct challenges unique to each situation. First, the UTR rally in Charlottesville was a permitted event, which allowed law enforcement and other planners to prepare. They had weeks to gather intelligence, interact with the permit holders and other community members, and prepare a plan designed to protect public safety and constitutionally protected speech. And yet, Charlottesville city officials devised a faulty operational plan, failed to coordinate with other agencies, and did not provide adequate information to shape community expectations.

Planners had no such advance warning before January 6. There was no permit and no engagement between law enforcement and participants. Although there was intelligence suggesting that some people planned to march to the Capitol, the number of participants and specific plans were hard to discern, and the Capitol Police had no official advance notice. January 6 was more of a moving target than Charlottesville. While the failure to create a secure perimeter was more understandable given the lack of planning, the consistent intelligence available prior to January 6 should have motivated the USCP to be more prepared for the worst-case scenario that ultimately unfolded.

The primary challenge for law enforcement at the UTR event was the potential for interpersonal violence among people with strongly divergent views. The UTR playbook called for provocation — doing and saying things designed to elicit a violent response and justifying violence in return. The anti-racist counter-protesters were diverse in their planned tactics but united in their desire to confront the racist speech that would take place at the Lee statue. Planners knew that these conflicting groups would intersect and had to find ways to keep them separated. Not only did they fail to achieve that goal, but their misguided plan and tactics actually thrust the conflicting groups toward each other — a recipe for disaster.

The threat at the Capitol wasn't interpersonal violence but rather violence directed at the joint session of Congress itself. The available intelligence indicated that Antifa and BLM groups that had clashed with Trump supporters at earlier events were not planning to attend the January 6 event. According to documents our committee collected, leaders of those groups told their followers to stay away from Washington on January 6.[5] The only public gatherings officially planned for that day were the president's speech on the Ellipse and other Stop the Steal rallies. And although intelligence did suggest possible attacks on the Capitol, the Capitol

Police did not devise a plan to repel that violence until the rioters had already overwhelmed them.

((•))

Before the Unite the Right rally in Charlottesville, police agencies gathered substantial evidence that showed that violence was not only possible but also likely. Similarly, multiple agencies obtained intelligence suggesting that people were planning to attack the Capitol in an effort to prevent certification of the election. Instead of preparing to meet the violence plainly predicted by the intelligence, police leaders in both instances planned to execute soft approaches more suited to peaceful demonstrations.

In Charlottesville "there was a wealth of accurate information to inform both planning for and response to these events," our report found.[6] Charlottesville Police Department intelligence efforts ahead of the UTR rally ran through the investigations unit. Each detective in the unit was assigned specific people and groups to research. Most individuals they tried to contact were unreachable, and the groups had no formal leadership structure. So detectives ended up focusing more on open-source information — including social media, internet posts, and news reports — for the information that would go into the intelligence reports they submitted to the CPD's command staff. The Virginia Fusion Center and the FBI also provided intelligence in writing and in verbal briefings suggesting that the event could and likely would turn violent.[7]

As mentioned previously, local progressive activists were also conducting their own similar open-source intelligence gathering, efforts that included infiltrating the private Discord server used to plan the event. They shared this information in what became known as the "Solidarity C'ville Dossier" with city council and law enforcement on July 17, 2017, in a publicized meeting. Their findings included a Facebook post by one militia member that said, "I can assure you there will be beatings at the August event" and that his men "will finish them all off," referring to Black Lives Matter activists, and a Daily Stormer post from a user named Extermina-judios (Exterminate Jews) calling for "some military guys there to crack skulls" of Antifa and [N-words].[8] As our report summarized, "the information gathered in advance made clear to CPD and VSP planners that this event was going to be well-attended and potentially violent . . . They could not have been reasonably surprised by what occurred on August 12."[9]

Despite numerous clear warnings of violence, police leaders devised an operational plan woefully inadequate to protect public safety at the UTR event. As set forth in detail in the Charlottesville report, the CPD operational strategy called for officers to mass behind bicycle rack barricades in five zones immediately around the park in which the UTR rally was scheduled to take place. Each zone had approximately twenty officers assigned to it — some from CPD and some from the Virginia State Police. The officers were all in regular summer police uniforms rather than riot gear. Their tactical equipment was stored some distance away, in vehicles and inside buildings. Several specialized assets and equipment — a CPD SWAT team with an armored vehicle and several VSP field force units equipped with full body armor, helmets, and shields — were positioned remotely and hidden from public view. There was to be no police presence along routes of ingress and egress toward the park. These areas were completely unmonitored.[10]

When altercations broke out well before the scheduled start time of the UTR rally, officers followed orders that called for them to allow the unrest "unless it was so serious that someone will get killed."[11] CPD chief Al Thomas watched the violence unfold from his perch in the command center and said, "Let them fight, it will make it easier to declare an unlawful assembly," according to his personal assistant, Emily Lantz.[12] An unlawful assembly declaration would provide the basis to clear the area before the event began. Instead of moving toward the interpersonal conflict in an effort to stop it, officers withdrew from the bicycle racks to obtain and don their riot gear.

Once the declaration of an unlawful assembly was made, it took officers more than an hour to actually begin dispersing the crowd. Given the plan's shortcomings, it took considerable time for CPD officers to access their riot gear and prepare to move the crowd and for the VSP field force units to arrive at the Lee statue. As the officers geared up, UTR adherents continued to brawl with anti-racist counter-protesters in the surrounding streets. And when officers finally began clearing the park, the poor execution of the dispersal of the park pushed the UTR attendees right into the waiting arms of the counter-protesters, resulting in more violence unimpeded by police.

Perhaps the biggest operational failure of law enforcement in Charlottesville was the failure to prevent vehicle access to the Downtown Mall, which resulted in the murder of Heather Heyer and dozens of serious injuries. In their encrypted chats on Discord, protesters had openly suggested using a vehicle as a weapon directed at counter-protesters. On July 18, for example, someone on a Discord group forum focused on the UTR event posted a photo of vehicles surrounded by crowds. Another user replied, claiming that in North Carolina "driving over protesters blocking roadways isn't an offense." The user then posted a meme showing a combine harvester that could be a "digestor" for multiple lanes of protesters, saying, "Sure would be nice."[13] While it is unclear if CPD or other officers had monitored this specific intelligence, the use of vehicles as weapons during mass demonstrations is a standard risk for which police should have prepared.

The only provision put in place to prevent vehicles from plowing into demonstrators was for a single officer to stand next to a small wooden barricade at Fourth and Market Streets, where vehicles typically cross the downtown pedestrian mall. CPD officer Tammy Shifflett was given that assignment, despite the fact that she was a school resource officer who did not typically work on patrol or carry a weapon. After the unlawful assembly was declared, Officer Shifflett feared for her own safety as crowds surged away from the park past her post on Market Street. Just steps from her location, a group of white supremacists beat DeAndre Harris with wooden clubs and poles. Officer Shifflett asked to be moved from the intersection, and CPD and command staff agreed to her request. That left the Fourth Street crossing completely unguarded, blocked only by the small sawhorse barricade. Less than two hours after Officer Shifflett's departure, James Fields drove his Dodge Challenger through that intersection into a large crowd of anti-racist counter-protesters.

When we confronted police planners in Charlottesville about the disconnect between the intelligence that suggested the likelihood of violence and the relatively passive operational plan to meet it, Captain Victor Mitchell of the Charlottesville Police Department, who was tasked with crafting the operational plan for the deployment of police assets, was remarkably candid. He told us that he approached the UTR event much as any other large gathering in Charlottesville. He likened the August 12 event to the annual Wertland Street Block Party, an informal social event organized by UVA students. Captain David Shifflett, the CPD ground commander at UTR, similarly compared preparations for August 12 to planning for previous events of a very different nature: speeches by world leaders like President Obama and the Dalai Lama. Captain Shifflett also admitted that neither he nor anyone else at CPD reached out to police officials in other communities where gatherings by some of the same racist organizations had descended into violence, such as Pikeville, Kentucky; Berkeley, California; or Portland, Oregon. Mitchell and Shifflett's candid admissions revealed that planners had looked at August 12 as a free speech event that called for relatively passive positioning of law enforcement assets.[14]

As our report explained in great detail, the law enforcement failures in Charlottesville eroded trust in police and local government, which remains a lasting legacy of the UTR event.

(•)

As in Charlottesville, law enforcement had ample warning of the violence that occurred at the Capitol on January 6. US Capitol Police monitored numerous open-source channels on which people articulated their expectations for the march to the Capitol. The final report of the select committee details the ample specific advance intelligence that was available to law enforcement. I will not restate that evidence here, other than to summarize its specificity regarding potential violence and the Capitol as the intended target.

Many people likened January 6 to the American Revolution, as they believed that the certification of President-elect Biden's election represented tyranny which must be resisted. In numerous postings, people declared their intent to bring weapons to the Capitol and to storm the building. They distributed maps of the tunnels beneath the Capitol complex. "If we occupy the capitol building," one Trump supporter posted, "there will be no vote." Another argued that the goal should be to "surround the enemy" and "create [a] perimeter" such that no one was allowed to leave until President Trump was "readmitted for another 4 years." This same user posted a diagram with arrows indicating where the "Capitol Access Tunnels" were located.

In advance of January 6, social media content included talk of kidnapping and executing members of Congress, with users writing that they needed to bring "handcuffs and zip ties to DC" so they could enact what they saw as "citizen's arrests." Others openly discussed hanging members of Congress rather than arresting them, arguing that "gallows are simpler and more cost effective, plus they're an American old west tradition too."[15]

The available intelligence clearly showed that this would not be a typical Trump rally but rather an organized effort to breach the Capitol building and prevent the transfer of power. As the final January 6 report summarized in the first appendix: "By the late afternoon of January 5, 2021, Capitol Police Assistant Chief for Intelligence Yogananda Pittman urged Capitol Police Chief Steven Sund to convene a 'brief call' to discuss 'a significant uptick in groups wanting to block perimeter access to the Capitol tomorrow starting as early as 0600 hours.'" Chief Sund remembered discussing those indications and the preparations Capitol Police already had "in place, and [that] everybody seemed fine with utilizing the resources we had." Chief Sund added that, by that time, he had already deployed "all the available resources."

Like the police in Charlottesville, the US Capitol Police used bicycle racks to mark a perimeter around the Capitol. They were not affixed to the ground and were vulnerable to being used as weapons against the police. USCP officers were positioned along the racks in numbers insufficient to repel the large crowds that overran the barricades. These barricades did not completely surround the Capitol complex — some areas weren't protected with the inadequate racks or guarded by officers at all. At the Peace Circle, Officer Edwards and four others stood along the bicycle racks as the Proud Boys easily pushed past them and surged toward the Capitol. There was no riot gear, no specialized units, no monitoring of routes of ingress or egress.[16] This plan would likely have been sufficient if protesters had respected the physical boundaries and exercised their free speech rights in a nonviolent way. It was woefully insufficient to repel violence.

USCP failed to pre-position any personnel from other agencies at the Capitol. Rather than utilize officers from the Metropolitan Police Department or other agencies, the Capitol Police alone staffed the perimeter. Even though the intelligence suggested the possibility of an attack on the Capitol, they failed to request that the DC National Guard be deployed in advance. Chief Sund testified that he asked that the National Guard be on standby on January 6, as he believed the USCP had sufficient assets alone to manage the crowd.[17]

As the crowd became violent at the Capitol, USCP did call for reinforcement. Hundreds of Metropolitan Police Department officers joined USCP in attempting to repel the angry mob approaching the Capitol. MPD officer Michael Fanone was on his way to an undercover narcotics purchase when he heard a distress call for reinforcements at the Capitol over his police radio. He put on his MPD uniform for the first time in ten years and drove to the Capitol, without any direction from MPD or USCP command staff. He soon joined a group of officers protecting a basement entrance, relieving officers who had been physically resisting a much larger crowd of rioters attempting to penetrate the building. The crowd pulled Officer Fanone into their midst, assaulting him with a Taser and beating him severely. "I was swarmed by a violent mob," he testified before our committee. "They ripped off my badge. They grabbed my radio. They seized the ammunition that was secured to my body. They began to beat me, with their fists and with what felt like hard metal objects. At one point I came face to face with an attacker who repeatedly lunged for me and attempted to remove my firearm. I heard chanting from some in the crowd, 'Get his gun' and 'Kill him with his own gun.' I was aware enough to recognize I was at risk of being stripped of, and killed with, my own firearm. I was electrocuted, again and again and again with a Taser. I'm sure I was screaming, but I don't think I could even hear my own voice." Officer Fanone lost consciousness and was ultimately pulled back behind police lines, badly injured.[18] His experience was not uncommon. At least 140 police officers were injured resisting the violence of the rioters in and around the Capitol building on January 6.[19] The Department of Justice has since said that this day was "likely the largest single-day, mass assault of law enforcement officers in our nation's history."[20]

The situation inside the Capitol building was chaotic and volatile. Officers were ultimately overwhelmed, unable to prevent rioters from streaming inside the building. Rioters roamed the halls and penetrated offices, destroying and defacing property and removing items as trophies. They chanted "Where's Nancy" and "Hang Mike Pence," looking for those and other elected officials whom they believed were complicit in the injustice of the "stolen" election. They penetrated the Senate chamber just moments after senators were evacuated by Capitol Police officers. An angry mob surged to the doors of the House chamber as members of Congress cowered inside, donning gas masks. At one point, rioters came within approximately forty feet of Vice President Pence as he was rushed to a loading dock beneath the Capitol building.[21]

Much like Captain Mitchell in Charlottesville, US Capitol Police chief Steven Sund expressed a false confidence in adequate preparation before January 6. In testimony before the select committee, Chief Sund explained that USCP "expected demonstrations" and "a large crowd . . . focused on the Capitol." He further said, "It was no different than I think what we had anticipated in the previous two rallies."[22] He also noted his own personal experience handling crowds in his previous job with the Metropolitan Police Department, saying, "In that role, I handled a lot of the major events, demonstrations in Washington, DC." Despite the clear intelligence suggesting violence, Chief Sund prepared for a peaceful demonstration with a large crowd. Like Captain Mitchell in Charlottesville, Chief Sund fundamentally miscalculated the amount of force that would be required to respond to the march at the Capitol.

These examples demonstrate that neither Charlottesville nor January 6 were intelligence failures. The disconnects between the intelligence and the operational plans are striking and represent colossal failures that connect UTR and January 6.

((•))

There are several reasons for these disconnects. First, the available intelligence was not adequately shared among the various agencies that were responsible for gathering information about the events. There was no comprehensive effort to consolidate the information gathered by numerous agencies and create a complete portrait of the threats. Such failures have been a recurring problem that afflicts law enforcement in America, which features a multitude of local and federal agencies working across a crazy quilt of jurisdictions.

The US Capitol Police was the agency primarily responsible for defending the Capitol before and on January 6. Its intelligence analysts monitored social media posts and open sources in an attempt to assess the risk of violence. Documents reviewed by the select committee show that they specifically predicted that the focus of the violence was the joint session rather than interpersonal violence among attendees. Tellingly, Chief Sund admitted in testimony before the select committee that he did not read these internal reports.[23]

Other agencies gathered similar intelligence warning of violence at the joint session. The Metropolitan Police Department, United States Secret Service, FBI, and other police agencies all possessed such intelligence. The FBI actually created a mechanism for internal sharing of tips and leads about the Capitol, labeling it CERTUNREST. They directed field offices to pass intelligence surrounding January 6 to this internal system, but this was an internal FBI process. The CERTUNREST tips were not put into a comprehensive report detailing the threat of violence or otherwise shared with other agencies before January 6. The Secret Service intelligence was similarly siloed and not passed along to USCP or other agencies. Agencies tasked with monitoring open-source channels for law enforcement gathered but failed to share information about the joint session. The DC Homeland Security office created internal reports explicitly warning that protesters were planning to occupy the Capitol, though they failed to pass those reports on to their federal counterparts.[24] Similarly, the Office of Intelligence and Analysis of the federal Department of Homeland Security monitored intelligence in advance of January 6 that predicted violence, though they failed to accurately record, consolidate, or share that information.[25]

Police agencies were similarly disconnected in their intelligence-gathering function in advance of the Unite the Right rally in Charlottesville. Even though they did not have a dedicated intelligence unit, Charlottesville Police detectives monitored open-source channels and gathered a large amount of information suggesting that violence was likely. The Virginia State Police similarly possessed such information, though they did not share it with CPD or other agencies. As with their operations plan, they hoarded that information and used it solely to inform their own independent approach to the event. The FBI received information about plans for UTR in advance of August 12 but did not provide it to CPD or others. The bureau was concerned that sharing their information would jeopardize sources within the white nationalist world. Despite its consistency and urgency, intelligence that accurately predicted violence in Charlottesville remained siloed and disconnected.

The failure to share information among agencies is a recurrent problem in American law enforcement. Despite persistent efforts, agencies have hoarded rather than shared information. The 9/11 Commission made this observation in their final report, noting that the wall between intelligence gathering and law enforcement needed to be lowered or removed. The 9/11 report specifically led to the creation of a new federal agency, the Department of Homeland Security (DHS), with information sharing as part of its mandate. DHS funding has enabled the creation of Fusion Centers in every state in the US. These entities gather intelligence about threats to public safety from federal, state, and local agencies and endeavor to aggregate it for participating agencies. Unfortunately, these centers are underfunded and inconsistently staffed. FBI field offices do not always participate in their local Fusion Centers, or else they share information selectively due to their concern for compromising sources.

The Office of Intelligence and Analysis (I&A) of DHS was designed to fulfill a similar information-sharing purpose at the national level. Rather than become a clearinghouse for comprehensive, accurate information about threats to public safety, however, I&A has been mired in politics. During the Trump administration, DHS leadership instructed I&A to focus on Black Lives Matter and other racial justice groups, which shifted resources away from monitoring the white nationalist groups that ultimately proved much more dangerous. "This political targeting was enabled by expansive intelligence authorities and a lack of meaningful checks on discretion," wrote the Brennan Center for Justice in an analysis of DHS on the occasion of its twentieth anniversary.[26]

The failure to aggregate intelligence is not a resource issue. We spend millions of dollars at all levels of government on personnel and processes to monitor open-source threat streams. Almost every police organization, from small local departments to massive federal agencies, monitors social media and other sources of information about people and events that threaten their respective areas of jurisdiction. Agencies have accurately shifted their intelligence-gathering capacity to new, electronic tools used by nefarious actors, while not abandoning old-fashioned methods like human sources.

Despite the resources devoted to intelligence gathering, police agencies still fail to work together to aggregate, assess, and share this treasure trove of information. Imagine a race car driver knowing about only one or a few of the other cars in a race. It'd be impossible for her to defend against a range of challengers that might come up behind or alongside her or to plan a way to overtake the lead position. American law enforcement agencies are like that driver. A lack of basic and readily available information renders them unaware of various nefarious actors and events that threaten public safety.

If law enforcement is to take full advantage of the resources they devote to intelligence gathering, they must find more effective ways of aggregating that intelligence across agencies. The federal government could lead this effort by designating a lead agency responsible for consolidating information about domestic threats and creating intelligence products for state and local partners. The Fusion Centers could serve this purpose, though only if the FBI and all relevant agencies agree to fully participate in their processes. DHS Intelligence and Analysis could be the central repository of real-time information about emerging threats to homeland security. I&A should be fully funded and depoliticized, two crucial qualifications that have been difficult to achieve since the creation of DHS. Law enforcement agencies at all levels need to change the culture of exclusivity that leads to turf battles, duplicative investigations, and disconnected enforcement activity. Absent these changes, American law enforcement will continue to be hamstrung by ineffectiveness and fall short of its potential to protect public safety.

((•))

Another reason for law enforcement's failure to operationalize intelligence in Charlottesville and for January 6 was deference to the First Amendment, which contributed to the failure to pursue leads derived from open sources. The FBI and other agencies placed undue restrictions on their use of information gathered from social media and other open forums due to concerns that investigative activity may chill free speech and association rights. In my view, these self-imposed restrictions are overly protective and severely hamper these agencies' abilities to prepare for events that raise serious potential for violence.

To ensure the uniform application of policy and protection of fundamental rights, the FBI has created a detailed list of internal rules and restrictions that govern the investigative activities of agents. The FBI's Domestic Investigations and Operations Guide, commonly called the DIOG, sets forth those rules. The DIOG provides that FBI agents must "ensure that all investigations and intelligence collection activities are conducted within constitutional and statutory parameters and that civil liberties and privacy are protected."[27] The DIOG provides that agents may "conduct no investigation based solely on the exercise of First Amendment rights (i.e., the free exercise of speech, religion, assembly, press, or petition)."[28] The DIOG goes on to say that information obtained from open sources like social media sites must be "specific and credible" regarding the possible violation of criminal law for the FBI to use or respond to it. If the information is deemed to meet this subjective standard, an agent may open a "preliminary assessment" and take investigative action such as recordation in an FBI database, surveillance of a subject, or a consensual interview. Absent that level of specific, credible information on violations of law, the FBI does nothing with such information.

A practical example illustrates the restrictive nature of these rules and how they disadvantage agencies in preparation for mass demonstration events. If an FBI agent monitors a user post on Facebook of a man holding an AR-15 machine gun with a caption suggesting that "January 6 is 1776. Be there, will be wild," that agent likely can do nothing with that information. It is clearly protected speech, as it does not directly threaten an identified individual or incite imminent violence. As a result, strict adherence to the DIOG prevents the agent from taking investigative action based on that Facebook post. She may not record that information and consolidate it with other intelligence in advance of January 6. She cannot monitor the postings, movements, or associations of the person who posted the photograph. She may not approach the person and inquire about the weapon, his plans to travel to Washington, or his intentions on January 6. Because this information was obtained via an open source and is protected by the First Amendment, agents are unable to use it in any meaningful way.

When asked at a congressional hearing after January 6 whether the FBI has the ability to monitor publicly available social media posts, Director Wray indicated that the answer was "complicated." He explained that FBI agents are "not allowed . . . to just sit and monitor publicly available social media and look at one person's posts just looking to see if maybe something would happen just in case. That we're not allowed to do."[29] Jennifer Moore, the FBI agent who supervised the intelligence branch of the Washington Field Office before January 6, made a similar point in testimony to the select committee. She used the example of the social media traffic about the tunnels under the Capitol building as an example.

> So we would brief, hey, our social media exploitation is seeing an increased talk of the tunnels around the Capitol. Are you seeing specific threats to the tunnels? No. So without that specificity, like, just talking about, like, hey, did you know there's a tunnel system under the Capitol. Hey, the tunnel is going on the east, the west, the north and south side. I can't action that . . . without it being very specific violence towards the tunnels, we can't take action or do that next step where we open it . . . and go out and try to interview that poster.[30]

She later summarized it this way: "They're not saying anything that's not First Amendment protected activity."[31]

The DIOG restrictions exist for a reason: They were formulated as a response to the FBI's historic violations of civil liberties. In the 1970s, the Church Committee of the United States Senate (named after the chairman, Senator Frank Church, a Democrat of Idaho) found that the FBI had improperly investigated civil rights leaders and anti-war protesters. The section of the committee's final report focusing solely on domestic surveillance, Book II, totals 404 scathing pages detailing the overreaches of the US government.[32] It describes how the FBI specifically targeted civil rights leaders, student activists, and others engaged in peaceful protest using the code name COINTELPRO. Agents improperly wiretapped, surveilled, and monitored Dr. Martin Luther King and others over the course of the COINTELPRO investigation. The bureau also used disinformation to stoke discord within civil rights and anti-war groups, attempting to disrupt their organizations and hamper their effectiveness. These tactics were illegal and exceeded the lawful authority of the FBI. The committee called the program "covert action designed to disrupt and discredit the activities of groups and individuals deemed a threat to the social order."[33]

While the historic excesses of the FBI are shameful and deserved the forceful response they prompted, the agency has arguably overcorrected and hamstrung its ability to respond to a shifting landscape of information sharing. The DIOG's restriction on taking any action based on open-source information unless it justifies the opening of a preliminary investigation is overly restrictive and hampers the FBI's ability to effectively prevent violence. Agents must be able to monitor and catalog protected speech if it suggests potential involvement in violence or other threats to public safety. They should aggregate that information and compare it with other intelligence regarding organizations and events. They should also be empowered to consider potential investigative steps based on that information. One person posting a picture of himself with an AR-15 and declaring his intention to travel to the Capitol is much less a public safety threat than fifty others doing the same. Agents should also be empowered to approach individuals based on their social media posts and conduct consensual interviews.

Allowing FBI agents to monitor and pursue open-source information in this fashion would not unduly infringe upon anyone's First or Fourth Amendment rights. The Supreme Court has made clear that the Fourth Amendment does not prevent the government from obtaining information from public sources, as the individuals sharing such information have no reasonable expectation of privacy. The court articulated this principle in the seminal case of *United States v. Katz*, which held that the placement of a listening device on the exterior of a telephone booth violated the Fourth Amendment.[34] In *Katz*, the court observed that "what a person knowingly exposes to the public, even in his own home or office, is not a subject of Fourth Amendment protection. But what he seeks to preserve as private, even in an area accessible to the public, may be constitutionally protected."[35] The court went on to hold that "the capacity to claim the protection of the Amendment depends not upon a property right in the invaded place but upon whether the area was one in which there was a reasonable expectation of freedom from governmental intrusion."[36] If someone posts information on a public site like Facebook, X, Instagram, or other platforms, he has no reasonable expectation that the information will be private and protected from governmental monitoring. The posting of material on social media is akin to utterance of that information on a public street. When people express their views, describe their experiences, or declare their intentions in a public fashion, they are explicitly inviting others to consume that information. Consistent with *Katz* and its progeny, law enforcement agents should have the unfettered right to consume and respond to that information just like any other person.

Katz and the cases that apply this principle demonstrate that the DIOG restrictions go beyond the requirements of law. Rather than using the clear standards of Fourth Amendment protection to govern investigative activity, the FBI exceeds those standards and handicaps agents' ability to gather useful information from open sources. The reason for this restrictive policy is the desire to avoid investigative steps that may have a chilling effect on free speech and association. The theory is that Americans may be less inclined to engage in protected speech or associate with others with similar views if their speech could draw law enforcement scrutiny. But the public's right to privacy and free speech must be balanced with the government's need for useful information. Both of these interests and policy goals are legitimate and should be factored into the rules that govern investigative activity by law enforcement.

I believe the DIOG's balancing of these fundamental rights goes too far to protect the possible impact on free speech and severely handicaps the agency's ability to understand and prepare to meet the myriad threats evident in open sources. Agents should be able to monitor, catalog, and aggregate open-source information. They should be able to conduct surveillance or consensual contacts with individuals whose protected speech suggests the potential for violence. Information shared on social media explicitly invites wide distribution. Accordingly, I do not believe governmental actors should be restricted from using that information to prepare to meet viable threats to public safety.

Today's information landscape has dramatically evolved since the DIOG was promulgated. Law enforcement must adjust its standards to fit new channels of information sharing and fully maximize their intelligence-gathering potential. Failure to do so will continue to hamstring the FBI and other agencies and unduly restrict their ability to prepare to meet the threat of violence at mass demonstration events.

((•))

The third and final reason for the consistent failure of law enforcement to anticipate and prepare for the evident threat of violence at extremist gatherings, including Charlottesville and January 6, is racial bias. The participants in the UTR rally and at the attack on the Capitol were largely white and perceived by law enforcement to be supporters of law enforcement. The relatively passive response to the advance intelligence suggesting the strong potential for violence at each event is strikingly different from the heavy-handed responses to the summer 2020 protests that followed the murder of George Floyd, in which many protesters of color were involved. These opposing attitudes demonstrate how race affects the assessment of danger and leads law enforcement agencies to underestimate the threat of violence from white men and overly estimate the potential for violence at demonstrations involving a significant presence from people of color. Failure to recognize and address this systemic dynamic will ensure that we continue to repeat it.

The Unite the Right rally organizers and attendees were almost exclusively white men. The organizing principle of the event was the advocacy of a white nationalist ideology. While the various organizations and individuals who were part of the UTR coalition had slightly different approaches, views of racial superiority motivated participation. Attendees openly discussed the prospect of conflict with anti-racist counter-protesters and came to the event prepared for such violence, wearing helmets and carrying clubs, poles, and other weapons. Law enforcement was keenly aware that a large number of angry white men would be descending on Charlottesville prepared to engage in violence.

Similarly, the threat of violence at the Capitol was presented largely by white men. While the organizing principle on January 6 was the participants' belief that the election had been stolen, many in the crowd that stormed the Capitol subscribed to racist ideologies. Indeed, some of the same people who marched in Charlottesville in 2017 were also at the Capitol on January 6, including members of the Proud Boys. Jason Kessler, the main organizer of the UTR event, is a former Proud Boy. Famous alt-right personality Tim Gionet, aka "Baked Alaska," was at Charlottesville and also participated in the January 6 attack. He livestreamed two different entries into the Capitol building, later pleaded guilty to misdemeanor charges, and was sentenced to two months in prison.[37] Nick Fuentes, leader of the white supremacist group the Groypers, also demonstrated at both events. He first rose to prominence in the wake of Charlottesville, and by January 6, 2021, had become a well-known movement leader.[38] Many other rioters displayed symbols of white supremacy, like Confederate flags, and even brought them into the Capitol building.[39] Officer Harry Dunn, one of the US Capitol Police officers who testified before the January 6 committee, described hearing racial slurs directed at him by people in the crowd. "You hear that guys? This N**** voted for Joe Biden" and "Put your gun down and we'll show you what kind of N**** you really are" were among comments directed at Dunn, who is Black.[40]

The Proud Boys and the Oath Keepers, the two groups most closely affiliated with organizing the violence that occurred at the Capitol on January 6, have repeatedly embraced race-based activities and white supremacist positions. Enrique Tarrio, the Proud Boys's ostensible leader, had been arrested in December 2020 for destroying a Black Lives Matter banner at a church in downtown Washington, DC. Members of the Proud Boys openly declare their devotion to "Western chauvinism" and their advocacy of white supremacy. In the words of the Anti-Defamation League, "The Proud Boys are a right-wing extremist group with a violent agenda. They are primarily misogynistic, Islamophobic, transphobic and anti-immigration. Some members espouse white supremacist and antisemitic ideologies and/or engage with white supremacist groups."[41] Jason Van Tatenhove, a former member of and spokesperson for the Oath Keepers, described the group's embrace of racist ideology in testimony before the January 6 committee. He left the group when he heard members denying the Holocaust. "The straw that broke the camel's back, really, was during a — it was actually just a social setting, in a grocery store up in Eureka, Montana," he told the committee under oath. "Where some close associates and some longtime members of, kind of, the core group of Oath Keepers were having an open discussion, and that discussion revolved around the subject matter of whether or not the Holocaust was a real, legitimate piece of history. And that, for me, was — I just couldn't abide by it. And so I left that conversation, went home, and told my wife I didn't care how we were going to break away but that we were going to find some way to do it, that I just could no longer be involved in any way in a group that was heading this direction."[42] Members of both groups were convicted of seditious conspiracy for their advocacy or use of violence at the Capitol, including Tarrio.[43]

As in Charlottesville, open-source intelligence made plain that the intent of white male participants to use violence. The Oath Keepers organized a stash of weapons in northern Virginia, preparing to use them in Washington, DC, if President Trump invoked the Insurrection Act.[44] The Proud Boys organized their followers to gather at the Ellipse and march to the Capitol, targeting the Peace Circle as a vulnerable breach point.[45] Numerous individuals unaffiliated with those or other groups discussed carrying weapons and converging on the Capitol with the specific intent of violently preventing the transfer of power.

The relevant comparison here is not between Charlottesville and January 6, as those events were strikingly similar in the racial composition of the crowd and the passive response from police. To fully understand the role of race in the law enforcement response, we need to compare the police preparation for violence in Charlottesville and at the Capitol with the much more aggressive response by law enforcement to the racial justice protests in the summer of 2020. After the murder of George Floyd in Minneapolis in May 2020, large crowds of protesters gathered at events around the country. These protests focused on the persistent trend of police violence against unarmed Black people and broader issues of racial justice. While the crowds of people at these events were diverse, there were large numbers of Black participants.

General William Walker was the commander of the District of Columbia National Guard in 2020 and 2021. In two interviews before the select committee, he was asked about the difference in police and military response between the summer 2020 demonstrations and the January 6 gathering. He described the willingness of civilian and military leadership to actively deploy the National Guard in the summer of 2020 to protect people and property in Washington, DC. He contrasted that assertive response with the reluctance among military leadership to use the National Guard at the Capitol. They were also much less communicative with General Walker as to operational planning in advance of January 6.

General Walker's observations about the DC National Guard are representative of a nationwide pattern of police response to the racial justice protests in the summer of 2020. National Guard units were deployed in numerous cities that summer. According to news reports, deployments totaled a stunning forty thousand troops mobilized during a major global pandemic when travel was still restricted.[46] In Washington, the DC National Guard clamped down on a protest outside the White House that led to an extreme frustration within their own ranks, which are 60 percent people of color, and thrust the National Guard into the spotlight.[47] A National Guard helicopter flew low over the crowd assembled in protest in front of Lafayette Park and the White House, which caused fear of military action among the crowd.[48] Similarly, police agencies used tactical equipment, armored vehicles, and specialized units to prepare for the summer 2020 protests. They erected fences and barriers to protect government buildings and private property. And, as the *New York Times* reported: "In Philadelphia, police sprayed tear gas on a crowd of mainly peaceful protesters trapped on an interstate who had nowhere to go and no way to breathe . . . Los Angeles officers were issued highly technical foam-projectile launchers for crowd control, but many of them had only two hours of training; one of the projectiles bloodied the eye of a homeless man in a wheelchair. Nationally, at least eight people were blinded after being hit with police projectiles."[49]

Law enforcement agencies took a heavy-handed approach to the racial justice protests in the summer of 2020. Police agencies used the many tools available to protect public safety, even when the intelligence in advance of the protests predicted violence with less specificity than that gathered prior to UTR and January 6. After-action reports in nine major cities, reviewed by the *New York Times*, all found that the departments did not handle events properly and needed more training on how to manage large protests.

What explains the difference between the police responses to these similar events that occurred close in time? General Walker offers an answer:

So, I'm African-American. Child of the Sixties. I think it would have been a vastly different response if those were African-Americans trying to breach the Capitol. As a career law enforcement officer, part-time soldier, last 5 years full time, but a law enforcement officer my entire career, the law enforcement response would have been different. You're looking at someone who would be stopped by the police for driving a high-value government vehicle. No other reason ... I've had to talk with my five children, and getting ready to have it with my granddaughter. The talk ... of what to do to survive an encounter with the police ... As a human being, as an African-American, I think it would have been a different response by law enforcement on January 6 ... I know that from experience ... It would have been ... a lot more heavy-handed ... I think it would have been a lot more bloodshed if the composition had been different. [50]

General Walker's perspective has been echoed by countless other Black Americans; his lived experience cannot be denied. Law enforcement seems to continually mis-assess danger in this country depending on the race of the individuals who present a threat of violence. They overestimate the prospect of violence presented by Black men and other people of color. They underestimate the prospect of violence presented by white men. This pattern persists in both directions and will continue to hamper law enforcement effectiveness unless we acknowledge it.

The essence of policing is the exercise of discretion. Whether it is a patrol officer deciding whether to stop a vehicle or a pedestrian on the street or an agency evaluating intelligence in advance of a mass demonstration event, police continually assess the possibility of violence or other threats to public safety. The exercise of that discretion is inherently subjective. It incorporates the decision maker's life experience, including their subconscious judgments about danger. Like all human beings, police officers and agency leaders cannot avoid bringing their own biases into decisions they make, particularly when those decisions are snap judgments informed by emergency events.

The contrast between the approach by law enforcement to the summer of 2020 demonstrations and the two events that are the subject of this book demonstrates that implicit racial bias almost assuredly informed the failure to prepare to protect public safety in Charlottesville and at the Capitol. The threats at Unite the Right and the day of the joint session of Congress were presented by white men who were wrongly perceived as less likely to behave violently and lawlessly than those protesting the murder of George Floyd and racial injustice. Assessments by law enforcement agencies were undoubtedly influenced by the fact that the summer 2020 protesters were explicitly critical of police. The murder of a Black man by police officers had precipitated the marches, and the Black Lives Matter movement was broadly critical of police track records in majority-Black neighborhoods and attitudes toward Black citizens. The antipathy of the crowds toward police undoubtedly informed the enhanced level of preparedness by police to prevent violence. In contrast, the crowds in Charlottesville and at the Capitol were perceived to be supportive of law enforcement, which also influenced preparation.

The evidence shows, however, that racial composition of a crowd and its perceived attitude about police are poor predictors of violence in mass demonstration events. While the summer 2020 racial justice protests presented public safety challenges, they ultimately were not infected by violence among protesters or against police. The heavy-handed police preparation arguably made the events potentially more, not less, dangerous. And yet law enforcement prepared for the UTR rally and the attack on the Capitol as if they were free speech events despite substantial, specific advance intelligence to indicate that violence was being planned and weapons were being carried and even amassed. The issue of racial bias makes police agencies markedly less effective, because — again — race is not an accurate predictor of violence. Objective assessment of intelligence that specifically predicts violence provides much more accurate information on which to base operational planning. Police agencies need to endeavor to play it straight when assessing intelligence, recognizing the subjective filters that may skew and hamper their assessments of danger.

While race definitely warps police assessment of danger, bias is more likely to be latent than conscious. In the investigations I led into both Charlottesville and January 6, we found no evidence of explicit support for the violent protesters among police officers at any level. To the contrary, the officers and command staff we interviewed expressed a strong desire to quell violence and frustration at their ultimate inability to protect public safety. We did not find officers or police officials who sympathized with the noxious ideology of the UTR organizers or the intent to disrupt the joint session of Congress. Nonetheless, flawed operational plans were insufficient to meet the threat plainly predicted by the intelligence.

This shows that the bias that infects these flawed plans is not overt, and that it does not register with members of the law enforcement community, which makes it much more difficult to recognize and counteract.

Given that this phenomenon of implicit bias is not obvious, it is essential that police agencies acknowledge its existence and work to counteract its effects. The United States Department of Justice took an important step in this direction during the Obama administration by requiring all federal law enforcement agents to participate in implicit bias training. From the director of the FBI down through the ranks of all federal agencies, all personnel were required to attend programs that flagged this issue.[51] While that was an important step in raising consciousness about implicit bias, it is insufficient. Repeated, ongoing discussions of the factors that influence discretion are necessary to counteract the impact of ineffective, often self-defeating factors. This must become a prioritized part of the culture of all law enforcement agencies, not just a onetime training program that is quickly forgotten. Institutional law enforcement has been reluctant to take on this issue, given how difficult it is for individuals to discuss and address unconscious biases of any sort. Continued reluctance to acknowledge the problem and change our culture will ensure the continuation of the problem of implicit bias. We cannot turn away. All Americans are entitled to equal rights and equal protections under the law. The fact that our investigations into Charlottesville and January 6 did not find conscious bias among law enforcement planners is a hopeful sign. The evidence may show that unconscious bias is a powerful factor, but it also shows that our police forces and military are overwhelmingly made up of people who want to uphold the rule of law and treat people right. As citizens in a democracy, we have an obligation to give them the tools, and the training, to be able to do their jobs well.

DIVISION

From the outside, the violence that took place in Charlottesville in 2017 and at the Capitol on January 6, 2021, looks like manifestations of partisan division. By choosing to call their rally Unite the Right, the racist organizers in Charlottesville purposely classified the event as a conflict of left versus right, appealing to conservatives to band together. The attack on the Capitol had a similarly partisan impetus; in advance of January 6, the former president told his followers that "radical, leftist Democrats" had stolen the election from him and, by extension, them. At first glance, framed in such ways, these events seem to suggest that America is a country divided along political lines — red versus blue, left versus right, conservative versus liberal.

After spending time talking with participants on all sides of the conflicts in Charlottesville and at the Capitol, however, I've become convinced that the divide they represent is not left versus right, but rather insider versus outsider. These events each began with a core impetus that attracted attention but then metastasized well beyond the issues that initiated them. What began as a rally to protest the removal of Civil War statues in Charlottesville became a broad forum for people with differing perspectives to express their collective anger at systems they believe are hostile to their interests. The primary motivator for the attack on the Capitol was the widespread fallacy that the election had been stolen. However, people in the crowd that day were also frustrated with systems of governmental control ranging from diversity programs to gun restrictions to COVID masking and vaccine mandates. Both events became broad forums for expressing anger at the government and other American institutions.

Charlottesville and January 6 reveal that the true division in this country is no longer political but rather cultural. Americans are less motivated by political ideology than by their faith (or lack thereof) in institutions. The people who showed up to protest in Charlottesville in 2017 and in Washington in 2021 were united in their belief that traditional American systems do not reflect their values, work in support of their welfare, or better their lives. They distrust government, the mainstream media, higher education, and science. They are united more by their cynicism about these pillars of American society than by politics.

The original permit application for the August 12 protest in Charlottesville indicated that the organizers intended to convene a group of approximately four hundred at a "free speech rally in support of the Lee Monument."[1] The event was to take place at the foot of the statue of Confederate general Robert E. Lee, which stood in a prominent location in a park in the center of town, surrounded by benches, walkways to and from the surrounding sidewalks, and large oak and maple trees. The Lee statue and another Civil War statue of Confederal general Thomas "Stonewall" Jackson occupied very prominent places in Charlottesville. The Lee statue was next to the central public library, just one block north of the city's iconic pedestrian mall commercial district. The Jackson statue was on a prominent hill in a tranquil park, immediately adjacent to the county courthouse. The Jackson statue dwarfed a very small rectangular plaque just steps away that marked the location where African men and women were auctioned as slaves in the 1800s.

As discussed in chapter 1, the UTR permit was filed at a time when the City of Charlottesville had embarked on a very public process to consider removal of the two statues, which drew national attention. A campaign event by a candidate for governor of Virginia in support of keeping the Lee statue was interrupted by a large crowd of demonstrators. A group funded by a nonprofit organization called the Monument Fund joined with the Virginia Division of the Sons of Confederate Veterans in challenging the city's ultimate decision to remove the statues. They invoked a 1904 Virginia statute that prohibited anyone from taking any action to "disturb or interfere" with the statues, which the courts interpreted to include removal, destruction, or alteration.[2] A circuit court judge granted an injunction in the lawsuit that prevented the city from moving forward with plans to remove the statues until the case could be resolved. This litigation ensured that the future of the statues would remain a live controversy throughout 2017.

Many people around the country paid close attention to the statue controversy. Jason Kessler and Richard Spencer decided to use the ongoing debate as an impetus to bring together a group of conservative organizations in a public show of force. The goal was not just to support the Civil War statues but also to promote a white supremacist ideology. Anger was the animating emotion behind the Unite the Right rally — anger at the systems of American democracy that the participants believed had strayed from their historic foundations of white Christian nationalism.

Kessler and Spencer were successful in piecing together a diverse coalition. While the two of them shared a core belief in white supremacy, they had differing organizational ties, views of history, and visions for change. Kessler had attended some gatherings in Charlottesville of a group of the Proud Boys — a loose affiliation of self-proclaimed Western chauvinists located throughout the country who advocate for a return to a male-dominated, racially homogeneous hierarchy.[3] Spencer claims to have originated the term *alt-right* to describe the white supremacist movement he desires to lead. He advocates for a white racial empire to replace the pluralistic societies in America and Europe. He has openly praised Adolf Hitler and embraced the label of neo-Nazi.[4]

The alt-right coalition that Kessler and Spencer assembled in Charlottesville for the UTR event reflected a shared belief in white supremacy and the threats posed by an increasingly diverse America. The assembled groups differed quite markedly, however, in their respective manifestations of that belief, their views of history, and the specific targets of their enmity. Adherents of Identity Evropa focused largely on the diminution of white power through immigration and diversity. The organization is particularly active on college campuses, speaking out against diversity programs.[5] The League of the South, as its name implies, advocates for a return to pre–Civil War white supremacy in a free and "Godly" southern state. It is a social and religious movement, advocating a return to a conservative Christian culture.[6] The Traditionalist Worker Party embraces Nazi ideology and espouses a white nationalist view of Christianity.[7] Vanguard America embraces the Nazi ideology of "blood and soil," advocating for a racially pure society (blood) exclusively occupying a geographic region (soil).[8] Many of the participants in the UTR event and the preceding torchlit march at the University of Virginia chanted "blood and soil" as they marched through Charlottesville. All told, anti-hate organizations estimate participants from at least fifty different hate groups traveled from at least thirty-nine states to demonstrate in Charlottesville in August 2017, all with slightly different motivations.[9]

While Spencer and Kessler attracted participants from these and other groups to attend the UTR rally, they also appealed to people who did not affiliate with any particular group. About two years after the rally, researchers at the ADL's Center on Extremism identified 330 of approximately 600 UTR participants and found the following breakdown of affiliations:

Alt-right: 91
Traditional white supremacists: 90
Neo-Nazis: 51
Racist skinheads: 30
Militia/111%: 22
Other: 22
Unknown: 14
Far-right media: 10

After President Trump's comments about "good people" on "both sides," multiple news outlets tried, with varying degrees of success, to track down individuals who demonstrated in Charlottesville just to support the statues — in other words, who had no intention to provoke violence and were not affiliated with any hate groups. The *New York Times* quoted a Kansas retirement home worker named Michelle Piercy as saying, "Good people can go to Charlottesville." The *Times* wrote that Piercy "drove all night with a conservative group that opposed the planned removal of a statue of the Confederate general Robert E. Lee" and was not there specifically to foment violence.[10] However, the *Washington Post* found that Piercy was actually affiliated with the American Warrior Revolution (AWR), a militia group that attended the rally.[11] Ostensibly billed as a rally in support of the statues, the UTR event metastasized into one of the largest gatherings of hate groups and white supremacists in modern history.

There is lingering controversy in Charlottesville over how "local" the Unite the Right rally was. To some, the horrific events of that day were perpetrated by the invasion by outsiders who chose Charlottesville as a forum to express their noxious views in front of the controversial Civil War statues. I've heard people in Charlottesville say that August 12 "wasn't us" and that the ideology on display that day does not reflect the values of our community. To other residents of Charlottesville, Unite the Right was definitely "us." They saw an endemic ideology of white supremacy that infects their daily lives emerge into the open. While they recognize that there were outside influencers who came to Charlottesville, they firmly believe that the event reflected the racism that has been palpable within this community for years. The truth lies probably somewhere closer to the middle. Nonetheless, the simmering disagreement about whether this was "us" or "them" reflects the racial fissures and deep division that continue to exist in Charlottesville.

While the UTR rally attracted participants with differing views and a wide array of motivations and objectives, they shared a common anger at the current state of America and its institutions. While some directed their enmity at Jewish people and others vociferously denounced people of color, what united them was their anger at the government. Despite their ideological differences, members of the League of the South fought against Antifa counter-protesters alongside the Proud Boys and Identify Evropa, joining forces to rage at what they perceived to be efforts to "erase history" and take America in a dangerously pluralistic direction. The crowd was aligned in their shared view that the government favored the people they despised by facilitating immigration, promoting diversity, and ensuring equal access and opportunity.

On August 11 and 12, 2017, the pervasive anger among the UTR participants was palpable. They chanted hateful slogans, hoping to antagonize anti-racist counter-protesters. They dressed for battle, wearing helmets and protective gear and carrying poles, clubs, and shields. They confronted anti-racist counter-protesters with both angry words and physical force, roaming the streets of Charlottesville in provocation. In contrast with the interfaith gatherings that coincided with UTR, the tenor of the participants was intense and vitriolic. These people came to express rage at a system that they believe has left them behind. They were angry and weren't going to take it anymore.

((•))

Planning for the January 6 insurrection began on December 19, 2020, when President Trump issued his now infamous "will be wild" tweet. This was the first reference to any sort of protest at the joint session of Congress that convenes every four years on January 6, two weeks before the inauguration.

President Trump's followers saw his December 19 tweet as a call to arms and immediately began organizing for a "big protest." The Oath Keepers began preparing for violence, recruiting members to come to Washington and stockpiling weapons. Led by Stewart Rhodes, the Oath Keepers planned to take up the president's call to arms in an attempt to prevent the certification of the "fraudulent election" and preserve American democracy. Rhodes attempted to contact the White House and suggest that President Trump invoke the Insurrection Act, which Rhodes believed would justify allowing citizen militias to enforce laws.[12] When he was unsuccessful at directly contracting anyone at the White House, he posted an open letter on Facebook and on the Oath Keepers' website. "Act Now! Do NOT Wait for January 6!" it read.[13]

The Proud Boys similarly prepared for violence. Enrique Tarrio and others recruited self-proclaimed members of the Proud Boys group from around the country to come to Washington for the "big protest." As a federal jury found in Tarrio's criminal trial, the Proud Boys were "specifically conspiring to oppose by force the lawful transfer of presidential power," in the words of Attorney General Merrick Garland.[14] One group of Proud Boys worked together to breach the police barricade at the Peace Circle while others marched in stack formations to enter the building at two different locations. They believed that President Trump had called them there to prevent the transfer of power.

Much as in Charlottesville, there were a large number of people at the Capitol on January 6 who were not affiliated with any organization. For most such individuals, their motivating desire was to prevent the certification of an election that they sincerely but misguidedly believed had been stolen from President Trump. The December 19 tweet that originally announced this "wild" protest on January 6 included a link to a report authored by White House adviser Peter Navarro "alleging election fraud 'more than sufficient' to swing victory to Trump." The president and a host of co-conspirators continually reinforced this unsubstantiated message of election fraud in the days and weeks prior to January 6.

Between the November election and January 6, "Stop the Steal" messaging took many forms. The president himself repeatedly claimed that the election had been stolen from him by "corrupt" election workers determined to prevent his hold on the White House. He cited a long list of specific claims of election fraud, all of which were unfounded — suitcases full of duplicate ballots being scanned in Georgia; the counting of a significant number of ballots from deceased, incarcerated, and other ineligible voters in Pennsylvania; tampering with vote-counting machines in Michigan; and other claims of blatant voter fraud. He repeated these claims consistently throughout this period, refusing to concede the election and continuing to challenge the validity of President-elect Biden's victory.

Each of the claims the president repeated was investigated by numerous local, state, and federal officials, and no evidence was found to support them. Indeed, Attorney General Barr had authorized United States attorneys and FBI agents around the country to investigate specific, credible allegations of voter fraud as soon as they surfaced rather than waiting until the election had been certified as had been prior DOJ practice.[15] Attorney General Barr and other officials at the Department of Justice informed President Trump that these claims of voter fraud were false. Other claims were rebutted by recounts conducted by state officials. Georgia secretary of state Brad Raffensperger, for example, told President Trump in a recorded phone call on January 2 that his office had conducted several hand recounts of every ballot cast in Georgia, all of which reinforced the reliability of President-elect Biden's victory in the state.[16] Despite being informed repeatedly that the specific claims of fraud he cited in speeches and social media posts were false, the president continued to repeat those claims.

The false claims of election fraud were also perpetuated in fund-raising solicitations sent by the Trump campaign and Republican National Committee. Ads claiming the election had been stolen and asking people to donate to an "election defense fund" were delivered via text message and email to Trump supporters whose contact information appeared on the same lists that the campaign had used prior to the election. The claims in these ads were not verified as accurate before being sent. If President Trump had made a claim of election fraud in a public statement, that allegation was deemed sufficiently reliable to be used in a solicitation. "You know, without looking at all of the fundraising emails that went out, it's hard for me to say that, you know, every single fund-raising email was unverifiable," Trump attorney Alex Cannon told our committee. "And it's also my understanding that, you know, everything that was put out in this campaign, both pre-election and post-election was predominantly messaging based on either the President's Twitter feed or something that the White House had put out . . ."[17] These appeals were incredibly successful, generating almost $250 million between the election and January 6. In reality, there was no "election defense fund." Rather, the money raised through these efforts went to President Trump's Save America leadership PAC.[18]

The culmination of the Stop the Steal messaging came on the morning of January 6, during President Trump's speech on the Ellipse. In that speech, the president continued to recite many of the same false claims of election fraud that his own Department of Justice and others had investigated, rebutted, and specifically informed him were false. The president encouraged his followers to "fight like hell" to prevent the election from being stolen. "We fight like hell," he said, voice booming over the crowd. "And if you don't fight like hell, you're not going to have a country anymore." He invoked the prospect that Vice President Pence had the authority to reject the electors submitted by certain states, despite the vice president's consistent prior explanations that he had no such authority. He encouraged the crowd to march to the Capitol, where the joint session was then convening. "We're going to walk down Pennsylvania Avenue. I love Pennsylvania Avenue. And we're going to the Capitol!" He told the crowd he would join them on this march in protest of the fraud that he continued to suggest had infected the election. "We're going to try and give them the kind of pride and boldness that they need to take back our country."[19]

Many people interviewed by the select committee cited the president's words on and before January 6 as motivation for their participation. Stephen Ayres, whom I introduced in the chapter on social media, testified that he came to Washington because the president had invited him.[20] As discussed in previous chapters, this view was amplified by dozens of participants in the attack on the Capitol, all of whom explained that they were there because they believed President Trump's "Big Lie" of election fraud and accepted his invitation to protest the certification.

The underpinning of the Stop the Steal narrative is the allegation that individual election officials acted illegally to steal the election from President Trump and thwart the will of the people. The Stop the Steal argument rests upon a willingness to accept without evidence the claim that election officials in various states conspired to commit an anti-democratic fraud on the American people. President Trump stoked this propensity to believe that the government would act nefariously to thwart democracy by criticizing election workers and state officials by name, calling them corrupt and criminal, which resulted in death threats against them in multiple states.

The idea that the system is rigged is a far-reaching criticism that is fundamental to the worldview of those who embraced the "Big Lie." It is this broadly cynical view of government that drew a diverse audience to the Capitol on January 6. The "Big Lie" of election fraud may have been the primary motivator, but it was fueled by multiple, long-standing strains of anti-government sentiment. In 2022, researchers from Harvard University investigated the motivations of 417 defendants charged with federal crimes for their role on January 6 and collated the results into a working paper published by the Technology and Social Change Project (TaSC) at Harvard Kennedy School's Shorenstein Center on Media, Politics and Public Policy. The research found that while the largest percentage of rioters were there because of their belief in President Trump and the "stolen" election (about 42 percent), others had different motivations ranging from a demonstration of frustration with the status quo to wanting a violent overthrow of the government.[21]

For example, many people at the Capitol had organized or participated in the UTR rally in Charlottesville. Nick Fuentes, a prominent white supremacist pundit, attended the January 6 event but did not enter the Capitol.[22] Tim Gionet, a white supremacist troll known as Baked Alaska, is facing federal charges after he allegedly streamed live video from inside the Capitol.[23] Gabriel Brown, a Proud Boy supporter and livestreamer, has been charged with destroying media equipment outside the Capitol.[24] These individuals were motivated by the same racist ideology that inspired their actions in Charlottesville. Former marine Tyler Bradley Dykes carried a tiki torch in the Friday-night march in Charlottesville and later served time for a felony conviction in connection to his actions that weekend. After he was released from custody, he stormed the Capitol on January 6. He has pleaded guilty to two felony counts of assaulting, resisting, or impeding officers.[25] Their specific variety of anti-government ideology stemmed from their white supremacist views and belief that the government jeopardized their white privilege.

Other people who participated in the attack on the Capitol were there to protest COVID restrictions like mask and vaccine mandates. They made up 2.16 percent of rioters in the Harvard study. Dr. Simone Gold was a prominent anti-vaccine activist who pleaded guilty to trespassing at the Capitol on January 6. According to her guilty plea, Gold was part of the mob outside the Capitol and watched as a police officer was assaulted and dragged to the ground. Once she got inside, she gave an impromptu speech decrying COVID-19 vaccine mandates and government lockdowns.[26]

The Harvard research also found small percentages of people citing other motivations for their attendance on January 6, including QAnon, religiosity, wanting to be part of a historic event, and even just simple curiosity.[27] It's important to note that the sample for these researchers were those who were charged with federal crimes. There were likely other, and perhaps less strong, motivations among those who did not infiltrate the Capitol and thus are not facing charges.

The broad anti-government views of the rioters at the Capitol is reflected in the rhetoric and iconography that was used to promote and participate in the event, and that is still used to defend or excuse it. Many rioters compared the attack on the Capitol to the American Revolution. The Proud Boys circulated a document called "1776 returns" before the riot, which included operational plans for violence on January 6. In addition to the Capitol, the targets identified in the memo for such violence included the Supreme Court, CNN, and congressional office buildings.[28] Representatives Marjorie Taylor Greene and Lauren Boebert explicitly compared January 6 to 1776.[29] Some rioters carried the Betsy Ross flag with thirteen stars in a circle and the Gadsden, more commonly known as the "Don't Tread on Me," flag with a segmented snake, both created during the American Revolution.[30]

Christian nationalism was also a prominent motivator for those in the crowd who believed the US has moved away from what they see as its Christian origins. Rioters could be seen in the crowd holding up Bibles, crosses, and signs that featured religious messaging.

As in Charlottesville, cynical views of the government were widely expressed at the Capitol. Election fraud, like the removal of Civil War statues, may have been the initial impetus to gather, but the event evolved into a much broader cause. There could be no more direct manifestation of extreme anger at the government and a feeling of disenfranchisement from "the system" than an attack on the iconic Capitol building while members of Congress were inside.

((•))

We are a country divided by politics. There are red states and blue states, with policy priorities that differ widely in each. While the California legislature pursues regulation of carbon emissions and the elimination of cash bail, their counterparts in Florida pass laws that ban certain books from public school classrooms, restrict abortion rights, and prevent gender-confirmation surgery. Americans who live in blue states have different levels of taxation, public safety regulation and spending, and restrictions on personal liberty from those who live in red states. In 2021, the year of January 6, "37% of Americans described their political views as moderate, 36% as conservative and 25% as liberal."[31] This political divide is a long-standing feature of American government and is reflected in our representative government, particularly in presidential election years. The Electoral College system created in the Constitution gives each state a certain number of electors corresponding to their number of elected representatives in Congress.[32] The vast majority of electors are from non-competitive states, as most states in the past several election cycles have reliably voted for either a Republican or Democrat for president. As a result, presidential elections are decided by a small number of Americans in swing, or "purple," states. Even within those states, the number of people whose votes could go either way and tip the balance is relatively small.

Divides within our political process reflect the deeper disagreement about the efficacy of government. Within the Democratic Party, a significant number of voters believe that capitalism is oppressive, is unfair to workers, and perpetuates wealth disparity in America. Bernie Sanders and his Democratic Socialist followers reflect this view. They advocate for the rights of workers, the redistribution of wealth, and the provision of basic services like health care for all Americans. Other Democrats believe that the government should do more to stem the climate crisis and impose a "Green New Deal" of restrictions to protect the planet. These voices clash within the party with more moderate Democrats who share broad policy goals but do not support more fundamental changes to the system proposed by those on the progressive left. This debate within the Democratic Party played out during the 2020 presidential primaries, when President Biden defeated more progressive challengers like Senator Sanders and Senator Elizabeth Warren. The divide continues today with internal policy discussions that require compromise to achieve consensus and implement legislation.

There are similar divisions within the Republican Party, where mainstream conservatives clash with far-right proponents of more radical change. This dynamic played out dramatically in the election of Speaker Kevin McCarthy at the beginning of the 118th Congress. It continues to manifest in debate over government funding, with members of the Freedom Caucus advocating for more extreme budgetary reductions. These divisions also play out in electoral politics, where some Republicans have been willing to criticize former president Trump and have consequently been defeated in subsequent elections.

I worked closely with Republican representatives Elizabeth Cheney and Adam Kinzinger on the January 6 select committee and saw firsthand how their principled positions on the attack on the Capitol led to their marginalization and ultimate abandonment by Republican colleagues. Representative Cheney, once the third-ranking Republican in the House of Representatives, lost to a Trump-supported challenger in a primary election. Representative Kinzinger was ostracized by his Republican colleagues and received death threats due to his support for impeachment and his committee service. Despite their conservative credentials and principled positions on issues like abortion, immigration, foreign policy, and the size of the federal budget, Representatives Cheney and Kinzinger were no longer welcome in the Republican caucus. As with the Democrats, disagreements among Republicans complicate any efforts to establish where the fault lines exist in American politics, let alone draw simple conclusions about the left/right divide.

These intra-party disputes do, however, provide more evidence of the insider versus outsider division in America described earlier. With both parties, tensions exist and conflicts arise largely between institutionalists who believe in incremental change and those who want more immediate, fundamental change. Far-left Democratic Socialists and far-right members of the Freedom Caucus arguably have much in common in this regard: They believe the traditional system of government is broken and needs radical reform. While they disagree on what specific changes should be made, they stand in opposition to traditional elements within their own parties.

((•))

Many commentators have noted, and bemoaned, the fact that the manner in which Americans consume information has become remarkably siloed. We can't agree on basic facts surrounding important issues because we aren't viewing the same news and opinions — not even close. This development both reflects and reinforces the division between those who want to rely on and support institutions and those who reject them. While Republicans watch Fox News and read the *Wall Street Journal,* Democrats tune in to MSNBC and read the *New York Times.* In the stories they highlight and the opinions they present, many conservative sites focus on the alleged weaponization of the criminal justice system, the perceived dangers of diversity programming, and skepticism about the impact of climate change. Liberal sites have a fundamentally different view of these same issues and call for increased accountability in the criminal justice system, proactive measures to promote equity and inclusion, and sounding the alarm about the dangers of climate change.

These contrasting sources of information do not simply present differing views on policies. They thematically reinforce a broad perspective about the efficacy of systems. Liberal outlets urge the government to use its authority to make the world more just and productive. By contrast, conservative outlets promote the traditional view that the government's social justice and economic initiatives are fraught with unintended consequences and often misguided, or even darkly suggest that US governmental authority is tyrannical. These sites subtly or explicitly suggest winners and losers, what's right and what's wrong. This is intentional, as it allows each source to gain market share by appealing to people who share its perspective. These approaches might reflect and cater to divergent worldviews, but they are also, perhaps primarily, business models. The media landscape is highly competitive, with more and more outlets vying for the attention of consumers of information. News is also more nationalized, as newspapers and television networks in small communities increasingly disappear or reduce costs. As a result, the old saw "All politics is local" has been turned on its head. Now it seems all politics is national. As a result, more Americans get their news from sources that reinforce rather than challenge their perspective on important issues, which reinforces our tribal divisions and ideological separations.

I find myself falling prey to this pattern of siloed consumption of information that reinforces my perspective. I listen to NPR while driving to work and read the *Times* and the *Washington Post* every day. I watch and sometimes appear on cable news — MSNBC and CNN, never Fox News. I understand that the choices I make reflect a value system. I believe those sources emphasize reliable facts and circumstances and strive to uphold journalistic ethics. I don't often lift my head from those sources to evaluate news coverage from different perspectives. The result is a circular feedback loop — what I read reinforces my views, which makes me read more and strengthens those views.

Higher education is another institution that is riven by division. Colleges and universities have been at the forefront of efforts to prioritize equity and inclusion for decades, and they have created new areas of research and scholarship that extend beyond traditional definitions of academic rigor. Administrators have attempted to create communities that celebrate diversity and reflect the pluralistic student bodies on their campuses. Critics of higher education have suggested that this effort has evolved in ways somehow hostile to certain groups, whether they be white students, conservatives, Jewish students, or others. They point to a woke culture that promotes self-censorship by discouraging the expression of "incorrect" points of view, undermining constructive discourse on campus and diminishing the value of the educational experience for all students. To these observers, higher education is broken. They believe college no longer creates a path toward knowledge and prosperity but rather arbitrarily indoctrinates students into a culture of enforced liberalism.

This divergence of opinion about colleges and universities is another manifestation of insiders versus outsiders. Our differing understandings of higher education go beyond policy disputes and become more about the efficacy of the institution, broadly speaking. While some people continue to see colleges as places that advance knowledge and create opportunity, others see them as indoctrination machines that promote beliefs at odds with traditional American values. The core divide is belief in the institution versus cynicism about its direction rather than liberal versus conservative beliefs.

We have also seen the divide of insider versus outsider in Americans' differing views on scientific issues like COVID-19 and climate change. The pandemic fundamentally altered life in America like few events in the nation's history. It created a host of challenges for government at all levels and required the unprecedented regulation of our daily lives so as to prevent even more widespread death and illness. Closures of schools and businesses, compulsory masking and social distancing, and ultimately vaccine mandates all stemmed from scientific decisions designed to protect public health. Decision makers responsible for these rules relied on experts to provide advice about a new virus, without reliable long-term understanding of the threat it posed.

Americans had widely divergent responses to COVID restrictions and public health measures imposed during the pandemic. While the weight of scientific opinion supported the efficacy of public health mandates for measures such as masking, social distancing, and vaccination, there were contrasting voices that resisted restrictions and gave credence to social media and political messaging not supported by data or public health officials. While some believed Dr. Anthony Fauci, who served as the director of the National Institute of Allergy and Infectious Diseases from 1984 to 2022, and their local public health officials, others speculated about the motives and trustworthiness of the government, pharmaceutical companies, the liberal media, even powerful private-sector individuals like Bill Gates who were trying to help.

What could have been a global event that reinforced our shared humanity became another manifestation of our core divisions. Our bodies' biological responses to the virus were agnostic to the opinions we held about it. Responsible studies have found that hundreds of thousands fewer people would have died from COVID had there not been so much hesitancy around common-sense public health measures.[33] The science wasn't seriously in dispute. Lack of belief in that science stemmed from distrust of the messengers. Cynicism about the system prevailed over facts and scientific inquiry.

Climate change is another area where the scientific community and its standards have been disputed and even rejected. There can be little doubt that greenhouse gas emissions have affected the earth's climate and threaten the health and safety of people around the world. Despite there being a clear scientific consensus, many people point to snowstorms as evidence that the planet is not warming and suggest that changes in global temperatures are cyclical. One result of such skepticism is to elevate entrenched economic interests over long-term health of the planet, favoring fossil fuel extraction and consumption, for instance, over the development of alternative sources of energy. As with the pandemic, climate change skeptics do not trust the messenger and question the motivation of those who are sounding the alarm.

The divisions that are revealed in how we consume information, how we view higher education, and how we respond to scientific findings also appear in our perception of the events in Charlottesville and at the Capitol — and all point to a core division in America between those who believe in institutions and those who distrust them. The participants in the UTR rally and the rioters at the Capitol were united in anger at the government and other institutions they believe do not protect their interests.

I don't mean to suggest that skepticism about institutions is a bad thing. American history is full of examples of people whose criticism of institutions ultimately improved them and made this country more equitable and just. From the American Revolution to the civil rights movement, intentional violations of law have exposed injustice and motivated important steps toward freedom and equality. My point here isn't to criticize strong opposition or even rejection of systems. Rather it is to point out that our core divisions center on the question of whether American institutions should be respected and regarded as vehicles that can serve the common good and as a means to settle our differences civilly, even when reforms are needed or when the political opposition happens to be in the majority, or whether they should be feared, rejected, even destroyed.

If we are to remedy this core divide, we must accurately assess it. While political polarization is undoubtedly a pressing issue, it does not alone explain the sharp divides that erupted in violence in Charlottesville and at the Capitol. Our divided politics is a symptom of this core dynamic, not a cause. Americans don't disagree because they are Democrats and Republicans but rather because some trust in the traditional systems of information, education, and control and some do not. Until we acknowledge this dynamic, we will be unable to restore America to a country with a common set of core values around how to settle our differences.

"THERE IS NO CAVALRY COMING"

S oon after former president Trump won enough delegates to secure the 2024 Republican nomination, former attorney general Eric Holder reacted to that news on X (formerly known as Twitter) by posting the following message: "There is no cavalry coming. No miracle solution. No saviors. In the end, we, the American people — not any of our institutions — have to save our democracy by voting in defense of that democracy this fall. We are the cavalry. The responsibility is ours."[1]

Holder's words were meant as a wake-up call to Americans who have assumed that the former president's attempt to return to the White House would be stopped — by Republican primary voters, aggressive reporting, criminal courts, the Constitution, or some other "savior." He wanted to disabuse those people of the false hope that our institutions operate as independent guardrails to prevent a dangerous outcome and protect democracy. The only effective means to ensure what Holder calls "the defense of . . . democracy" is us — the people of this country. We are the only saviors available and ultimately will be responsible for democracy's protection or its disappearance.

As I read the attorney general's words, it occurred to me that they apply to a much broader conflict in America than just the 2024 presidential election. The issues that informed the political violence in Charlottesville in 2017 and at the Capitol on January 6, 2021, and the resulting division they reveal will not be remedied by any one savior. In particular, our current system of government at all levels is not equipped to bring Americans together and diminish the division that roils our nation. Rather than constructively address the pressing issues facing our democracy, our current system protects incumbency, discourages compromise, and reinforces the cynicism described above. Gerrymandered districts diminish true competition. Unlimited campaign spending protects special interests. The result is ineffective government that reinforces skepticism and exacerbates the political and cultural differences between Americans. As Holder observed, the institutions of our federal, state, and local governments are not equipped to reduce division, heal America, and protect democracy.

Holder's words "we are the cavalry" were meant as motivation to everyone who believes that the former president presents a threat to democracy to vote against him. Rather than waiting for an external check on the possible outcome that a candidate who has expressed contempt for election results and the rule of law could gain power, Holder urged Americans to be that restraint by participating in the democratic process.

Holder's diagnosis and recommended remedy has applications beyond the 2024 election. This book will be published well after November 2024, and yet regardless of that election's outcome and its aftermath, I write with confidence and alarm that there will be a pressing need for America's citizens to do all that we can to preserve and protect democracy. The threats we face are bigger than any one politician, and our deep division will remain regardless of who prevails in the fall election. Given that persistent reality, we need to turn to organic solutions that promote constructive dialogue, encourage community and common purpose, and unite Americans around a common set of values. This cannot be done by relying on elected and appointed government officials to step into the breach personally or to enforce guardrails through the courts or law enforcement agencies, but rather it must be achieved by regular people exerting a collective will in favor of fairness and democratic processes over partisan outcomes. "We are the cavalry. The responsibility is ours."

((•))

From the time I was a young lawyer, Eric Holder has been a role model and inspiration to me. In the fall of 1993, Holder was the newly appointed United States attorney for the District of Columbia. He stepped into that position at a time when the crime rate in Washington, DC, was on a disturbing increase. Crack cocaine had been introduced into DC and other urban communities just a few years before, which fueled competition among drug sellers that was often enforced with gun violence.[2] According to a 2002 National Drug Intelligence Center threat assessment, "The District had more drug treatment admissions to publicly funded facilities for cocaine abuse than for any other drug from 1994 through 1999, and that number increased approximately 510 percent from 363 in 1996 to 2,225 in 1999."[3] The situation became so untenable that the mayor of Washington, DC, Sharon Pratt Kelly, asked President Clinton to deploy the National Guard on the streets of Washington to augment the resources of local law enforcement.[4] While the president did not accommodate her request, he did authorize the hiring of new assistant United States attorneys (AUSAs) to help increase the pace of criminal prosecutions.

Unlike other American cities, because of its unique position as a federal territory rather than a state, Washington, DC, has no local district attorney. The US attorney and their assistants are charged with investigating all crimes that occur in the city and prosecuting criminal violations in both local and federal courts. The US attorney functions as both the local and federal prosecutor, a status unique among federal districts around the country.

Eric Holder's primary responsibility when he became US attorney was to hire these new AUSAs and deploy them as part of a strategy to combat the surge in violence. I was fortunate enough to be one of the first new prosecutors he hired. US Attorney Holder swore me in as an assistant United States attorney on April 25, 1994. After administering the oath of office and saying hello to my wife, he led me into his spacious corner office at 555 Fourth Street NW, just a block away from both the DC and federal courthouses. He told me that he did not have a long list of rules that I must follow as I approached my new responsibilities as a prosecutor. He explained, however, that I would have immense discretion to make decisions that directly and significantly affected the lives of many people, and that there was one rule that I must heed at all times: "Do the right thing." He encouraged me to always follow my core sense of justice and belief in what is right. He said that the right thing might not always be the most aggressive from a prosecutorial standpoint and that it would sometimes result in disappointment among those with whom I worked. He told me that he had hired me because he believed in my ability to be fair, to exercise good judgment, and to do justice.

I have recalled that advice from my first day on the job many times throughout my career. Holder was correct that doing the right thing sometimes led me to say no to agents or victims if I had misgivings about how evidence had been obtained or otherwise believed we couldn't prove a case. Sometimes the most important tests of a prosecutor's judgment are reflected in decisions *not* to pursue cases. I would come to learn that the right thing is often reduced to telling the truth, even when that truth is unpopular and difficult to hear.

Almost fifteen years after that afternoon on US Attorney Holder's couch, we ended up working together again at the Department of Justice. On February 3, 2009, Holder was appointed attorney general of the United States.[5] Several months later, President

Obama nominated me to serve as United States attorney for the Western District of Virginia, and I was confirmed by the Senate. I approached the privilege of serving as US attorney with the example Eric Holder had set for me in mind and tried to emulate his priorities, his judgment, and his leadership in my own district. I gave every AUSA whom I hired the same instruction I'd received: "Do the right thing."

Sometime in 2010, a group of newly confirmed US attorneys was invited to the White House for a brief meeting with the man who had appointed us all — President Barack Obama. We assembled in the ornate East Room of the White House and waited for the president to greet us. He walked into the room with the attorney general by his side and proceeded to give us advice very similar to what Holder had told me years before: "You're not my lawyers, you're the people's lawyers." The president told us that he did not want us to make decisions with a view toward what would benefit the administration or forward any political agenda. Rather, he instructed us, we should at all times make decisions and set priorities based on our belief in what is best for the people of our districts. He reminded us that doing the right thing meant separating politics from justice. AG Holder looked on, nodding in agreement as the president reinforced our independence.

I was reminded of both of these events at the outset of my work on the January 6 committee, and especially in my phone call with committee chairman Bennie Thompson. During that initial conversation, Chairman Thompson told me that he was familiar with my work as a US attorney and with the report I had authored in the wake of the Charlottesville events in 2017. He said that he wanted me to pursue the January 6 investigation in a similar fashion — gathering the facts and telling the truth about what happened. Specifically, Chairman Thompson explained that he wanted this investigation to "follow the facts, wherever they lead." I believe I told him about Eric Holder's advice to me as a young

AUSA and assured him that I would pursue our important work with that same commitment to doing the right thing.

The ideals expressed by these three men — Eric Holder, Barack Obama, and Bennie Thompson — embody the very best of government. They all inspired me to be guided by facts and evidence, not politics. They encouraged me to tell the truth, no matter how inconvenient that truth might be. They prioritized ethical behavior and a commitment to fairness over convictions or predetermined outcomes. They appealed to my core sense of what is right and wrong and identified that ideal of justice as the necessary foundation of my work.

Ironically, my career led me to focus on moments when others in government did not do the right thing and instead failed spectacularly to protect democracy. Our investigations of both the Charlottesville events and the January 6 attack on the Capitol described dysfunctional government. Both investigations include sharp criticisms of governmental officials at all levels who fell well short of the high standards of professionalism and justice described above. These leaders acted out of self-interest and failed to meet the moment. From Charlottesville police chief Al Thomas to former president Trump, the reports we issued reveal repeated failures of public leaders to protect core values of free speech, public safety, and the peaceful transition of power. The system didn't work in Charlottesville or at the Capitol. To the contrary, these events will go down in history as colossal failures of government.

((•))

Several systemic factors have contributed to broad governmental dysfunction and have reduced my faith in the ability of our elected officials to protect democracy. Our current system protects incumbency and discourages compromise in several significant ways. The result is a representative government that reflects the core divisions within America as opposed to our common interests and values, and that fails to address the pressing issues of the day. This dysfunction in turn reinforces the public's cynicism about government and increases the sense of an insider versus outsider division.

Under our constitutional system, the conduct of elections is a power reserved for the states. Article I, Section 4, of the Constitution provides that "the Times, Places and Manner of holding Elections for Senators and Representatives, shall be prescribed in each State by the Legislature thereof." Pursuant to this provision, state legislatures conduct elections for both federal and state offices. They set the rules that govern elections in each state and have ultimate legal authority over the results.

One facet of the states' power to conduct elections is the drawing of legislative districts. Under Article I, Section 2, of the Constitution, representatives "shall be apportioned among the several States . . . according to their respective number" and revised every ten years. The state legislatures control the process of drawing the lines that govern their representatives in Congress as well as their own state legislative districts. These legislative processes typically result in revised district maps every ten years, incorporating data from the most recent US Census. Legislators evaluate population growth or decline, changing demographics, and other census data to reconsider the number and nature of individual districts within each state. State legislators may delegate the authority to draw these lines to others, though in most states the legislature retains ultimate authority to accept district lines and control the redistricting process.[6] In addition to census data, the legislators consider existing districts, including the current representatives who occupy those districts and how they may be affected by changes to the lines. Some districts must be redrawn in ways that change the number of legislators apportioned to each state. According to the Constitution, each state will have at least 1 representative, and then an apportionment calculation divides the remaining 385 seats among the states. Congress has power over the method used to calculate apportionment.[7]

Because the process of redistricting is controlled by politicians with direct and personal interests in the outcome of the process, it is no surprise that it broadly protects incumbency. The vast majority of legislative districts in Congress and in state legislatures are designed to achieve a predetermined ratio of party control. This phenomenon is called gerrymandering, a term that harks back to 1812 when the Massachusetts legislature redrew state senate districts to favor the party led by Governor Elbridge Gerry.[8] The word has come to refer to the partisan manipulation of geographic boundaries that define districts for elected representatives.

Gerrymandering reflects a clear partisan lean and results across the country in districts made up largely of either Democratic or Republican residents. The maps drawn or approved by legislators reflect the approximate ratio of party control in each state. If the Republicans control the state legislature, they will supervise a redistricting process that reinforces that control. Democrats similarly protect their interests when they control state legislatures. They do this by drawing districts that are designed to be "safe" for one party or the other rather than being truly competitive. The legislators who draw the maps sometimes go to extremes, producing districts that seem illogical and disjointed.

According to the Princeton Gerrymandering Project, thirteen of the fifty states fail a redistricting report card designed to reflect whether each district is fairly and equally distributed based on metrics of partisan fairness, geographic features, partisan composition, and minority composition.[9] And according to a 2023 study by Harvard researchers published in the *Proceedings of the National Academy of Sciences*, the 2020 redistricting led to more so-called safe seats that protect incumbents. "Gerrymandering does end up reducing electoral competition," researcher Kosuke Imai said. "As a result, there are a lot more incumbents being elected. And electoral outcomes tend to be less close than the predicted margins."[10] The result is very little true competition in the vast majority of elections for Congress and state legislators — the legislative bodies designed by our founders to most directly reflect the views of the voting public.

As each district is gerrymandered to reflect population data that ensures the control of one party or the other, there is little chance of an upset or a particular district changing from one party to the other. Republican districts stay Republican, and Democratic districts repeatedly send Democrats to Congress and the state legislature. At both the state and federal levels, districts that "flip" from one party to the other are exceedingly rare. According to the Brennan Center for Justice in 2022, "There are now fewer competitive districts than at any point in the last 52 years." After the most recent redistricting cycle, "we saw the percentage of competitive congressional districts fall even further to just 14 percent."[11]

The fact that legislative districts are reliably within the control of one party or the other pushes our politics to the extreme. The strongest threat to reelection faced by members of Congress typically comes from within their own party. The most likely way a member of Congress in a safe district will lose is if they are outflanked to the extreme by a primary challenger.

The district in which I live reflects this phenomenon. The Fifth District of Virginia is gerrymandered to be a safe Republican district. While the district includes the liberal college town of Charlottesville, the vast majority of it is rural and conservative. The Fifth District has been represented by Republican members of Congress consistently since 2010. In 2018, Republican Denver Riggleman was elected to represent the Fifth District. Riggleman was a libertarian who believed in limited government. Consistent with the philosophy that government should not restrict personal choice or limit individual freedom, he was a supporter of gay marriage. In 2020, Riggleman officiated at the wedding of two gay men who had been volunteers in his campaign. Later that year, Bob Good, a self-described "Biblical conservative" who cited Riggleman's support for gay marriage as the impetus for his campaign, defeated Riggleman in the Republican primary. The Democratic candidate in the Fifth District in 2020 was Charlottesville resident Dr. Cameron Webb, a Black physician with both law and medical degrees. Webb supported gay marriage and other progressive policies and had strong support in Charlottesville. Nonetheless, Good resoundingly defeated Webb by approximately twenty thousand votes. Despite his credentials and strong, well-funded campaign, Webb had almost no chance to win due to the gerrymandered nature of the Fifth District.

The protection of incumbency reflected in our gerrymandered redistricting process has the practical effect of discouraging compromise. If a member of Congress or a state legislature can only lose to a more extreme candidate within his or her own party, that legislator has little incentive to work with members of the other party. The threat of a primary challenge pushes elected officials in both parties toward more partisan positions. Rather than working toward compromise solutions to difficult problems, members of legislative bodies retreat to their respective partisan positions and demonize their opponents. Compromise is actually risky, as it opens up members on both sides to a potential challenge from a more partisan candidate within their own party.

The refusal to compromise or work toward bipartisan solutions fueled by gerrymandered districts has led to paralysis in government. So many important issues are mired in this partisan divide, which results in no meaningful change in policy. Politicians and policymakers across the ideological divide agree that we need to do more to fix an immigration system that is underfunded and ineffective. Nonetheless, Congress has been unable to pass legislation to address clear problems. Similarly, voters in both parties believe that gun violence is an issue that needs to be addressed, but the two parties' official positions on access to firearms prevent meaningful reform. While we often agree on what problems need to be remedied, we disagree so strongly on possible solutions that legislators hold fast to core partisan positions in order to protect their political flanks rather than engage with goodwill in a give-and-take process.

In Virginia, control of our closely divided state legislature has recently changed hands several times. Out of forty senate seats and one hundred House seats in the Virginia General Assembly, only a handful were actually competitive in the previous election, according to the Associated Press.[12] Virginia is not unique, as the lack of political competition at the state level is common across the country. And as in Congress, political polarization in state legislatures hampers compromise and prevents bipartisan solutions.

I saw the effect of political polarization over the course of both investigations on which I worked. The two Republicans on the January 6 committee, Vice Chairwoman Liz Cheney from Wyoming and Representative Adam Kinzinger from Illinois, both left Congress as a result of their involvement in the select committee's bipartisan investigation of former president Trump. Representative Cheney was defeated in the Republican primary by a more conservative state legislator who repeatedly cited her work with Democrats as a sign that she was out of touch with Wyoming. "Liz Cheney betrayed us because of her personal war with President Trump, who won Wyoming by massive majorities twice," Harriet Hageman said when she announced her primary campaign against Cheney, whom she had previously supported.[13] After her win, Hageman said of Cheney, "She's still focusing on an obsession about President Trump. And the citizens of Wyoming, the voters of Wyoming sent a very loud message tonight. We have spoken."[14] Representative Kinzinger chose not to seek reelection in Illinois in part because his seat had been redistricted to become more conservative. He drew the ire of conservatives within his own party because of his work on the select committee and his vote to impeach President Trump following January 6.

Similar pressure to avoid intra-party challenges influenced decision makers in Charlottesville in advance of the Unite the Right rally. Charlottesville is a predominantly Democratic city and has repeatedly elected Democratic city councilors. While there are no gerrymandered districts in Charlottesville, the city has the same lack of real political competition that infects the Virginia legislature and the US Congress. In the days leading up to August 12, 2017, Charlottesville community members repeatedly urged the liberal councilors to deny the UTR permit and prevent the rally from taking place. Rather than acknowledge the core legal reality that the First Amendment protects hateful speech and explain to their constituents the city's inability to deny the permit, the councilors took the ill-advised and tardy step of trying to move the event away from the Lee statue. The ACLU's predictably successful challenge in federal court of the city's unsupported attempt to move the rally and failure to protect free speech rights resulted in confusion and a lack of information available to the public about the Unite the Right event. The councilors may have been motivated by good intentions — wanting to protect the community from intentionally provocative and hurtful speech — but those noble desires led them to take action without factual or legal foundation. Rather than prepare to meet the difficult public safety challenges presented by the UTR rally and inform community understanding and expectations for August 12, the councilors capitulated to the community's understandable but uninformed desire to prevent the event from proceeding.

No member of the city council told our investigators that their decision to deny the permit and move the rally away from the Lee statue was motivated by fear of partisan challenge in an upcoming election. To the contrary, they each explained that they were reflecting the will of the people and attempting to prevent harm.

Nonetheless, a desire to accommodate the overwhelming majority of their supporters rather than uphold the rule of law led them to make a poor decision. While some councilors publicly articulated the city's First Amendment obligation to accommodate the hateful speech,[15] their decision to give in to public pressure and move the event to a park outside of town was a reflection of their monolithic perspective. It is impossible to determine if political diversity among council members would have made a difference in the formulation of a plan for the UTR event that could have protected both free speech and public safety, but the absence of disparate voices seems to have contributed to a lack of will for trying to do so.

There are several steps we could take to diminish the polarization that infects our current politics. One obvious way to make government more effective would be the creation of a system that encourages rather than eliminates true political competition. Instead of designing districts to protect incumbents, we could draw them to consistently reflect geographic and community boundaries, contiguous areas that share common features, rather than artificial groupings designed to ensure partisan control. A more objective approach to drawing lines based purely on census data would result in districts that may vacillate between Republican and Democratic control over time. The officials elected in these less partisan districts would have much more incentive to compromise and work with counterparts across the aisle.

To minimize the risk of political considerations influencing the redistricting process, we should remove legislators from the granular work of drawing district boundaries. Consistent with their Article I power to manage elections, state legislatures could delegate the authority to draw district lines to outside experts — judges, citizen panels, or academics. Some states have done just this, creating nonpartisan redistricting commissions or other processes designed to minimize the impact of politics on this crucial process. Most states that have done this also ban commissioners from running for office in the districts they draw. Others ban legislative staff and/or lobbyists from serving on the commissions.[16]

In November 2008, California voters passed the Voters FIRST Act, authorizing the creation of the California Citizens Redistricting Commission to draw new district lines, taking the job out of the hands of the California State Legislature and transferring it to the citizens. According to the commission's website, "The Commission must draw the district lines in conformity with strict, nonpartisan rules designed to create districts of relatively equal population that will provide fair representation for all Californians." It is made up of five Republicans, five Democrats, and four unaffiliated members, chosen through a lengthy process involving public applications and a lottery.[17]

California is one of nine states (in addition to Alaska, Arizona, Colorado, Idaho, Michigan, Montana, New York, and Washington) whose state legislature has no ultimate control over the redistricting outcome. Other states, like Virginia, have redistricting commissions but have not bestowed them with complete independence. Rather, the commissions send proposals to the state legislature for approval.[18] According to the American Bar Association, "The record of redistricting commissions has been mixed, with some succeeding in drafting and implementing plans and others failing. Looking at the national landscape, commissions have failed for numerous reasons, while functional commissions have all shared the same qualities." Those qualities include a tie-breaker vote in case of a Democrat and Republican draw on any decisions, non-politically-appointed members, and, importantly, final and ultimate control over the district lines. "As Washington, D.C., and individual states look toward reforming the redistricting process," the ABA writes, "they should keep these lessons in mind."[19]

The ABA designates the commissions in California, Colorado, and Michigan as "Gold Standard" commissions from which other states can learn. They have received positive feedback on redistricting efforts and share the qualities of independent non-politically-appointed commissioners and the power to actually implement the lines they choose, not having to defer to their state legislatures.[20]

For many years, there has been a national effort to require independent redistricting commissions for all states. The effort was included in the omnibus election integrity bill called the For the People Act, which passed the House in 2019 during the 116th Congress but was not given a vote in the Senate. The bill was reintroduced at the beginning of the 117th Congress as HR 1 and S 1. This bill would have required each state to have a fully independent fifteen-member redistricting commission composed of five Republicans, five Democrats, and five independents. Despite its inclusion of numerous other reforms to the election process, it did not have enough support to pass.[21]

Another way to push back against the deleterious effects of partisan gerrymandering is the use of ranked choice (RCV) and top-two voting processes, both of which diminish the importance of party affiliation by eliminating separate primaries for the major parties. With RCV, all candidates and voters are eligible to participate in a single primary election. Voters rank their first, second, and third choices for each office. If one candidate is ranked first on a majority of ballots, they are declared the winner. But if no candidate receives a majority of first-choice ballots, then the candidate with the lowest number of votes is eliminated and that person's ballots are distributed to the remaining candidates. This process continues until one candidate has received a majority of voters' first, second, or third votes. California, Maine, and Alaska use RCV systems to select congressional and state legislative candidates, and some jurisdictions around the country use RCV for local elections. All told, as of the 2022 election, ranked choice voting was used in sixty-two jurisdictions, ranging from Alaska and Maine to New York City and Cambridge, Massachusetts.[22]

Primary elections are similarly nonpartisan in a top-two election system. In states that use this process, the two candidates who receive the most votes in the nonpartisan primary election advance to a runoff in the general election, regardless of their party affiliation. The general election may have two Republican or two Democratic candidates in a particular district, depending upon the results of the primary. California, Nebraska, and Washington used a top-two primary system as of September 2023, while Alaska and Louisiana used a variation on the format.[23]

By diminishing party control of primary elections, ranked choice and top-two voting systems give voters a wider array of choices in elections even within gerrymandered districts. In a primarily Democratic district, there could be a ranked choice contest between a Democrat who favors compromise with Republicans and another Democrat who favors a more absolutist approach to particular problems. All voters, not simply Democrats, would have the chance to vote for these candidates and weigh in on the relative utility of each approach. These nonpartisan systems give more voters power to influence elections and ultimately choose candidates who more closely reflect their positions. Legislators are therefore more directly accountable to all of the constituents they represent, creating incentives to address rather than avoid important and complicated issues.

Both ranked choice voting and top-two systems lead to measurably positive results on metrics ranging from voter satisfaction to increased incentive to compromise among candidates. For example, voters in states that routinely use RCV report overwhelming satisfaction with the system in surveys.[24] According to a 2020 study in the Minneapolis–St. Paul area, implementing RCV in 2009 and 2013 caused a 10 percent increase in voter turnout, and even greater increases for precincts with higher poverty rates.[25] Turnout rates have continued to climb, all the way to a stunning 54 percent participation of eligible voters in a 2021 municipal election. "It's a pretty phenomenal turnout . . . Every voter felt like their vote counted, and indeed it did," Jeanne Massey, executive director of the pro-RCV organization FairVote Minnesota, was quoted as saying in the *Minneapolis Star Tribune*.[26] A different study in 2021 found especially high turnout rates among younger voters in RCV cities, which the researchers were able to attribute to "great campaign civility," another common, measurable result of implementing RCV voting.[27] "Findings suggest RCV acts as a positive mobilizing force for youth voting through increasing campaign contact," the research summarized.[28]

Research also suggests top-two primary systems can even result in more moderate candidates entering a race. Christian Grose, academic director of the USC Schwarzenegger Institute for State and Global Policy, compared election results of US House of Representatives members in the three states that have a top-two primary system: California, Louisiana, and Washington. He also examined any effect on those states' legislative races. Interestingly, Grose examined the lawmakers' votes over fifteen years to examine the effect over time. He found that "the top-two primary led to less extreme behavior by members of Congress in the three open primary states."[29] He explained further in a 2020 research article that "legislators elected in the top-two primary system are more moderate than those elected in closed primary systems," in part because "the threat of a same-party general leads legislators to moderate as they may face a same-party general election challenge in the future."[30]

((•))

Another key factor that protects incumbents and diminishes compromise in government is money. There are few meaningful limits on campaign donations in our political system, which results in substantial sums of money flowing to candidates for office. Incumbents receive the large majority of these contributions, most of which are given by corporations, unions, or groups with a vested interest in particular issues. Together with gerry-mandered districts, the steady stream of campaign dollars protects incumbents and diminishes compromise and competition.

In two seminal cases, the United States Supreme Court has ruled that spending on campaigns is a form of free speech protected by the First Amendment. In 1976, the court ruled in *Buckley v. Valeo* that campaign contributions are a form of expression protected by the First Amendment. Accordingly, any restriction upon the fundamental right of free expression would be subject to "strict scrutiny" and must be justified by a "compelling governmental interest."[31] The court essentially applied a balancing test — evaluating whether restrictions on political spending were justified by the interest such limits were designed to protect. The opinion described that public interest as "encouraging citizen participation in political campaigns while continuing to guard against the corrupting potential of large financial contributions to candidates." Applying strict scrutiny, the court in *Buckley* overruled an overall cap on spending by candidates for federal office and their campaign committees. This ruling ensures that candidates for federal offices and independent advocacy groups can spend unlimited amounts to support campaigns, without restriction. The court also ruled that candidates can spend an unlimited amount of personal funds on campaigns.

In 2010, the court again recognized campaign spending as protected speech in *Citizens United v. Federal Elections Commission*.[32] In *Citizens United*, the court considered the constitutionality of a complete federal ban on campaign contributions by corporations or labor unions. That ban was based on two distinct policy benefits. First, a ban on corporate campaign spending prevented the "corrosive and distorting effects of immense accumulations of wealth that are accumulated with the help of the corporate form." Second, the law had an anti-corruption rationale, designed to prevent expenditures being given as quid pro quo for commitments from candidates.[33] The court rejected both policy rationales and invalidated the prohibition on corporate giving. Again applying strict scrutiny, the court found that the policy interests supporting the ban were insufficient to overcome the free speech rights of corporations and unions.

Since the Supreme Court invalidated limitations on spending by corporations, nonprofit political action committees have been incorporated to solicit money to support an array of causes and facilitate unlimited spending on campaigns. Section 501(c)(4) of the Internal Revenue Code makes contributions to social welfare organizations tax-deductible, which further incentivizes contributions to these nonprofit corporations. These special interest groups are colloquially known as Super PACS. They cannot legally coordinate with campaigns, as such coordination would violate FEC regulations that survived *Citizens United.* They are, however, free to purchase television advertising, engage in direct mail and door-to-door advocacy, and provide additional support to candidates for office. Unlike official campaign organizations, they need not disclose their donors to the FEC, which allows contributors to these issue advocacy groups to remain anonymous.

Since *Citizens United* was decided in 2010, there is virtually no restriction on the ability of individuals and special interest organizations to support political campaigns. Wealthy donors are able to pour unlimited amounts of money into Super PACs, which funnel that money into advocacy efforts on behalf of particular candidates who support particular issues. Though these efforts must officially be disconnected from campaigns, that separation is difficult to police and enforce. Mitt Romney came under fire at a presidential debate in 2012 for calling a Super PAC that supported him "my Super PAC."[34] He later had to walk back the comments, promising, "I haven't spoken with any of the people that are involved with my super PAC in months."[35] Hillary Clinton also came under fire for large Super PAC donations in the 2016 campaign and had to defend against allegations of involvement at a presidential debate, saying, "It is not my PAC."[36]

Stephen Colbert famously made a mockery of this aspect of Super PAC law by creating his own, real Super PAC in 2011 called Americans for a Better Tomorrow, Tomorrow. The FEC even signed off on it as a legitimate Super PAC. The group raised $1.2 million by early 2012 and supported real political candidates in the Iowa and South Carolina presidential primaries, an effort that included outrageous commercials and public statements. The bit revealed the loopholes — which Colbert called "loop-chasms" — in how campaign finance laws operate, ultimately winning the comedian one of the highest honors in journalism, the Peabody Award.[37]

The nonprofit group OpenSecrets is a nonpartisan research organization that tracks campaign spending. OpenSecrets estimates that in the election immediately following *Citizens United*, campaign spending by 501(c)(4) Super PACs increased by 53 percent from the previous election cycle.[38] In 2020, Super PACs spent a record $3,427,543,995 to support federal election campaigns. The vast majority of the money raised and spent by Super PACs goes to support incumbents. In the 2022 election cycle, the top fifty recipients of Super PAC donations in Congress were all incumbents, ranging from Republican representative Cathy McMorris Rogers, who received $3,344,596, to Democratic representative Pete Aguilar, who received $1,446,952.[39]

Super PACs invest their campaign spending in candidates whose votes in Congress demonstrate support for the special interests they were created to advance. The Club for Growth is a conservative organization that supports "reducing income tax rates and repealing the death tax . . . the full repeal of Obamacare . . . regulatory reform and deregulation . . . and expanding school choice."[40] In 2022, the Club for Growth spent $69,864,090 on political campaigns through various Super PACs and other organizations it controls.[41] The vast majority of this spending went to support incumbent Republicans who champion those issues. Similarly, the League of Conservation Voters Victory Fund promotes environmental stewardship and the mitigation of climate change. The LCV Victory Fund spent $33,303,633 on political contributions in 2022, all of which went to support incumbent Democratic candidates or to oppose Republicans.[42]

Their ability to spend unlimited amounts of money on campaigns gives Super PACs enormous influence over our politics. Members of Congress run for office every two years. They are incessantly raising money to ensure they have the resources to fund their never-ending campaigns for reelection. These members understand that access to the tremendous sums of money provided by special interest groups is dependent on supporting particular policies favored by the Super PACs. As a result, they have a disincentive to compromise with members who oppose those policies — the almost certain loss of financial support from Super PACs. Republicans have little incentive to work with Democrats on commonsense restrictions on access to firearms, as they risk losing the support of the National Rifle Association and other pro-gun groups that provide millions of dollars to Republicans through Super PACs. Similarly, Democrats are reluctant to work with Republicans on regulatory reform as they risk losing the support of well-funded labor unions who spend millions supporting pro-union Democrats via Super PACs. Money in politics perpetuates gridlock and discourages members from compromise solutions, as any perceived retreat from absolute support for a particular position jeopardizes the special interest money that funds campaigns.

The undue influence of money in politics is not a partisan issue. Republicans and Democrats have benefited from the Supreme Court's ruling in *Citizens United* and now greedily solicit and receive large contributions from Super PACs. According to OpenSecrets, outside organizations spent $1,266,011,505 on "conservative" candidates and causes — about 55 percent of the total Super

PAC and outside group spending in that cycle. Other organizations spent $935,436,195 on "liberal" candidates and causes, about 40 percent of the total.[43] This data shows that both parties have adjusted to this Wild West of campaign finance and benefit from the lack of regulation on spending.

Remedies to the outsized influence of money on our politics are hard to identify given the Supreme Court recognition of political contributions as a form of protected speech. However, some innovative solutions are being implemented primarily at the state and local levels. While the court has ruled that the Constitution forbids a total ban or undue restrictions on political contributions, some states provide public funds to offset those from Super PACs and outside donors. For example, Connecticut, Arizona, and Maine offer full public financing for candidates for both legislative and statewide offices.[44] State laws provide public funding for candidates who reach a particular threshold of support, as reflected in primary votes, contributions, or other metrics. The Connecticut law enhances public support for candidates in "party-dominant" districts, an incentive designed to counter the impact of gerrymandering.[45]

Minnesota has been offering some level of public financing for candidates since 1974, an initiative that was a response to the Watergate scandal and what it revealed about the corrosive impact of fundraising on electoral politics. The state has a two-part system composed of direct public subsidy payments and a political contribution refund program. Put simply, candidates for statewide office can get partial grants if they agree to spending limits, and then the donors can have up to 50 percent of their contribution refunded by the state.[46]

In addition to public funding programs, both Connecticut and South Carolina restrict the campaign finance activities of lobbyists. South Carolina limits registered lobbyists from donating to any candidate for a body the lobbyist has previously lobbied. A lobbyist also can't host fundraisers or ask for campaign contributions from others. In Connecticut, lobbyists can only donate up to $100 to the campaigns of candidates for most offices, and likewise cannot host fundraisers or act as a "bundler" for donations.[47]

Programs in other states focus on regulating coordination between donor entities and candidates, including one in California that widens the definition of *coordination* to include a litany of activities. For example, a donation is illegal "if it is made at the request, suggestion, or direction of, or in cooperation, arrangement, consultation, concert or coordination with the candidate or if the candidate participated in making any decision or had any discussions with the creator, producer, or distributor of the communication, the person paying for that communication, regarding the content, timing, location, mode, intended audience, volume of distribution, frequency of placing the communication." In other words, as the Campaign Legal Center puts it, it limits the kind of wink-and-nod coordination that usually flies under the radar.[48]

Other novel programs include what New York City calls its matching funds program. Since 1988, candidates for city offices have been able to agree to campaign spending limits and increased financial oversight in exchange for six-to-one matching funds for every dollar raised by small donors (under $175).[49] As the Brennan Center for Justice writes of the program, "By pumping up the value of small contributions, the New York City system gives [candidates] an incentive to reach out to their own constituents rather than focusing all their attention on wealthy out-of-district donors, leading them to attract more diverse donors into the political process. This is markedly different, they explained, from how they and other candidates conduct campaigns at the state level."[50] This allows challengers and candidates who do not benefit from Super PAC contributions to compete financially with more generously funded incumbents. The small-donor matching fund does not violate *Citizens United* or otherwise restrict the ability of special interest groups to influence elections. It does, however, provide somewhat of an offset to special interest money. A bill to enact small-donor matching funding has been introduced in Congress, though it faces little prospect of success given the lack of zeal by either party to change the current system.

The City of Seattle has developed a novel program that provides "democracy vouchers" to city residents, who can use those vouchers to provide support to candidates for local office, and the city council has allocated $3 million to it. The goal of the democracy voucher system is to "increas[e] transparency, accountability, and accessibility for how Seattle elections are financed."[51] The Supreme Court rejected a challenge to the voucher program in 2019, and it will go into effect in 2024.[52]

These public finance systems don't eliminate the influence of Super PACs and outside money in politics. They do, however, level the playing field somewhat. While *Buckley* and *Citizens United* protect the rights of corporations and Super PACs to pump unlimited sums into political campaigns, candidates who receive public funds may not be nearly as beholden to the special interest organizations, and in turn they may be more free to compromise in service to their constituents. There is still a lack of measurable evidence with which to assess the effect of these reforms. The Brennan Center notes, however, that "if anything, matching fund programs are likely to reduce polarization by encouraging candidates of all kinds to seek new donors, many living in their own districts."[53]

((•))

The institutional protections of incumbency inform my view that government is not equipped to heal our core national divide and reinstitute faith in our institutions. Rather than heal the division between insiders and outsiders that I have identified and examined in this book, the current system actually exacerbates it. The rules that govern campaigns and our political process create cynicism in government and reinforce the view that our institutions are broken.

The protection of incumbency is a major reason our elected officials appear paralyzed, unable to pass legislation or find consensus solutions on a range of issues that concern and frustrate a majority of voters across the political spectrum, like environmental protection, gun violence, and immigration. School shootings persist without policy solutions to make them less common. Our southern border continues to experience a surge in migrants from other countries as we argue over barriers and asylum rules. Carbon emissions escalate without agreements on how to reduce our dependence on fossil fuels and protect our planet.

Rules that reduce incentives to compromise promote absolutist thinking and rhetoric. If incumbents in safe districts can only lose to more extreme primary opponents, their politics become more extreme. Special interest money flows to incumbents, rewarding legislation or obstruction on behalf of the powerful few while diminishing political competition. And our two major political parties have a vested interest in perpetuating this broken system because each benefits from the current rules.

If our leaders continually fail to address the most important issues facing this country and the world, they will become less and less legitimate in the eyes of the people whose interests they are supposed to represent. The fact that the current rules result in both Democrats and Republicans almost never losing reelections leads to widespread cynicism among the electorate. The institutional class of elites is the perceived enemy, rather than one side or the other.

I fear that our current system of government strays a long way from the core principles I learned from Eric Holder, Barack Obama, and Bennie Thompson. Rather than doing the right thing, the men and women we elect to positions of authority too often do the safe thing for their own careers and for their parties. In contrast with Eric Holder's direction to do what's right even if unpopular, legislators retreat to their partisan corners and resist working with, or even being cordial to and respectful of, their political adversaries. In direct contradiction to President Obama's direction to me and other US attorneys to avoid politics in the exercise of our prosecutorial discretion, elected officials prioritize politics over principle and leave important issues that require compromise unaddressed. Rather than "following the facts wherever they lead," as Chairman Thompson directed me to do, our leaders are trying to make facts conform to political narratives. Good government has become a secondary concern to maintaining power, which understandably leads Americans to lose faith in our institutions.

Over the course of the January 6 investigation, I learned that democracy depends on individual decision makers. It relies upon our elected officials' willingness to put the public interest over self-interest, follow the rules, and remain faithful to the immutable principles set forth in our constitution and laws. Vice President Pence did that on January 6 when he refused to accept the slates of fake electors submitted by various states. Georgia secretary of state Brad Raffensperger did that when he resisted President Trump's entreaty to "find 11,780 votes." Officer Caroline Edwards did that when she bravely defended the Capitol as rioters assaulted her and surged toward the building that is home to our representative democracy. These individuals represent the best in government and remind us that good people can and do emerge in crises. We need to do more to encourage others to follow their footsteps, remaining faithful to the rule of law even when it reduces their power or jeopardizes their safety. The future of American democracy depends on our ability to choose the right thing over the easy thing. It is to those solutions that we turn next.

"IT'S HARDER TO HATE UP CLOSE"

In her bestselling memoir, *Becoming*, Michelle Obama wrote that one of the central lessons she learned about America over the course of her tenure as First Lady was that "it's harder to hate up close." She described meeting people in different regions of the country, from all walks of life. Some were fans, and some were critics. She explained that she often found common ground with others regardless of their political or cultural perspective, or their opinions of her and her husband, simply by spending time with them. "When voters got to see me as a person, they understood that the distorted pictures of me were untrue," she wrote. Mrs. Obama believes that when people take the time to listen to one another, barriers fall and their shared humanity emerges. Her simple but powerful message suggests that basic human connection is the best way to combat hatred, acrimony, and division in America.

Our hatred is palpable these days, and it's stimulated by many of the factors that have been explored in this book — a profit-driven social media apparatus that curates the information we receive and pushes us into echo chambers, governmental authorities who seem to protect the interests of a privileged few, and leaders who exploit and exacerbate the differences among us for political gain. It often seems we are surrounded by voices that reinforce our firmly held convictions. We infrequently interact with or have a chance to learn from people who have opinions or experiences very different from our own, which in turn breeds mistrust and misunderstanding. We tend to fear what we don't understand, and to be judgmental of people different from us. In other words, we hate from a distance, not up close.

Division leads to two fundamental reactions, both of which are destructive in ways that threaten our democracy. Some people get angry at those who are different from them and institutions they perceive to be broken. Their anger manifests in many forms, even violence. Charlottesville and January 6 were spasms of this anger that led to violence fueled, at both events, by people whose rage had reached a boiling point. They were prepared to take extreme measures and risk their safety and liberty in support of strongly held views. They physically assaulted people, causing death and destruction. They also undermined the sense of security of everyone who was present at those events.

Other people have a passive response to the division in our society and their own sense of frustration and distrust — apathy. Rather than get angry and prepare to defend their perspective with violence, they retreat and disengage. These people don't believe it matters if they vote because they feel as if our elected representatives are "all the same." They don't talk or listen to people outside their insular, like-minded circles, as they either are not interested in furthering their understanding or don't want to risk conflict. These people allow their apathy to pull them away from our institutions. They disengage from the processes they believe are broken — government, education, media. They don't get angry, they just stop paying attention.

Anger and apathy are very different reactions to the common problem of cynicism about our institutions. Violence is an obvious threat. You can see it play out, as anyone who has watched footage of Charlottesville and January 6 knows. Apathy is more insidious. It cedes power to the people and groups who take action even at times when their opinions and priorities are clearly in the minority. Anger and apathy may have very different immediate effects, but they are both powerful forces eroding the quality of our democracy. Given their power, they are the central hurdles we must overcome if we are to heal the division that currently afflicts this country. We must recognize, call out, and overcome both our anger and our apathy.

While the challenge presented by the twin threats of anger and apathy is formidable, there is a powerful remedy that has the potential to overcome both forces. As Michelle Obama says, we need to come "up close," pay attention and engage. I'm convinced that if far more people vote, we will have a better, more responsive government. If far more people make an effort to think critically and educate themselves about pressing issues, our democracy will be stronger. If we listen to each other rather than yell at each other, we'll all be smarter. The remedy is us, actively participating and working to protect democracy. Like the police officers who defended the Capitol on January 6, we need to run toward the problem, not away from it. If we can find the will and the methods to do that, we will emerge from this challenging time stronger and more unified than ever.

((•))

Imagine for a minute a very different sort of Unite the Right rally. What if a group of people motivated by their odious views of racial superiority gathered for a peaceful event. They organized speeches that proudly proclaimed their sense of historic primacy and articulated their shared belief that America has somehow deviated from that tradition. They wore shorts and carried water bottles rather than putting on body armor and carrying shields. They gathered in solidarity to express their collective will rather than to provoke hostility. What if their goal was persuasion rather than confrontation? The anti-racist counter-protesters might still have tried to disrupt this rally, but it would have been a much different event.

Of course, that wasn't the way UTR organizers and attendees approached August 12, 2017, in Charlottesville. Instead, anger was everywhere that day. The event was never intended to be a peaceful protest or a gathering where people made speeches and attempted to recruit followers to their ideology. It was a belligerent mob determined to provoke confrontation. UTR organizers recruited attendees by appealing to their fears, not their hopes. The people who were persuaded by that message came to the event to fight, not to learn or to persuade.

Communications among organizers and attendees that were reviewed as part of the investigation I led demonstrated a determination to provoke opposition and prepare for violence. Eli Mosley was designated UTR's chief of security, and he organized armed groups to escort speakers to and from the event. Many people prepared in advance for violence by gleefully predicting confrontation and expressing a desire to fight, injure, and maim their opponents. They even posted memes about their violent intent in their Discord chats, which were meant to be humorous. One is a photo of John Deere harvesting equipment with the caption "Introducing John Deere's New Multi-Lane Protester Digestor." The poster wrote, "Sure would be nice." The same user suggested putting a "6-8 inch double threaded screw in 2 3 ft axe handles. [If] shit gets real unscrew the bottom and go to town." As the rally drew closer, more and more participants posted photos and selfies of themselves "battle-ready," with their shields, masks, and weapons. At least one selfie featured Trump lawn signs in the background, and in another the poster was wearing a MAKE AMERICA GREAT AGAIN hat.[1]

The crowd that marched in Charlottesville chanted several slogans that reflected their anger and were designed to provoke a violent response. "Jews Will Not Replace Us!" reverberated through the grounds of the University of Virginia on Friday, August 11, and bounced off the walls of buildings in downtown Charlottesville on Saturday, August 12. Those words reflect a warped anti-Semitic frustration with Jewish people and their success. The chant was periodically modified to "You Will Not Replace Us," directed at the diverse gatherings of anti-racist counter-protesters who confronted the rally participants. "Blood and soil," a key slogan of Nazi ideology under Hitler that promoted the vision that only Aryans — members of the so-called master race — should live in Germany or the lands it conquered, similarly echoed through the UTR event. All of these words were chanted at high volume, delivered with vehemence and strong emotion.

The clothes worn by the UTR rally-goers and the items they carried similarly reflected their anger and desire for confrontation: helmets, body armor, flagpoles with sharpened ends, clubs, and shields. They marched in military formation, sending a clear message of preparedness for conflict. The combination of their warlike appearance and their provocative words revealed their true intent — to provoke onlookers to violence, in turn justifying physical confrontation.

The ultimate act of anger that occurred in Charlottesville was the murder of Heather Heyer. James Fields, who had been photographed earlier on August 12 with a shield bearing the insignia of the white nationalist group Vanguard America, drove his Dodge Challenger into a large, diverse crowd of anti-racist counter-protesters. He was later convicted in state court of premeditated murder and pleaded guilty in federal court to a hate crime.[2] While his actions were thankfully unique on August 12, they reflect the extreme antipathy that the UTR participants manifested in Charlottesville.

The anger expressed by the UTR attendees provoked an angry response, as it was designed to do. The organizers intended conflict all along, though they wanted their violent acts to be cloaked in the faux justification of self-defense. This was made extremely clear in the federal civil lawsuit *Sines v. Kessler*, which held the rally organizers responsible. As Judge Norman K. Moon wrote in his opinion, "Kessler himself told others on Discord to 'bring picket sign post, shields and other self-defense implements which can be turned from a free speech tool to a self-defense weapon should things turn ugly.' And, in the days leading up to the event, he met in person with Defendant Cantwell to plan 'unlawful acts of violence [and] intimidation.'"[3] Rally organizers chose a liberal college town like Charlottesville for this intended show of force, mindful that their event would draw a significant opposition that would likely match their anger and intensity. Those elements created a climate where violence was expected and in their view justified. To some in the crowd that day, the UTR rally was meant to be the first battle in a race war that would continue across the country — a spark to ignite a broader conflict. Outspoken white supremacist Chris Cantwell had even said on a podcast in January 2017, months before the event took place, "Some of us got to be fucking cannon fodder for the race war."[4]

The people who marched to the Capitol on January 6, 2021, were also angry. They had been led to believe that the 2020 presidential election had been stolen from former president Trump and that their actions were necessary to prevent an illegitimate election from being certified. Many people at the Capitol believed that they were patriots acting in accord with ancestors who had rebelled against British rule in the American Revolution. They were every bit as angry as those who marched in Charlottesville, though for different reasons.

As in Charlottesville, there was ample discussion of the potential for violence in advance of January 6. As recounted above and cataloged in great detail in the seditious conspiracy trials that have ensued since that day, many people planned to use violence to interrupt the joint session of Congress. They were determined to prevent the certification of President Biden's election by any means necessary, including pushing through the resistance of police and breaching the building. The Proud Boys and the Oath Keepers prepared for battle, not for a peaceful demonstration. Motivated by their outrage at nonexistent election fraud and the perceived injustice of a stolen election, they were determined to overcome resistance with violence. Oath Keepers founder Stewart Rhodes felt that "the time for peaceful protest is over" and created an invitation-only Signal group to plan their violent assault, including creating the quick reaction force of firearms stored in Virginia.[5] Many, many other participants also expressed a similar, excited desire to participate in violence. As we summarized in the committee's final report on January 6: "Kenneth Grayson predicted what would eventually happen on January 6th, when on December 23, 2020, he wrote on Facebook that President Trump called people to Washington, DC through his December 19th tweet and then added 'IF TRUMP TELLS US TO STORM THE FUKIN CAPITAL IMA DO THAT THEN!'"[6]

Some demonstrated their intent on January 6 by circulating pre-printed flyers that proclaimed "#OccupyCongress" over images of the United States Capitol. Robert Gieswein, a Coloradan affiliated with the Three Percenters and who was among the first to breach the Capitol, said that he came to Washington, DC, "to keep President Trump in."[7]

President Trump's speech on the Ellipse on the morning of January 6 further inflamed the crowd. He used violent images, telling the crowd to "fight like hell and if you don't fight like hell, you're not going to have a country anymore."[8] He told his supporters, "We will never give up. We will never concede. It doesn't happen," which suggested to them that there was still a chance that they could prevent the election from being certified. He encouraged those in the crowd to "make [their] voices heard" and told them to march to the Capitol as the joint session was convening. The president's words incited the crowd to do all they could to prevent a perceived injustice. While the president did add "peacefully and patriotically" to his exhortations, the clear intent of his words was to stir the crowd's anger and rally support for a march to the Capitol specifically intended to prevent the certification.

A large number of people were moved by the president's words and took them literally. As Trump's speech wound down in the early afternoon of January 6, those who had been listening to it marched to the Capitol prepared to "fight like hell" to prevent the certification of President Biden's election. They weren't there to make speeches or conduct a free speech rally. To the contrary, many including the organized Proud Boys and Oath Keepers moved to the Capitol determined to use force to achieve their goals.

There could be no more direct manifestation of the anger that characterized the mob at the Capitol on January 6 than the chants of "Hang Mike Pence" that were heard throughout the attack. These angry words were shouted by numerous rioters after the vice president issued a statement declaring his intent to accept the certified slates of electors submitted by the states, as the Constitution required. For following the law, he was vilified as a traitor and threatened with death. Members of the crowd constructed a hangman's noose on the grounds of the Capitol, an ominous warning meant to convey their willingness to use ultimate force to achieve the crowd's goals. Chants of "Where's Nancy" — Speaker of the House Nancy Pelosi — as the mob marched through the Capitol and their possession of zip ties and other items that could be used to restrain were further manifestations of the group's anger at the elected officials who were gathered for the joint session.

As with Charlottesville, it's possible to imagine leaders of the January 6 protest taking a far less confrontational approach. If, for instance, President Trump had made more than an oblique reference to marching "peacefully and patriotically" to the Capitol and instead explicitly discouraged violence, the event could have been a political protest rally rather than a riot. The crowd could have gathered in the shadow of the Capitol at a stage on the National Mall, listened to speeches, and expressed their collective perspective on election integrity, just as other groups have done in that same space for many years. What if the crowd had expressed concern about the election and rallied support for their views rather than unleashing their rage about results that did not go their way and storming the Capitol?

Charlottesville and January 6 were not events designed to win "hearts and minds" or otherwise influence public opinion. They were rather gatherings of angry people, largely white men. They were not "free speech" events, but riots. It is impossible to watch troubling scenes from both well-documented events and not understand the crowd's vehemence and antipathy toward institutions.

Beyond Charlottesville and January 6, there are many other examples of anger surfacing quickly in today's America fueled by similar dynamics: the insider–outsider divide and mistrust of government institutions and democratic processes. The global COVID pandemic, for example, stoked anger at institutions and furthered division in this country. Some people resented government public health mandates and the restrictions on their lives and liberty. They doubted the information they received from authorities and demonized the messengers of the cautious advice provided throughout the pandemic. Division over this topic continues to this very day, with opportunistic politicians and activists engaging in revisionist history based on perceptions, not facts, and using rhetoric intended to incite, not inform. Rather than trusting the experience of Dr. Anthony Fauci and the other professionals tasked with navigating our national response to an unknown new pathogen, many people ascribed sinister motivations to him and other government officials doing their best in the face of an overwhelming challenge. At the same time, people who wanted to place their faith in the experts who held positions of authority resented those who refused to abide by masking, social distancing, and vaccination mandates. They themselves were angry that people were endangering others and taxing our health care system in unreasonable ways.

The national reaction to the pandemic surprised me. At the outset, I thought it could be an opportunity to reinforce our shared humanity and become a unifying force in this country. Much like 9/11, it presented a common enemy that had the potential to highlight how much Americans have in common. That expectation proved to be naive and unrealistic, as the pandemic became yet another wedge used to separate us. It prompted anger rather than sympathy. It resulted in people being suspicious of others' motivations and gave them reasons to resent and demonize rather than coming together in shared suffering and sacrifice. Something that had potential to unify ended up stoking division — a sad reminder of the polarized times in which we live.

There are numerous examples of significant events and issues that demonstrate and reinforce anger at our institutions. *New York Times* columnist Frank Bruni wrote a book on this subject called *The Age of Grievance* in which he details the many manifestations of American anger, and the fact that it comes from both sides of the political spectrum.[9] He points out that while grievance has fueled social change throughout American history, it seems these days to be particularly personal. "Not all grievances are created equal," he writes. "There is January 6, 2021, and there is everything else. Attempts by leaders on the right to minimize what happened that day and lump it together with protests on the left are as ludicrous as they are dangerous . . . But it's also true that on both sides of the political divide, there's a quickness to grievance, a tendency among many people to identify themselves and interpret events in terms of past, current, and looming hurts . . . It's not so much bipartisan as it is pan-partisan or supra-partisan, and it's getting worse."

I don't mean to suggest that opposition to institutions is somehow inherently destructive or misplaced. As Bruni notes, American resistance to injustice has motivated many important changes in law and life throughout our history. There is, however, a fundamental difference between the productive dissent that motivated the civil rights movement and today's palpable anger at institutions. What we are experiencing today is reflexive anger, not necessarily one motivated by a specific goal or cause. It is reactive, not proactive. For instance, people with disparate motivations came together in common cause against a system they believe fails to protect their interests and rights in Charlottesville and in the attack on the Capitol. Resistance to institutions was the cause around which they rallied, not some broader legal, social, or policy objective. Anger at institutions is ultimately self-fulfilling and also self-perpetuating, as it undercuts the ability of institutions that depend upon democratic participation and compromise to be effective. Anger separates us, which makes democracy less productive, which furthers anger and skepticism. Many people are trapped in this cycle today and find numerous examples of dysfunctional institutions that reinforce their anger.

((•))

Not everyone who believes our institutions are broken is outraged. As I discussed earlier in this chapter many of those who have lost faith in our democracy are more apathetic than angry. Their response to the problems they observe is to withdraw rather than engage. To these cynics, the system is irretrievably broken. They don't believe their personal participation matters, as the problems are too large and intractable for them to make a difference.

There are lots of examples of the ways apathy can be more damaging to our democratic system than eruptions of anger or even political violence. A surprisingly low number of people in this country actually exercise their right to vote. In the 2020 presidential election, about two-thirds of eligible voters actually cast a ballot.[10] A total of approximately 154 million people voted in that election.[11] That means about 77 million Americans who were eligible to vote failed to participate — a shockingly high number. Of those 77 million, about 12.8 million were registered to vote yet did not. The US Census Bureau conducted a survey of eligible voters who did not participate. The results show that "not being interested in the election" was the primary reason people did not vote, followed closely by dislike of candidates and campaign issues, and being too busy or having a conflicting schedule.[12]

When so many Americans choose not to register to vote or cast a ballot, it gives those who do participate disproportionate clout. More specifically, their votes are worth one-third more than they would otherwise be. The enhanced value of each vote gives outsized power to more extreme perspectives and policy positions. People whose vote is motivated, for example, by a desire to support a progressive cause like the Green New Deal may represent 15 percent of the vote in a particular election. We don't know whether the one-third of voters who did not participate support the Green New Deal in the same proportion. Similarly, 25 percent of the voters in a state election may be motivated by the desire to outlaw abortion in that jurisdiction. That percentage of voters doesn't mean that a quarter of the people in that state support a complete abortion ban, as the large number of non-participants may have a different view. In short, lack of participation cedes political power to people with special interests.

Apathy also makes people less motivated to stay informed about issues that directly affect their own lives and the well-being of others. In August 2022, only 38 percent of Americans indicated that they follow the news "all or most of the time," according to a Pew Research Center survey.[13] Another 19 percent follow the news "only now and then," and 9 percent said they "hardly ever" follow the news. These figures are down about 15 percent since 2016, when 51 percent of Americans indicated that they followed the news "all or most of the time" and only 5 percent said they "hardly ever" consumed news.[14] Distrust of the news media is particularly acute among Republicans. In 2022, 37 percent of self-identified Republicans followed the news "all or most of the time," a 20 percent drop from 2016 when 57 percent of Republicans indicated that level of interest in news. Among Democrats, the percentage that follows the news "all or most of the time" dropped 7 percent between 2016 and 2022.

The Pew findings demonstrate that declining interest in news is fueled largely by distrust of the media among a wide array of Americans. Gallup has been polling Americans regarding their "trust and confidence in the news media" every year since 1974. In 2022, 38 percent of Americans responded "none at all" to the question of whether they had such trust and confidence. This percentage is up sharply in the past four years and up substantially since the 1970s.[15] The distrust in media reflected by the Gallup findings skews younger and Republican, as those groups tend to be more skeptical about the veracity of television, radio, and newspaper reporting.

Americans are not only withdrawing from news and politics but also participating in other forms of civic and community life to a much lesser degree than in previous years. Church attendance in the United States, for example, declined more than 10 percent between 2000 and 2023. According to a recent Gallup survey, only three in ten Americans regularly attend a religious service of any kind.[16] This decline is evident across denominations and regions of the country and, as with a lack of interest in news coverage, is particularly marked among younger adults. Union membership has declined by 50 percent in the past thirty years,[17] as has membership in professional and civic organizations.

A recent poll conducted by the *Wall Street Journal* and the University of Chicago found declining rates of belief in institutions that have motivated Americans for years. For example, only 38 percent of survey respondents indicated that "patriotism" is very important to them, down from 70 percent in 1998.[18] Only 39 percent said religious faith is very important to them, down from 62 percent over that same span. Only 27 percent of survey respondents indicated that community involvement is very important to them, down from about 50 percent in 1982. These responses reflect the core reality of cynicism among Americans and reflect our lack of community connection and increasing polarization.

Widespread withdrawal from endeavors that enhance community leads to increasing isolation among Americans. The bipartisan Joint Economic Committee of the United States House of Representatives published a report in 2019 that revealed the percentage of Americans who reported talking with neighbors at least a couple of times per month declined from 71 percent to just more than 50 percent between 2008 and 2018.[19] According to a 2023 Pew study, "A narrow majority of adults (53 percent) say they have between one and four close friends, while . . . some 8 percent say they have no close friends," and younger generations report having fewer friends than older generations.[20] As independent journalist Anne Helen Petersen writes on this topic, her specialty, "My theory is that retirees have more time, sure, but they're also just generally more practiced at the infrastructure of community and friendship. They're not the peak 'joiners' that their parents were in the postwar period, but they grew up in households that were much more likely to have strong connections to religious and community organizations in some capacity."[21] In other words, the new norm for Americans is loneliness.

Some of the isolation we are experiencing is a reflection of our access to and use of technology. People can shop, obtain entertainment, and communicate without directly interacting with other people in real time. Our ability to access basic services via technology decreases time spent in communal settings. Even before the rise of the internet and smartphones, the loss of "third spaces" — a term first coined by sociologist Ray Oldenburg in 1989 — was being widely studied and discussed as a growing, and concerning, phenomenon.[22] A third space is one that is not home (the first space) or work (the second place), but rather a third place where people socialize and build community: churches, bowling alleys, Elk lodges or American Legion halls — anyplace people regularly gather to interact with others in person can fit the bill. The problem has become greatly exacerbated since it was first identified and studied in 1989. Back then, the biggest challenges to third spaces were American zoning laws and automobile culture. Folks would go home and stay at home rather than go around the corner, down the street, or across the neighborhood to a gathering place. Technology changed people's habits for the worse, and in a post-pandemic world, fewer of these spaces even exist. Instead of finding ways outside of work and home to connect with others, many Americans withdraw into social media platforms and other electronic means of engagement.

These declines in participation reflect widespread alienation in America, not just from one another but also from the government that is supposed to serve, and reflect, us all. The University of Chicago study indicates that almost half of Americans (49 percent) feel "more and more like a stranger in my own country."[23] According to a study from nonpartisan research organization Public Agenda, nearly one in three adults feels "politically alienated": 34 percent of Republicans, 29 percent of independents, and 25 percent of Democrats.[24] Fully half of all Americans believe that "democracy is in crisis," a figure that has sharply increased over the past several years. "Politicians don't represent me. They are only responsible for corporations and large funders," one twenty-nine-year-old female Democrat respondent from South Dakota told researchers. "I don't believe any politician on either side. Everybody votes on party lines and with so much polarization, nothing ever gets done. Politicians are solely focused on their own interests," said a twenty-three-year-old female Republican from Oklahoma. The study found that 66 percent of Americans consider it a serious problem that politicians are more interested in blocking the other party than in getting anything done.[25]

This widespread feeling of alienation also has dangerous potential in terms of actual violence. The most startling of the University of Chicago study's findings was that 28 percent of voters believe that "it may become necessary at some point to take up arms against the government."[26] This view is held by one in three Republicans and one in five Democrats — a surprisingly high number of people across the political spectrum who are so disengaged that they are inclined to justify the use of force against the government. This finding shows that apathy and anger may actually be related in a continuum of cynicism about institutions. Apathy leads to alienation, which leads to desperation and potential violence. We risk slipping into a dangerous pattern of self-perpetuating dysfunction. The more we get angry or apathetic, the less functional our system becomes, which in turn reinforces cynicism about democracy and the value of participating in its processes or safeguarding its institutions.

((•))

According to Pew Research, 65 percent of Americans always or often feel "exhausted" when they think about politics.[27] This discouraging finding represents yet another step on the slippery slope toward national apathy. I can empathize. It's difficult to put forth effort when you know that many others aren't paying attention and those that are will strongly disagree with you in disagreeable ways. I have wondered whether any of the work I've done on the Charlottesville and January 6 investigations actually educated and informed people in ways that influenced their opinions. I hope the verified facts our work revealed have mattered, though I fear that in both instances we were largely preaching to the choir, speaking to people who were outraged by these horrific events and were more interested in having ammunition to support their opinions than in gaining understanding and growing.

I resist that feeling of exhaustion and continue to believe that the serious problems we face are neither permanent nor intractable. Despite having spent so much time immersed in the awful facts surrounding the Unite the Right rally and the January 6 attack on the Capitol, I remain hopeful about the future of our democracy. Even after spending years as a federal prosecutor focused on heinous crimes and brutal acts of violence, I believe people are essentially good and will choose to do the right thing the vast majority of the time. I have faith in our collective resilience, ability to learn from history, and fundamental humanity. That faith outweighs my concern about the ugliness and division that my work has revealed.

What informs my faith in our potential is the belief that the remedy to these problems is actually quite simple. We need to find ways to establish and maintain community and enhance the connection to one another. We have to appreciate that we are much more alike than we are different. By and large, we want the same things for our families and for our country, even if we disagree in a multitude of ways about the best ways to achieve them and about the role of government. We should emphasize the ways in which we are alike — our common aspirations, values, and priorities. Our nation is unique in its rich diversity of perspective, culture, and experience. We should celebrate that diversity and use it to enhance our understanding of the challenges we face.

I appreciate that the "simple" solution described above sounds both vague and unrealistic. How exactly can we come together, enhance community, and celebrate our diverse perspectives? Is that even possible given the statistics cited above about levels of anger and apathy in our nation, and the polarization that we have all come to expect? How we respond to and learn from Charlottesville and January 6 and the common threats to our democracy that persist today will determine the future of our country, and of each of us and those we love. Looking back at those two events, we first need to recognize and reinforce the positive forces that prevented worse outcomes, and then we need to hold accountable those whose actions threatened public safety. Looking forward, we need to use the lessons of Charlottesville and January 6 as motivation to promote community. Seen with clarity, Charlottesville and January 6 can light the path toward a better future — one we should all aspire to follow.

COURAGE AND ACCOUNTABILITY

T hroughout my years as a federal prosecutor, I witnessed both heart-wrenching tragedy and inspirational courage. I spent years immersed in the worst moments of people's lives. I asked robbery victims to recount the incidents in which their property was stolen, sexual assault victims to describe the abuse they suffered, and fraud victims to tell me how they were misled. I saw a range of emotions in these meetings — shame, sorrow, anger, and vengeance. Almost no one who came to my office was happy to be there. The people with whom I dealt were either profoundly affected by a loss they could not undo or reluctant to assist in holding others accountable.

In the midst of this tableau of tragedy, I also witnessed heroism, courage, forgiveness, and mercy. Witnesses came forward to describe the violence they observed, despite the very real risks their cooperation created for themselves and their families. I saw dogged detectives pursue every lead with determination to hold those responsible accountable. I saw overworked defense lawyers zealously defend their clients despite caseloads that far exceeded mine. I appeared before judges who carefully considered my arguments, tried to make just decisions, and endeavored to impose fair sentences. Out of the darkness in the cases that fill the dockets of criminal courts around the country, people find light, integrity, and purpose. Tragedy creates opportunities for heroism.

Perhaps no one embodies this reality more than Carol Watkins, the mother of a homicide victim in a case I handled as an assistant US attorney in Washington, DC. Carol's son Anthony Watkins was one of more than a dozen men murdered by a violent drug gang that I prosecuted in the early 2000s. Our star witness in the trial of the gang members responsible for these killings was a man named Oscar Veal, who functioned as a paid assassin for the gang and killed seven people. Veal pleaded guilty to all seven murders, including Anthony Watkins's, and agreed to describe each one for the jury, including the direction and compensation he received from the gang leaders. Ms. Watkins sat in court and listened as Veal described how and why he murdered her son.

At every criminal sentencing in federal court, victims have the right to present information to the sentencing judge about ways in which the crimes at issue have affected them. When Carol Watkins addressed the court at Veal's sentencing, I was braced for condemnation and expected her to ask the judge to sentence the man who killed her son to a lengthy prison term. Ms. Watkins turned and faced Mr. Veal — choosing to direct her remarks to him rather than the judge. In a hushed courtroom, she told Mr. Veal, "I love you. I pray for you. And I forgive you." Everyone was stunned. In a thoughtful, measured voice, she explained that her Christian faith prevents her from judging others, seeking vengeance, or passing judgment on people for the worst things they've done. To the contrary, she explained, her faith compels her to love and forgive those whose transgressions have harmed her. She told Mr. Veal and everyone in that hushed courtroom that she had to choose love over hate, as doing so was the only way she could continue to live in a world without her son.

I recall weeping as Ms. Watkins spoke that day, incredibly moved by her grace and compassion. Her act of forgiveness toward a man who had taken her son from her left an indelible mark on me. It represented the very highest form of human dignity, well beyond what I thought possible or could have summoned myself in that moment. She demonstrated that tragedy creates an opportunity to assert values. She showed me that trying times test our resolve, our perspective, and our ability to move ahead. Carol Watkins turned her loss into a test of her faith, her values, and her approach to life. I have aspired to follow her example in response to the tragedies in my own life.

The story of Carol Watkins is relevant to Charlottesville and January 6, because in studying those two tragedies, I found heroism, courage, strength, and fidelity to purpose. Any account of those horrific events must include an acknowledgment that there were numerous people who, like Carol Watkins, responded to darkness with light. These heroes countered the threats posed by the white supremacists in Charlottesville and the angry mob at the Capitol by adherence to core values — duty, bravery, and the rule of law. But for their heroic actions, the outcomes could have been far worse.

It is also important to acknowledge the legal responses to the events in Charlottesville and at the Capitol, which have led to important measures of accountability. The news media have widely covered thorough efforts by law enforcement officers at all levels of government to bring those who engaged in political violence to justice. Lesser known, however, are the efforts of civil plaintiffs to use the courts to provide accountability, raise awareness, and limit the potential for future lawlessness. One group has invoked a Virginia statute that prevents unofficial militia activity in a suit designed to prevent the white supremacy organizations that marched on Charlottesville from returning. Other plaintiffs have invoked federal civil rights statutes to hold the rally organizers accountable for the damage they caused. Similarly, civil cases have followed the attack on the Capitol. Not only have twelve hundred individuals been criminally charged for their involvement in the assault, but Capitol Police officers and other plaintiffs have sued Donald Trump for his role in inciting insurrection after losing reelection in 2020. These cases continue to wend their way through the courts, a slow-moving but potentially significant step toward holding people responsible for their actions.

While the heroism shown in Charlottesville and Washington and the steps toward accountability are significant, they do not address the systemic issues and conditions that allowed these threats to our democracy to coalesce in the first place, and are still ongoing. While good people prevented worse outcomes in these two crucial instances, their actions do not resolve the broader systemic issues that motivated each event. Accountability will not heal the underlying division in our society that these events revealed. America needs forward-looking solutions that are sweeping in nature. While law enforcement, advocacy groups, and victims of political violence should be lauded for their efforts to hold those for January 6 and Charlottesville accountable, it's up to we the people, of all political stripes, to address dynamics that pose the greatest threats to democracy and create the conditions for political violence.

((•))

As detailed above, the events in Charlottesville started with a local debate about the presence of Civil War statues in two downtown parks. A high school student, Zyahna Bryant, started the discussion by submitting a petition to the city council asking that the statue of Robert E. Lee be removed. In announcing the petition, Bryant wrote, "When I think of Robert E. Lee, I instantly think of someone fighting in favor of slavery. Thoughts of physical harm, cruelty, and disenfranchisement flood my mind."[1] Bryant was soon joined by a chorus of other local activists who similarly objected to the statue. Their efforts led to the creation of the Blue Ribbon Commission on Race, Memorials and Public Spaces, which gathered community input and considered the future of the statues. This group of local activists generated an important public discussion about not only the Civil War statues but also race, history, shared public spaces, and ultimately our values as a community.

As the UTR event came into focus, many people in Charlottesville prepared to counter the hateful speech they knew was coming their way. The Reverend Seth Wispelwey was one of those people. Reverend Wispelwey is an ordained minister of the United Church of Christ and an organizer of an interfaith group called Congregate C'ville, which brought together Jewish, Catholic, Protestant, and Muslim groups aligned in their common desire to counter the UTR participants. Reverend Wispelwey and Congregate C'ville organized nonviolent resistance training for anti-racist activists to prepare them to confront the permitted event with civil disobedience, risking arrest and assault. On August 12, 2017, the reverend was part of a diverse group of people who locked arms and attempted to block access to the park where the rally was to be held. He was pushed aside and assaulted. "If white supremacy is the governing and prevailing order, and white supremacists threaten violence and do violence and are looking for violence, you can't ignore it because it is the oxygen we breathe," he told journalist Nora Neus in her oral history book *24 Hours in Charlottesville* about why he decided to take action.[2]

Lieutenant Joseph Hatter of the Charlottesville Police Department was positioned just steps away from Reverend Wispelwey's attempted blockade of the park. Lieutenant Hatter was a zone commander, assigned to lead a group of officers stationed immediately across the street from the park where the permitted rally was to take place. On the morning of August 12, Lieutenant Hatter waded into the crowd to de-escalate conflicts between attendees. In one incident, "Lieutenant Hatter jumped over the barricade to de-escalate the tension between [a] flag-toting demonstrator and the crowd around him . . . Hatter spoke a few words to calm the demonstrator down," our report found. "This is the only instance we identified of a CPD officer leaving a barricaded safe zone to enter the crowd and de-escalate a potentially violent situation on August 12."[3] Rather than follow his supervisors' directive that he stay behind the barricades, Lieutenant Hatter attempted to prevent violence before it occurred. Upon declaration of the unlawful assembly, Lieutenant Hatter was called to lead his officers away from their assigned zone to don riot gear and prepare to disperse the crowd. During our independent review of these events, Lieutenant Hatter expressed his frustration: "We were prevented from doing police work," he told me. "People [were] getting hurt, and I'm standing around behind a steel fence."[4] His actions stand in stark contrast with the other CPD and VSP officers who stood by while violence unfolded.

After the unlawful assembly was declared and the park cleared, Heather Heyer was part of a group of anti-racist protesters who moved through Charlottesville looking to prevent confrontations between the alt-right attendees and local residents. She was in a large crowd at the intersection of Fourth and Water Streets when white nationalist James Fields drove his Dodge Charger into them. Heyer was killed, and many others were seriously injured. Heather Heyer sacrificed her life protesting against hate. There can be no greater example of fidelity to purpose and putting yourself at risk for your beliefs. "If you're not outraged, you're not paying attention," Heather posted on Facebook shortly before she died.[5]

Heyer's mother, Susan Bro, is another hero to come out of the events of the summer of 2017. She has picked up Heather's mantle of advocating for racial justice, establishing a foundation in Heather's name and speaking out against injustices in Charlottesville and beyond. "Before this, I was a government employee, so I kind of kept my opinions to myself, a little bit," she told the *Washington Post* with a laugh. "Heather and I were definitely on the same page a lot politically, and when we weren't, we would talk it out. Now people want my opinion, so fine, I have things to say. It's not that I never had them before. I've always had things to say, just nobody was willing to listen, and now people are asking me, and so I'm speaking." Ms. Bro has said that she wants to make her daughter Heather's death "count."[6]

In the aftermath of the UTR event, city manager Maurice Jones faced a dilemma. Criticism of CPD, the city council, and other parts of city government immediately followed the rally. Lawyers and insurers advised Mr. Jones to refrain from making any admissions or taking steps that could support litigation against the city. He ignored that advice and commissioned an independent review of the events of the "summer of hate" in Charlottesville. "As our City continues to recover from the rallies that brought great hate into our community, we must take time to reflect on our operational response to these tragic events," he said in his announcement.[7] Mindful of the risk that a review would reveal facts exposing the ineffectiveness or negligence of city officials, Mr. Jones believed that an independent review of the facts and circumstances of the UTR and other events was essential to healing and restoring public confidence in government. In announcing the review, he pledged that it would be fully independent and proceed with full access to city personnel and information. He further promised to disclose the results of the review to the public upon its completion. His willingness to launch a review and examine the city's failures was an example of effective leadership, and it led to the credible accounting of events that I have relied on for this book.

There are multiple examples I could cite of heroes whose actions on and around January 6 helped preserve democracy. Like Lieutenant Hatter, there were many brave men and women in law enforcement who risked their lives to protect others in the Capitol building. US Capitol Police officer Caroline Edwards, whose story is told in chapter 4, continued to protect the west front of the Capitol after receiving a concussion when rioters pushed past her at the

Peace Circle. She bravely described her experience to a national audience at the first prime-time hearing of the January 6 committee.[8] Metropolitan Police Department officer Michael Fanone was pulled into the crowd and viciously beaten by rioters, escaping only when he referenced his young daughter and pleaded for his life. Officers Daniel Hodges, Aquilino Gonell, and Harry Dunn joined Officer Fanone in describing their experience protecting the Capitol on January 6 in the select committee's first hearing in the summer of 2021.[9] There were hundreds of men and women who similarly repelled violence that day. But for their bravery and courage in the face of great danger, the insurrection may have been successful.

In the days before January 6, numerous state officials performed their duties with honor and fidelity to the rule of law, even in the face of extreme pressure from then president Trump and his co-conspirators. Election workers like Ruby Freeman and her daughter Shaye Moss counted ballots in Georgia with diligence and fairness. President Trump falsely accused them of fraud in multiple tweets, which resulted in threats to their lives.[10] As a federal judge later found, they were defamed by President Trump's lawyer Rudy Giuliani, who similarly accused them of surreptitiously miscounting votes.[11] In Pennsylvania, Al Schmidt was Philadelphia city commissioner and the lone Republican on a three-member municipal board tasked with overseeing the conduct of elections in that city. In a November 11, 2020, tweet, President Trump accused Schmidt of "refus[ing] to look into a mountain of dishonesty and corruption" in the counting of votes in Philadelphia.[12] Like Freeman and Moss, Schmidt was subject to vile death threats by Trump supporters. While Freeman, Moss, and Schmidt have received the most attention, false accusations of voter fraud led to similar threats to election workers around the country. Dozens of poll workers and ballot counters were vilified and threatened due to unfounded allegations.

Our elections in this country are facilitated by thousands of public servants, both paid and volunteer, who work diligently to conduct fair vote counts. You see some of them when you vote — the men and women sitting at tables, checking identification and providing ballots. Others are unseen — working in nondescript government buildings to keep track of voter registration, establish and maintain polling stations, facilitate absentee and mail-in voting, and broadly ensure that every eligible voter can cast his or her ballot in an impartial, nonpartisan process. The men and women who run our elections do so with honor and integrity, performing their important responsibilities largely in anonymity. Their careful adherence to law ensures that our elections are conducted fairly and impartially. The fact that some of them have been vilified due to the unfair criticism of the voting process makes their service even more heroic, as it puts them at risk.

Elected officials similarly stepped up to defend democracy in the days after the 2020 election. Georgia secretary of state Brad Raffensperger supervised the conduct of the 2020 election in his state. His office investigated numerous allegations of voter fraud and conducted three complete audits of the results, all of which confirmed that President Biden won the presidential election in Georgia. He explained all of this to President Trump in a telephone call on January 3, just three days before the attack on the Capitol. Secretary Raffensperger stood firm in the face of direct pressure to "find 11,780 votes." Like the poll workers described above, his rejection of false theories of fraud subjected Secretary Raffensperger and his family to vile threats. Arizona Speaker of the House Rusty Bowers, another Republican, similarly rejected President Trump's direct encouragement to take official action based on nonexistent voter fraud. Like Secretary Raffensperger, Speaker Bowers said no. These brave state officials stayed true to their duty to the Constitution, despite overwhelming public pressure from the president of the United States.

There were voices inside the White House who similarly tried to ensure a peaceful transition of power after the 2020 election. Foremost among those was White House counsel Pat Cipollone, who helped prevent his client, the president of the United States, from taking extreme action to pursue baseless allegations of voter fraud. Cipollone was one of several White House advisers who instructed the president that there was no basis to seize voting machines or appoint a special counsel to investigate voter fraud during a meeting on the evening of December 18.[13] He also strongly opposed the president's appointment of Jeffrey Clark as acting attorney general, telling the president in an Oval Office meeting on January 3 that doing so would not change the core reality of an absence of evidence of voter fraud and would result in mass resignations at the Department of Justice. On January 6, Cipollone opposed the president's proposed trip to the Capitol during the joint session and repeatedly encouraged him to issue a stronger statement directing his followers to leave the Capitol. "I felt it was my obligation to continue to push for that, and others felt it was their obligation as well," he told the select committee. "My view was that we should do as much as we possibly can as quickly as possible." In that same interview before the select committee, Cipollone explained that he seriously thought about resigning his position as White House counsel between the election and the inauguration of President Biden but was concerned about who might replace him.[14] He did not resign, and as a result, he remained a calm voice of reason in opposition to others pursuing an unlawful strategy to maintain power.

Vice President Pence is another hero of January 6. He repeatedly told the president that he did not have the legal authority to reject certified slates of electors submitted by the official authorities in each state. Nonetheless, the president privately berated him as weak, and publicly claimed that the vice president did have authority to unilaterally reject these certified slates of electors. Despite that pressure, the vice president remained faithful to his constitutional duty on January 6. His refusal to bow to that pressure led President Trump to issue a tweet during the attack on the Capitol alleging that he lacked courage, resulting in the crowd furiously chanting, "Hang Mike Pence." After coming within forty feet of the angry mob during his evacuation from the Senate chamber,[15] the vice president calmly worked (from a loading dock beneath the Capitol) with military and law enforcement leaders to ensure the resources necessary to disperse the crowd and resume the joint session. His actions on January 6 reflect a fidelity to duty and the rule of law above and beyond his personal safety and political self-interest.

Many of the heroes who helped preserve democracy on January 6 were lifelong Republicans, members of President Trump's own party, who put the Constitution over their political self-interest, and their country over their party. They recognized that maintenance of democracy depends upon adherence to certain immutable principles, like the people's right to choose their leaders. They stayed faithful to that core value on January 6, which prevented the anti-democratic outcome of a successful insurrection.

If not for the actions of the people described in this chapter and countless others who similarly protected democracy, you could be reading a very different story about these two events and living in a very different America. People often ask me what surprised me most about the two seminal events I was tasked with investigating. I frequently respond by citing the realization that democracy is earned, not given. The individual stories of courage outlined above show that democracy comes down to individual decision makers and their willingness to adhere to the bedrock principles on which this country was founded. Democracy comes down to us. Everyone who enjoys the freedom that comes with living in a democratic society has the responsibility to protect and defend the values that ensure that freedom. Thankfully, people responded to that challenge in Charlottesville and at the Capitol on January 6. Whether or not we will respond to future challenges with similar strength and courage depends upon no one other than us.

((•))

The legal response to Charlottesville started with arrests and criminal charges on August 12 and the days that immediately followed. Prosecutors had the benefit of ample video evidence showing assaultive conduct, which they used to charge numerous individuals who committed violent acts on August 11 and 12. The commonwealth's attorney for the City of Charlottesville brought assault charges against men who assaulted DeAndre Harris at a parking garage on Market Street on August 12 — an attack caught on video that left Mr. Harris with a severe head injury. Four men were charged with attacking Mr. Harris, and all were convicted at trial or pleaded guilty.[16] In addition, local authorities have spent the six years since the Unite the Right rally identifying, charging, arresting, and trying other people who marched with the mob on August 11 and 12. Many of these people were found by social media sleuths who managed to post photos and track down identities, aiding law enforcement immensely. But many of those cases took years to prosecute, or are even still ongoing.[17]

Members of the alt-right were not the only ones to face criminal charges after the UTR rally in Charlottesville. The local prosecutor also brought charges against several anti-racist counter-protesters for their involvement in violence. DeAndre Harris, the assault victim described above, was charged with unlawful wounding in a separate incident that same day. He was acquitted by a judge who found that he was protecting others when he used a flashlight to strike a white UTR attendee.[18] Donald Blakney was charged with malicious wounding when he lashed out at an unarmed UTR attendee who verbally assaulted him. He later pleaded guilty to a misdemeanor assault offense.[19] Corey Long aimed a makeshift flamethrower at alt-right protesters as they streamed out of Emancipation Park when the unlawful assembly was declared, resulting in charges of assault and battery and disorderly conduct.[20] Long contested the charges and was convicted of disorderly conduct when the assault victim failed to cooperate with the prosecution.[21] The prosecutor's decision to charge Harris, Blakney, and Long was criticized by many community activists in Charlottesville.[22] The prosecutor explained this decision by emphasizing his commitment to content-neutral application of the law, particularly when acts of violence are involved.[23]

The federal government also charged individuals with crimes, including civil rights offenses and violations of the Anti-Riot Act. James Fields, the man who drove into the crowd on Market Street and killed Heather Heyer, was prosecuted for murder by both the local prosecutor and the United States attorney for the Western District of Virginia. His actions were motivated by racial animus, which made the murder a federal hate crime. Fields was convicted in state court[24] and pleaded guilty to the federal crimes, resulting in a mandatory life sentence.[25] The US attorney also prosecuted several members of the Rise Above Movement (RAM) for violations of the Anti-Riot Act, a federal criminal statute that had not been used by federal prosecutors since the 1960s. The US attorney charged that these men traveled from California to Charlottesville with the intent to participate in a riot and commit acts of violence. This novel theory was successfully upheld in federal court, resulting in lengthy jail sentences for RAM defendants.[26]

Two significant civil proceedings similarly helped achieve accountability for the racist violence in Charlottesville. The Institute for Constitutional Advocacy and Protection at Georgetown Law Center brought a civil complaint against the various militia groups that participated in the UTR event. This suit resulted in a consent decree that prevents twenty-three separate militia or alt-right groups from returning to Charlottesville and engaging in "paramilitary activity."[27] A group of individuals harmed by the racist violence in Charlottesville on August 11 and 12 brought a federal civil rights case against several people who organized the UTR event and committed acts of violence. A federal jury found

Richard Spencer, Jason Kessler, Christopher Cantwell, and others guilty of conspiring to violate the civil rights of the plaintiffs and awarded the latter $23 million.[28]

The civil cases are important steps toward accountability and will help prevent anything like the UTR event from happening again. While the federal civil rights case may not result in the collection of anything close to the jury's award of $23 million in damages, the jury's finding that the defendants' actions in Charlottesville were motivated by racial animus is an important validation of the plaintiffs' position that UTR was a racist provocation more than a free speech event. The legal consequences imposed on the organizations and individuals that participated in the rally raise the stakes of future involvement in large-scale events that provoke violence, wherever they may be held in the United States.

The January 6 attack on the US Capitol has resulted in the largest criminal investigation ever undertaken by the United States Department of Justice. As of the date of this writing, over twelve hundred individuals have been criminally charged with offenses stemming from their involvement in the Capitol riot.[29] These charges range from misdemeanor trespassing on Capitol grounds to seditious conspiracy, which requires intentional use of violence to disrupt the lawful function of government. Of those whose cases have been adjudicated, all but three have been convicted or pleaded guilty.[30] Even now, more than three years after the attack on the Capitol, the Department of Justice continues to investigate and bring new charges.

Prosecutors at the state and federal levels have also brought charges against people who were not at the Capitol yet who allegedly committed acts that led to the January 6 attack. The most significant of those are the federal and state charges against former president Trump, in which he is alleged to have conspired to disrupt the joint session of Congress and prevent the transfer of authority. The select committee specifically referred evidence of these and other federal crimes to the United States Department of Justice and provided evidence to the special counsel evaluating these events.[31] Prosecutors in Fulton County, Georgia, have brought a racketeering case against the former president and eighteen other individuals alleging a conspiracy to prevent certification of the official results of the Georgia election.[32] In addition to Georgia, prosecutors in Michigan, Nevada, and Arizona have charged a number of individuals in those states with serving as fake electors and causing the submission of false electoral certificates to Congress.[33] These cases are pending at the time of this writing and will be resolved in the months ahead.

The events of January 6 have also resulted in civil litigation. A group of US Capitol Police officers and Democratic members of Congress have brought several civil actions against former president Trump and others for causing them harm during the January 6 attack. These cases are proceeding, as a federal appeals court has denied the former president's claims that he is immune from these suits.[34] Other individuals have brought defamation actions against Rudy Giuliani, Fox News, and others who have falsely alleged voter fraud.[35]

Beyond civil and criminal litigation, lawyers whose conduct facilitated the attack on the Capitol have been subjected to professional discipline, up to and including disbarment. John Eastman, Rudy Giuliani, Sidney Powell, and Jenna Ellis were all at one time lawyers who represented the former president and his campaign. Jeffrey Clark was the Justice Department lawyer who was prepared to take action without basis in fact or law as acting attorney general. All of them have been or are in the process of being sanctioned by the bars of which they were members, resulting in their inability to continue to practice law.[36]

All of these cases and disciplinary proceedings matter, as they provide a measure of accountability for the conduct that informed the attack on the Capitol. The legal responses also have a deterrent

effect, as they dissuade future rioters, fake electors, or other conspir-
ators from engaging in similar conduct. We've seen this deterrent
effect in operation at the various courthouses where the former
president has appeared for hearings. There are many people in
America who believe those proceedings are unjust and represent a
"deep state" effort to silence and punish the former president. Nonetheless, the number of people willing to risk their liberty to protest
those proceedings is negligible and undoubtedly reflects recognition of the strong legal response to the January 6 attack.

((•))

While the personal heroism we witnessed in Charlottesville and at
the Capitol prevented worse outcomes, it is not enough to protect
democracy going forward. I believe in the fundamental goodness
of people and expect that brave men and women will continue to
step up in times of crisis. Our history is full of examples of ordinary people doing extraordinary things and heroes who emerge
in trying times. We are fortunate to live in a country in which
every person has the opportunity to contribute to the health of
our democracy. While I have every expectation that our national
character will continue to reflect that heroism, we cannot rest on
that assumption without taking on the broader issues that threaten
our democracy.

While numerous individuals have been held accountable for
their acts at both events, the legal responses alone will not deter
similar actions and prevent future misconduct. Court decisions,
after all, have to do with responding to actions that have already
taken place. While accountability and justice matter, they must
be augmented by proactive solutions to strengthen democracy.
The final chapter of this book will now turn to the question of
forward-looking, systemic changes that can be made.

BALLOONS

One of the primary responsibilities of a United States attorney is relationship building. During my five years serving as US attorney for the Western District of Virginia, I spent a lot of time driving around Virginia, cultivating and maintaining relationships with a range of stakeholders who came into contact with the work of our office. I met with police chiefs, sheriffs, and other state and local law enforcement personnel. I met with elected officials, business leaders, and representatives of nonprofit and charitable organizations. My intention was to bring a holistic approach to public safety — a union of targeted enforcement, crime prevention, and reentry support for people released from prison. I analogized this vision of public safety to a three-legged stool and became an evangelist for the necessity of providing support for prevention and reentry programs in the communities in which we were targeting our enforcement efforts. I even carried a stool around in the trunk of my car to use as an illustration in sketching out this approach during these meetings.

One of the most poignant days I had during my time as US attorney was a visit to the campus of Virginia Tech in Blacksburg on April 16, 2010. It was the third anniversary of a campus mass shooting that took the lives of thirty-one people. I went to Tech to meet with the law enforcement leaders who responded to that awful tragedy as well as to attend various memorial services. I spent a lot of time with the federal agents from the Bureau of Alcohol, Tobacco and Firearms who had been among the first on the scene, and I heard them describe both the violence they witnessed and the emotional toll the incident had taken on them since.

That cool April morning started for me on the Virginia Tech drill field — a large grassy lawn in the center of campus in front of the building where the shooting took place. When I arrived at the drill field, I was part of a large crowd of hundreds, even thousands, of people who were gathered to participate in the Run in Remembrance, a 3.1-mile run through the campus, dedicated to the memories of the thirty-one victims. Each of us was given a balloon, either maroon or orange, the Virginia Tech school colors. We were instructed to move toward the starting line for what would be a silent start to the run. A cluster of thirty-one white balloons floated up over the quiet crowd of strangers. As the white balloons ascended skyward, runners in the crowd started releasing the maroon and orange balloons we'd been given. There was no direction to do so, but as more and more balloons rose, everyone released theirs. What ensued was absolutely beautiful — a sea of maroon and orange balloons rising up toward the thirty-one white balloons that had gone first.

I have told that story many times since 2010, as I think the symbol of the balloons rising over the drill field is the perfect illustration of how communities can come together in the wake of tragedy. The silent communication of the symbolic release was so meaningful, as it showed that a large group of strangers connected to one another through a common sense of purpose were linked by their shared humanity, their grief, and their desire to help one another recover from that awful tragedy. What united us was far more powerful and important than any differences — religious, socioeconomic, political — that might separate us in our daily lives.

I start this chapter with the balloon story because it presents a good analogy about what I believe is ultimately necessary to heal the division in America and preserve democracy. In response to the violence in Charlottesville and at the Capitol, we need to come together and connect rather than retreat to the warring tribes that so often define us. We need to focus on what we have in common, as those commonalities are far more significant than our differences. Ironically, one thing a majority of Americans share is a sense of frustration with the polarization gripping our politics and culture. We need to find ways to listen to, learn from, and respect one another, then ultimately recommit to some common values. We can't rely on elected officials, individual heroes, the court system, or any other outside source to mend what's broken in America. I've made the case in this book for my belief that a variety of dynamics in our political system have led us to a point where American democracy itself is at risk. We've lost sight of the fact that our democracy works only when people have faith in the institutions upon which we rely to settle our differences. The balance has tipped away from a system that works for the people, and the only way to correct the situation is for us to do it ourselves, to find ways to promote community over division.

Admittedly, coming together is easier said than done. I've explored in great detail in this book many forces at play in America that push us apart. An information landscape fueled by social media algorithms and for-profit news models keeps us in silos and reinforces our prevailing beliefs. We live in gerrymandered districts that see little political competition and almost no compromise. Primaries that are controlled by the two major political parties and fueled by special interest money reward extreme rhetoric and an unwillingness to compromise. So many of us are angry, or apathetic, or both. Any effort to heal our division will have to overcome these forces. Unity is upstream, so we'll have to struggle to achieve it.

Despite these odds and the forces arrayed against us, I believe America can come together and heal its current division. Doing so will require engagement, participation, and willingness to take personal responsibility for the maintenance of democracy. It will take a concerted, grassroots effort that inspires, motivates, and appeals to our hopes and aspirations. It will take attention and effort, rather than complacency. Healing will take sustained attention to what unites us, and a willingness to listen, compromise, and admit mistakes.

To fix our broken democracy, we should pursue three basic goals. First, we should do all we can to encourage people to participate and make it easy for them to vote, stay informed, and voice their concerns. Second, we need to find ways to teach and model constructive engagement, giving people the tools to sift information, pursue and consider alternative points of view, and listen to and learn from their fellow citizens. This should start early in public schools that help young people navigate the systems by which they receive information and encourage them to pursue the first goal of participation. Finally, we need to create systems for Americans to come together in common purpose — working together in service to their communities and finding ways to help one another. If we commit to pursue these three foundational goals, America will heal itself.

People across the political divide believe in the importance of contributing to the greater good, the benefits of pursuing knowledge, and the idea that community makes us stronger. The irony of the division I've seen in my work in Charlottesville and in Congress is that it is inconsistent with the fact that Americans share so many fundamental priorities. We have more in common than we do differences. Our shared values and goals make me optimistic about our nation's ability to come together around core principles of democracy — in other words, how we reach compromise solutions without political violence. While the events described above reveal the existence of strong disagreements, they do not alter the fact that all of us want to live in freedom to pursue happiness, create productive lives for our families, and live in a world that is fundamentally just and humane.

The Role of Government

As related above, the current reality of political polarization makes me pessimistic about the ability of government to address the problems and threats revealed by the events in Charlottesville and at the Capitol. This is particularly true with respect to fixing the processes of representative government itself, as both sides have a vested interest in the status quo. While a few state legislatures have implemented systems to draw competitive districts, the vast majority perpetuate the broken system of gerrymandered districts because it protects the territorial interests of both sides. Congress has been repeatedly unwilling to reduce the pernicious influence of money in politics, as both Republicans and Democrats rake in large amounts of special interest money that flows primarily to incumbents. Representative governments at all levels of our federal system are ill equipped to change the rules to encourage competition, as doing so would jeopardize the firm grip on power held by the decision makers.

Changing the rules that govern our governments will require an organic effort. Recognizing the reality of legislative inertia, voters in some states have been successful in using ballot measures and referenda to drive systemic change. Between 1985 and 2022, there were a stunning 402 ballot measures in California, one of the states that most frequently uses this method of direct governance. Of those, 231 were approved.[1] One ballot measure on reproductive freedom that passed in 2022 was Proposition 1, which established that "the state shall not deny or interfere with an individual's reproductive freedom in their most intimate decisions, which includes their fundamental right to choose to have an abortion and their fundamental right to choose or refuse contraceptives," and represents a significant use of citizen power. Similarly, Proposition 17, which was passed in 2020, restored voting rights to people on parole for felony convictions. In 2018, Proposition 1 authorized $4 billion in housing programs, and even farther back, in 1911, Proposition 4 granted women in California the right to vote.[2] Of course, elected officials make the rules that control the availability of the tools of direct democracy, and most states do not offer their citizens the option of advancing such ballot measures.

Beyond fixing their own rules and processes in ways that might increase compromise and reduce gridlock, representative bodies could pursue legislative initiatives to address the threats to our democracy revealed by Charlottesville and January 6. Both parties have an interest in evaluating the regulation of social media and considering whether we should create an obligation for platforms to moderate content. Similarly, both Republicans and Democrats want to ensure that law enforcement is effective at identifying and preventing active threats to public safety. Reforms like repealing or altering Section 230, which provides immunity for social media companies with respect to third-party content generated by its users, or creating a viable system of information sharing among law enforcement agencies raise complex risks and rewards; they will require thorough analysis of relevant facts and, of course, compromise. The necessity of compromise to achieve reform is what makes me pessimistic about Congress's ability to lead the way on these and other complex issues. While the lack of a partisan divide on the importance of addressing these particular matters creates the potential for real change, Congress has not shown the political will to take on complicated matters that require cooperation and compromise since the very act of reaching across the aisle has become suspect.

I am more optimistic about our government's ability to facilitate solutions that reflect core values common to Americans across the political spectrum. Perhaps Congress could come together to fund national service programs and encourage young people to devote time and energy to fixing the problems in their communities. A huge benefit of a national service program would be that it would bring together young people from disparate backgrounds and regions, as military service already does. As noted elsewhere in this book, people hate and distrust from afar, not up close. Living and working together toward common goals would foster understanding among young Americans in ways that would benefit them as individuals, and American democracy itself, for the rest of their lives.

Facilitating Participation in Public Life

The very essence of democracy is self-governance. The founding fathers understood that a government of, by, and for the people would have more legitimacy than a monarchy, as everyone governed has an opportunity to shape the rules by which they live. To maintain their status, elected officials must be responsive to those they represent, or not get reelected. In a real sense, they are representatives, tasked with giving voice to the priorities and perspectives of their constituents.

While this process makes sense in theory, it doesn't often work in practice. American democracy has been on a path for many years to increased polarization for reasons that I've explored at length. The success of the democratic process working in ways that promote the common good depends upon the willingness of people to hold their representatives accountable. Citizens must voice their concerns to their elected leaders and ensure that those views are reflected in the actions of those leaders. In my view, participation is a fundamental obligation of anyone who lives in a democracy. When people fail to voice concerns and do not vote, they cede their democratic authority to those who do. Our government becomes less representative and more prone to pursue the objectives of subsets of individuals who make their voices heard and are more susceptible to manipulation by a range of interest groups, misinformation, toxic algorithms, and other dynamics that threaten democracy. Low levels of participation in the political process makes our system less democratic, as it represents the interests and opinions of far fewer citizens than it should.

The first and most basic responsibility of citizenship is voting. Casting our ballot for leaders who manage our public schools, levy taxes, consider policy responses to emerging challenges, and navigate our country's place in world affairs is the obligation of every American. Failing to do so makes our government less responsive to the needs of the majority and cedes power to voices who protect special interests. Full participation, starting with voting, is the only way to ensure that government acts in the interests of all citizens.

To facilitate this core requirement of full participation, we must make it easier to vote. We have traditionally held elections on Tuesdays in November primarily during business hours. While this method works for most Americans, on any given Election Day a considerable percentage of eligible voters cannot physically travel to a polling station due to professional or family obligations, infirmity or illness, lack of transportation, or other factors. To accommodate those people, we should extend the window for casting a ballot to multiple days and locations.

While the traditional practice of voting in person should remain an option, we have the technological capacity to facilitate voting by other means. People should be able to vote by mail, using absentee ballots or other official forms to ensure reliability. In 2000, Oregon became the first state to conduct its presidential election entirely by mail.[3] The secretary of state delivers ballots to all registered voters, who must return their marked ballots by Election Day. Eight states have passed laws to allow elections to be conducted entirely by mail, while others allow mail-only elections in localities.[4] Almost all states allow some form of voting by mail if voters meet certain conditions.

In many other areas of American life, we use online platforms to express preferences and conduct important transactions. You can apply for a passport, purchase a firearm, or enroll in public school using online platforms. We could use similar secure, online processes to facilitate voting — both registering and voting itself. Over twenty states allow their citizens to vote online through secure portals controlled by elections officials.[5] Pursuant to the Uniformed and Overseas Citizens Absentee Voting Act (UOCAVA), members of the US military can cast their ballots online in local and federal elections. If those serving our country in uniform can cast secure ballots, that privilege could be widely extended to all citizens.

It is not only in the method of casting ballots that we should expand access. Many states disqualify categories of people from voting, including those with a felony conviction or certain mental disabilities. People who live legally in this country as permanent non-residents are ineligible to vote, and those who live in US territories like Puerto Rico, Guam, and the US Virgin Islands cannot cast ballots in presidential elections.[6] Regardless of the tremendous impact the executive branch of the federal government has on life in these territories, their residents have no voice in who makes those policies and how they are enacted or implemented.

These rules unduly restrict participation and disenfranchise many people affected by elections. Preventing felons from voting is the most pernicious example of denying individuals a voice and an opportunity for engagement with the political process, since they are among those most directly affected by the laws of this country. Disenfranchisement is one of the many onerous collateral consequences of a felony conviction. The loss of voting rights extends beyond the punishment imposed for the crime and serves no legitimate public safety purpose. It is a categorical exclusion of people who have been otherwise held accountable, unrelated to the facts and circumstances of their criminal conduct. As of 2022, about 4.4 million people lost their right to vote because of a felony conviction.[7] But even that high number is already a 24 percent decrease since 2016, because many legislatures have since recognized the fundamental unfairness of preventing felons from voting and now provide for automatic or discretionary restoration of rights.[8] The exact laws vary from state to state; however, all but nine states have some process for restoration, whether voting is restored after prison, after parole, or after probation.[9] And two states, Vermont and Maine, allow all currently incarcerated prisoners to vote.[10]

As a longtime prosecutor, I am very familiar with the effect of a felony conviction on someone's life even after they have served their sentence. I believe the imposition of onerous collateral consequences on people who have been held accountable and served their time is unfair and counterproductive for both the individuals involved and the larger communities in which they live. Communities are stronger when every member has the ability to be productive and reach their full potential. In pursuit of that goal, I started the Fountain Fund, an organization that provides low-interest loans to formerly incarcerated men and women and helps them reenter communities post-incarceration.[11] We help these individuals access capital to repay court-imposed debt, purchase job-related clothing or equipment, or start small businesses. I believe strongly that we are all invested in the success of returning citizens, as their contributions make our communities stronger. Governments should do more to provide reentry opportunities and help people achieve their full potential.

Participation in government extends beyond voting. There are some traditional models of collective decision making at work in the United States from which we can draw inspiration. For example, Americans have used Quaker meeting rituals and processes as a way of promoting civic engagement and communal decision making since the early days of this country. The decision-making process is conducted using horizontal leadership. Each person, dubbed a "friend," gets an equal say, and ultimately the group requires a consensus in the final decision. According to the American Friends Service Committee, "In making decisions Friends do not simply vote to determine the majority view, but rather they seek unity about the wisest course of action. Over time Friends have developed ways to conduct meetings that nurture and support this corporate discernment process."[12] Quaker meetings are not just a way of voting but rather a process of how to come to that decision.

This model has already been successfully applied to many modern, secular environments. For example, Quaker schools around the country apply the Quaker method to decision making within their communities, allowing students greater say and transparency in how their own community operates.[13] "The challenges associated with using Quaker processes in a Friends school are often about the time it takes to do justice to the process, as well as our willingness to be transformed by the experience," the Moorestown School writes. "Yet, by leaning into the use of the Quaker process, Friends schools give students the opportunity to try a different way of approaching decision making and give them a set of tools to use throughout their lives."[14]

What would it look like for town councils or other smaller, local-level governments to employ a Quaker model? Could a local school board, for example, implement a process of participatory decision making to decide big issues like the pursuit of particular programs or priorities or more discrete matters like the naming or renaming of a school? If every parent has an opportunity to voice their point of view in this communal process, the end result will reflect a broad consensus and consequently have enhanced legitimacy. Not everyone will necessarily agree with the decision, but they will have had a substantive opportunity to voice their concerns and influence the outcome. While this has not been tested on a formalized government level, activist movements including the Clamshell Alliance, an anti-nuclear group in the 1970s and 1980s, and the Occupy Wall Street movement of the 2010s have drawn from the Quaker model in their consensus decision making.

Jury service is another manifestation of citizen participation in government, and, similar to voting, it is infected with exclusions. Most states call people for jury service from voter registration lists, and some pull additional names from the pool of licensed drivers.[15] This process reduces the subset of potential jurors to those who have engaged with other processes of government, leaving large numbers of otherwise eligible citizens outside of the jury process. Almost all states prevent convicted or accused felons from serving on juries.[16] This exclusion suffers from the same fundamental lack of fairness as voting restrictions; these men and women have been held accountable for their crimes and should be able to fully participate in their communities and enjoy all the benefits of citizenship. Facilitating the participation of all citizens in jury service will make the criminal and civil justice systems more democratic.

Some local governments create councils, advisory boards, or other collective processes to collect feedback about specific issues. These panels are often voluntary, allowing individuals to apply to serve. A very timely example are police review boards, often called citizens' review boards, which have become even more popular since the summer of 2020 protests. More than 160 towns or cities currently have some form of civilian oversight established through legislation, according to the National Association for Civilian Oversight of Law Enforcement.[17] However, these police oversight boards have vastly different levels of power.[18] According to an ABC News story, "Oversight bodies often face challenges accessing police records, true independence from local politicians, and resistance from police departments and unions, experts say."[19] According to a 2016 report, only 6 percent of civilian oversight agencies have the power to discipline officers, only 40 percent have the ability to subpoena witnesses, and only 41 percent have the ability to subpoena records.[20] Despite these limitations, civilian review boards are an important way to provide accountability, allow for independent investigations, and provide feedback on internal policies and training procedures.

Civilian boards exist across all policy and interest areas. When I first moved to Charlottesville, I applied to serve on the Charlottesville/Albemarle Commission on Children and Families. I had very young children at the time and wanted to contribute to the support our local government provided to our youngest and most vulnerable neighbors. I learned a tremendous amount about my community and was privileged to have a voice in how its resources were deployed. Other popular citizen commissions focus on historic preservation, arts, parks and recreation, ethics, and other issues. Some larger cities, like New York City, have dozens of such commissions ranging from the Board of Health and City Planning Commission to the Climate Change Adaptation Task Force and the New York Public Library Board.[21] New York City also has general community oversight committees called community boards, whose purpose is "to encourage and facilitate the participation of citizens within city government within their communities, and the efficient and effective organization of agencies that deliver municipal services in local communities and boroughs." There are fifty-nine all-volunteer boards throughout the city, each comprising up to fifty members who are nominated by city council.[22]

Special interest panels are important mechanisms of citizen participation. Governments should look for ways to involve voices from within the communities they serve to help set priorities, guide policymaking, and inform budgetary decisions. These panels are easy to create and require little administrative process and few resources. They give participants a sense of pride in service and broaden the reach of elected officials. Citizen committees are a form of outsourcing that brings important perspectives into conversations about pressing issues, resulting in more representative and effective solutions.

When governments create commissions like the one on which I served, they should cast a wide net for members and ensure the participation of a diverse array of perspectives. These panels often attract people who are already the most informed and able to commit the time and energy to applying and serving. Citizen committees should not rely solely on self-selected volunteers but actively recruit individuals with deep experience and diverse points of view. Service on these panels should accommodate working men and women and others who have limited ability to contribute to such efforts. Citizen commissions need to reflect the communities they serve.

In addition to individuals making efforts to ensure that members of commissions and participants in ad hoc initiatives fully represent communities, the government can also use its resources to back and encourage more civilian participation. In 2011, the Obama administration launched a popular online petitioning platform called We the People, which allowed anyone to create and support petitions, which would then be reviewed by the administration.[23] This service yielded a number of successful petitions that led to tangible change on topics ranging from state laws banning conversion therapy to baseball legend Yogi Berra receiving the Medal of Freedom.[24]

We should do all we can to promote these mechanisms of citizen involvement and make it easy for all to engage, whether by serving on formal commissions or participating in ad hoc engagement efforts such as circulating petitions or launching letter-writing campaigns. Amnesty International hosts a Write for

Rights campaign in the days leading up to World Human Rights Day (December 10) in which people from more than 170 countries are encouraged to write letters and sign petitions for a variety of human-rights-related causes. The campaign netted a stunning 5.8 million letters and signatures in 2023. More important, perhaps, Amnesty International reported that "over 100 people featured in our campaign have seen a positive change in their situation," and the release from imprisonment of at least 48 people could be attributed directly to Write for Rights efforts.[25]

Living in a democracy provides both rights and responsibilities, and it is incumbent upon every American to find ways to participate. The privileges and freedoms we enjoy must be safeguarded through engagement, participation, and attention to the maintenance of those rights. My hope is that the events of Charlottesville and at the Capitol motivate Americans to commit to doing all they can to protect democracy. The simplest and most effective way to achieve that goal is to show up and participate in democratic processes.

Encouraging Constructive Dialogue and Engagement

In addition to encouraging full participation in the various manifestations of democracy, we need to give people the tools to manage the responsibility that comes with such participation. We need to find ways to encourage constructive dialogue among people across this country — within and among communities. We should devise and facilitate systems that help people look beyond the exclusive silos in which they live and get their information and seek out perspectives different from their own. We should help children learn to think critically and navigate the information ecosystem driven by algorithms, affinity groups, and the lack of content moderation among social media platforms. Most important, each of us should find our own unique ways to engage with our neighbors and participate actively in our democracy.

Like many things in life, critical thinking is easier if it's learned and practiced while young. As a threshold step toward creating a more engaged citizenry, we should start with the youngest participants in our democracy — children. Schools have the unique potential to promote the value of community simply by teaching kids how to evaluate information and engage with one another — in other words, teaching them not what to think, but how to think. By giving children the basic skills to navigate life in a pluralistic society, schools plant the seeds that nourish and protect democracy. They should rise to, not shy from, this awesome responsibility and prepare our kids to engage with one another and use the diverse sources of available information. Our schools should help students develop the skills necessary to sift what's true from what's false, to know the difference between verifiable facts and unsubstantiated claims. And they should encourage students to consider alternate perspectives before making decisions or solidifying points of view.

Social media literacy should be a fundamental part of school curriculum. Education about these platforms should start with clarity about how they operate — the practice of curated feeds that respond to prior engagement. We should help kids realize the echo chambers these algorithms create, making it difficult to find and consider alternative perspectives. Schools need to help students understand that traditional sources of news and information are governed by standards different from the free speech platforms of social media. We must prepare our children to navigate a world in which all manner of information is immediately available by pushing a couple of buttons on a device carried in your pocket. These lessons should focus on the benefits these devices and platforms provide as well as their risks. The risk is serious; the US Surgeon General has proposed adding a warning label to social media platforms, with a special emphasis alerting parents to the danger they pose to teenagers. Congress would have to approve such an action, but there is precedent, such as warning labels on cigarettes.[26]

Schools should also give our children a framework with which to approach the world. Teachers should expose students to alternative perspectives and ensure that curriculum involves diverse points of view. Schools need to establish mechanisms that encourage students to consider the views of people with whom they disagree and continually hone their opinions. High school students may not remember the specific math formulas or historical facts they are taught, but if they develop the foundational ability to think critically about the world, they will carry that with them forever.

One program tackling both social media and information literacy more broadly is the nonprofit News Literacy Project, whose mission statement reads: "People who are exposed to the News Literacy Project's programs learn how to identify what they can trust, share and act on, and they become better-informed, more engaged and more equal participants in the civic life of their community, their country and the world."[27] Some news organizations, including the *New York Times*, the Associated Press, NPR, Reuters, and many more, have partnered with the program, integrating their content and supporting its mission. The organization targets both educators and students with resources for use in the classroom and beyond. They run a free specialized online learning platform called Checkology, with specific lessons about media sources and bias, misinformation, and even conspiratorial thinking. One version of the platform is designed for younger students, while another has recently launched for adults and the general public, after it became clear how broad the need is.[28] And the program works: 87 percent of students correctly identified fairness as a standard of quality journalism (a 17 percent increase from pre-assessment), 85 percent understood that one of the appeals of conspiracy theories is the sense of community and belonging they provide (a 27 percent increase), and 71 percent of students could recognize when a social media post didn't provide credible evidence (an 8 percent gain).[29]

If there is any environment in which constructive discussion about pressing, complex issues should be possible, it is on college and university campuses. Students should hone their critical thinking skills at the undergraduate college level and emerge with the ability to question assumptions and learn from others. As I've discussed, I spent several years as university counsel at the University of Virginia, watching how the university's admissions team strives to recruit and retain a diverse student population. Elite schools like UVA attract students from all regions of the country and around the world with differing social, religious, and cultural backgrounds, and differing political opinions. This diverse group of promising young minds comes together in classrooms, dormitories, athletic fields, and dining halls. Many students come to places like UVA without prior exposure to ideas and experiences their fellow students have to share, and they generally choose relatively homogeneous work environments, neighborhoods, and social circles when they depart. For most American college students, their time on campus is the best opportunity they will ever have to develop an informed sense of the world's great diversity and their own contributions to it.

The forces of division outlined in this book affect college students as much as the rest of us, and that division prevents some students from embracing the full benefits of living and learning in a diverse college environment. Too many retreat to affinity groups that reinforce rather than challenge their opinions. For some, college is a credential more than an exploration, a way station on a preordained path more than an unpredictable journey to self-awareness filled with surprises and marked by personal growth.

To counteract the inertia and division that infects American society and to maximize the collective benefit of the aligned opportunities presented on campus, university leaders need to create systems to encourage critical thinking. This starts with recruiting students and faculty with diverse perspectives — both liberal and conservative. If a particular school, department, or other organization is one-dimensional, it has the tendency to teach more of an orthodoxy than a dynamic understanding of complex issues. Conversely, learning environments in which people with contrasting views can listen to and learn from one another produce more informed students, who are prepared to consider all sides of a situation. They will become freethinkers in college and for the rest of their lives, applying the ability to constructively engage when they leave campus and to appreciate the reality that thoughtful people of goodwill can hold conflicting opinions and yet still talk them through, work together, and get along.

At the University of Virginia, several programs aim to encourage respectful dialogue and teach students how to engage with diverse perspectives in a changing world. The university's Miller Center for Public Affairs and Karsh Institute of Democracy have teamed up to establish a series of programs called Democracy Dialogues, which bring together prominent scholars, government officials, and journalists with sharply contrasting views to discuss emerging issues.[30] Professor Mary Kate Cary, a former speechwriter for President George H. W. Bush, directs a program called Think Again UVA, which promotes intellectual diversity on campus. The four pillars of Think Again UVA are freedom of expression, viewpoint diversity, intellectual humility, and critical thinking.[31] Professor Cary regularly works with other faculty with divergent experiences and perspectives to help students come together and practice these core values. Many top universities now run similar dialogue programs, including Dialogue Vanderbilt, the Project on Civic Dialogue at American University, Harvard Dialogues, and Dean's Dialogue at

Yale, the latter of which hosted a candid conversation on Palestine and Israel shortly after the October 7, 2023, attacks. Some of these programs run dialogue groups themselves, while others provide grants and support for other dialogue-focused events.[32]

Even absent a specific campus program, students should pursue opportunities to engage with those with whom they disagree. Diverse perspectives are abundant on college campuses, and motivated students can and should challenge their own beliefs in exchanges with others of differing views. It is imperative for individual students to take responsibility for their own education by reaching beyond their cocoons of homogeneity. They should embrace their short-lived opportunity to live with and learn from people who come from different backgrounds and hold different views and who are also going through the same process of exploration, learning, and personal growth.

The obligation to seek diverse sources of information and constructively engage with others extends beyond college campuses, though finding and connecting with people with divergent perspectives is perhaps harder outside an academic setting. Interfaith America is one organization facilitating such conversations on a nationwide level through in-person summits and online courses and events, as well as campus and corporate consulting services.[33] Interfaith America says that a five-year longitudinal study of their on-campus program has shown that students involved in it are able to engage productively with others about religious diversity, a first step toward a "thriving, resilient democracy." "While polarization appears to dominate the nation, a majority of Americans want to live in a religiously diverse democracy — though they may lack the skills to unlock that diversity's potential," the organization writes.[34]

While programs like these create important opportunities for constructive dialogue, we cannot sit around and wait for some organized program to come into our lives before we seek to cultivate this crucial life skill. Democracy is stronger if all Americans embrace the opportunity to engage with their diverse peers. All of us need to challenge our assumptions, reach beyond our silos of common information and experience, and think critically. We can do this by seeking out alternative sources of news and information and talking with and listening to friends and neighbors who have different political views. Of course it can be difficult to confront perspectives that sharply differ from your own. But if we approach these encounters with curiosity and humility, we may learn something that enhances our understanding.

Pursuing the Common Good

In addition to facilitating dialogue among people who disagree and learning from one another, we need to promote opportunities for Americans to have common experiences. Shared service, collective endeavors, and group pursuit of common interests bring people together like nothing else. Reinforcing our shared humanity by working together is ultimately the most lasting and effective way to strengthen democracy.

I grew up playing team sports from the time I was old enough to run all the way into college. Sports taught me much about life beyond the fields and courts on which I played. Most important, they taught me how to work with others as part of a team and how to pursue the common goal of winning a game or a championship with a diverse group of others who were committed to the same goal. My high school football team in Fort Washington, Maryland, was, like my high school graduating class, about half white and half Black. We were extremely successful, going undefeated during my senior year until a tough loss in the state championship game. Part of our success stemmed from the personal closeness our team enjoyed off the field. We liked one another, supported one another, and were invested in one another's and the team's success. Some of my teammates lived in areas very different from my suburban street and faced challenges outside of school that I could only imagine. I didn't see some of my teammates in any of my classes, as they struggled in subjects in which I excelled. Outside football, we seemed to have little in common, yet we felt like brothers because we shared a very important, common purpose.

High school football was one of the most formative experiences of my life. It shaped me as much as anything else I did in high school, as it reinforced the power of shared experience. When people come together to pursue a common goal, their differences seem less significant and less divisive. Bringing people together in any group pursuit provides the impetus for them to see one another in ways they would not otherwise. Shared pursuits reveal our essential sameness.

The same thing can happen on a national scale if we create ways for Americans to come together in a common cause, shared service, and collective endeavors. One specific way to achieve this goal would be a national service program, providing opportunities for young people to work together in specific projects that benefit communities. National service programs increase civic engagement, benefiting both the beneficiaries of projects and those who are providing the assistance. There are many existing models of national service from which to draw inspiration. In its own words, AmeriCorps is a federal agency that "brings people together to tackle the country's most pressing challenges through national service and volunteering" in communities around the country.[35] The program offers paid and volunteer opportunities to people of all ages to serve on the local, state, and national level in areas of focus ranging from disaster services and education to veterans and military services.[36] And overall, its programs are successful. The AmeriCorps Office of Research and Evaluation (ORE) recently found a positive effect on measures across student literacy, school attendance, and environmental protection.[37]

The government can incentivize programs like AmeriCorps and other national service programs by providing benefits for those who participate. The Public Service Loan Forgiveness (PSLF) program forgives any outstanding balance from the Department of Education if you work ten years full-time at a nonprofit or government agency and make qualified payments toward your loans. AmeriCorps service counts toward this ten-year period.[38] Federal or state governments could similarly provide direct stipends, tax credits, tuition vouchers, or other forms of financial or other support for those who enroll in national service programs.

Retired general Stanley McChrystal served as commander of the International Security Assistance Force in Afghanistan. He has proposed a national service requirement as a condition of citizenship as a "big idea" designed to foster American unity and democracy.[39] McChrystal's proposal would require Americans to provide one year of service, doing things like tutoring students in under-performing schools, caring for elderly residents in nursing homes, or providing disaster relief in distressed communities. Military service would also count toward this requirement, though only as one of many options available for individuals to choose from. It is not surprising that a thirty-four-year veteran of the armed forces like General McChrystal would support this kind of effort, as the military, like my high school sports experience, is another example of unity achieved through common purpose. While imposing a mandatory service obligation may be difficult to achieve politically, some studies have shown that it would be popular.[40]

Nigeria is one of the only countries that requires national service, at least for all university graduates. They must participate in the National Youth Service Corps (NYSC) for one year;[41] "emphasis is placed in rural posting in the areas of Agriculture, Health, Education and Infrastructure."[42] Many countries require some form of military service. According to studies by the Centre for Economic Policy Research, "military conscription contributed to the formation of a shared national identity, boosting loyalty to the polity, and instilling patriotism."[43]

But a deliberate commitment to pursuing the common good should not be solely reserved for people enrolled in AmeriCorps or other similar programs. All Americans can implement this priority in their lives by seeking opportunities to work toward community or other shared goals and objectives. Schools, churches, neighborhoods, any number of various organizations all set goals for the benefit of their members. Participating in these collective efforts and working with others in pursuit of those goals has tremendous benefits beyond making progress toward achieving the goal that is being pursued. Coming together with our neighbors to build a playground, working with other parents to fund an after-school program, or joining a church group on a service trip to a faraway place all enhance our understanding of our place in the world and the people with whom we interact. These efforts connect us to something larger and represent an affirmative antidote to division in America.

((•))

The prospective reforms suggested in this chapter won't cure the division that afflicts our democracy. They will, however, mitigate its effects and limit its reach. Given the paralysis of government, we must all take on democracy as a common project and approach the maintenance of our democracy as a shared responsibility. The more people participate in the processes of government and the workings of their communities, listen to and engage with people with differing views, and pursue shared experience and common purpose, the stronger our democracy will be.

Despite the hard-earned lessons of my work on the events in Charlottesville and on January 6, I remain optimistic about our ability to protect democracy. The approaches outlined above really are quite simple, and therefore achievable, if we muster the will to overcome our own apathy. I believe people are fundamentally good, motivated largely by benign impulses, and influenced profoundly by the joy and pain of the people around them. While there are systemic impediments pulling us apart and profiting from the divide, there are more powerful forces — our humanity and our legacy of democracy — that will keep us together if we make the effort.

In 1888, German philosopher Friedrich Nietzsche wrote, "Out of life's school of war: What does not destroy me, makes me stronger."[44] The recent spasms of political violence in this country in Charlottesville and on January 6 were episodes of war — harbingers of American division and our dangerous potential to descend into conflict and division. Those events were America at its worst. Let us respond by reaffirming America at its best. We should see Charlottesville and January 6 as motivators and use them to make us stronger. Let them encourage us all to recommit to preserving American democracy.

ACKNOWLEDGMENTS

The first and most important person who helped shape this book is my incredibly talented researcher, Nora Neus. I met Nora years ago, when as a high school senior she interviewed for a Jefferson Scholarship at the University of Virginia. I was impressed with her then and watched her shine first as a student at UVA and then as a local journalist in my hometown of Charlottesville. When some years later Nora was recommended to me as a possible collaborator on this book, it seemed like a partnership destined to occur.

Nora provided invaluable assistance to me over the course of this project. Her thorough research added important examples, quotes, and factual support for my ideas and proposals. Many of the programs and remedies described in this book are the product of her diligence and creativity. Nora was much more than a researcher, however. She gave me substantive advice about tone, structure, and content throughout the drafting process. She reviewed every word I wrote, kept the narrative focused, and helped me avoid undue repetition. She encouraged me to add more of my own thoughts and perspectives throughout the book and helped me understand that my personal perspective and experience is the thread that holds these chapters together. I came to trust her judgment and appreciate her thoughtful advice. She is an accomplished writer in her own right and has tremendous potential to tell stories that matter. I look forward to continuing to watch her promising career unfold.

Chip Fleischer, a senior editor at Steerforth Press, was my second partner in the writing process. I found Chip through another UVA connection — a mutual friend who grew up with Chip in Kansas City suggested that we discuss a book about my experience with these two substantial investigations. Chip was the first person to believe in the commercial potential of this project and the prospect of its contribution to important discussions about democracy. I appreciate his confidence in me and this story and his willingness to commit his firm's assistance to making this book a reality. Like Nora, Chip reviewed every word of my draft chapters and provided thoughtful feedback on matters big and small, about both style and substance. His seasoned advice informed my approach to the book, and his careful guidance through the process has made it an immeasurably better product. I have made a lifelong friend in Chip and so appreciate his support.

I've been fortunate over the course of my life to have talented teammates who have helped me achieve success. The people with whom I worked on the Charlottesville and January 6 investigations are foremost on that list, as they performed extremely well under immense pressure. I was enriched by the lawyers and other professionals who contributed their efforts to these two intense and demanding undertakings. Neither this book nor the underlying investigative work that informs its conclusions would have been possible but for their excellent service.

In 2017, I was a partner at Hunton & Williams, an international law firm based in Richmond, Virginia. Many people who worked at the firm contributed to the Charlottesville investigation. Associates Trevor Garmey, Kevin Elliker, and Jon Caulder immediately signed on to the independent review team, setting aside other work and deploying to Charlottesville for long periods of time. Trevor managed the document review process, working with the city and other sources of information to ensure that we gathered and cataloged a large amount of relevant material. Trevor, Kevin, and John all helped interview witnesses, draft portions of the final report, and prepare my public presentations of our findings. Their commitment to ensuring accuracy in every word of the report gave our work immense integrity that has withstood the test of time. Associates Brittany Davidson, Suzanne Hosseini, Martha Condyles, and Britt Anderson lent their considerable talents to the review and contributed to the report in meaningful ways. Ye-Eun Sung and Barbara Butler were my assistants during the review process and ensured that I did not neglect any administrative task or other matter as we rushed to finish our work.

The Charlottesville review team also benefited from the expertise of police professionals who helped inform our conclusions. Rachel Harmon, a professor at the University of Virginia and former prosecutor with the Civil Rights Division at the Department of Justice, studies the police and helped us understand the complex issues facing law enforcement during mass demonstration events. Kim Dine, Eddie Reyes, and Chris Perkins were former chiefs who joined crucial interviews and helped inform our critical findings regarding CPD and VSP's approach to the Unite the Right event. The Police Foundation made Kim and Eddie available to our review without cost, in recognition of the public purpose of our work. I learned a tremendous amount about law enforcement from these experts.

My partners at Hunton & Williams supported our work and allowed me to take on the review, mindful of the financial loss it would entail. The firm established and staffed a 1-800 number and website to field community reports of information. Paralegals, research librarians, and others at Hunton pored over open-source video and other material looking for relevant information, all of which contributed to our findings. Our document management team at Cognicion hosted a large amount of data and brought their high standard of client service to this substantial project. I could not have been successful in the Charlottesville review without the support of the firm and its people, for which I am extremely grateful.

As in Charlottesville, I was part of a talented team of professionals who made the January 6 committee a success. Foremost among them were the lawyers with whom I worked on the investigative team. This diverse and experienced group joined the committee staff from various places, many taking substantial pay cuts and leaving family behind as they came to Washington. Their commitment to the truth was unwavering, which is the main reason for the success of our investigation. Soumya Dayananda, Sean Tonolli, John Wood, Dan George, Candyce Phoenix, and Amanda Wick led the five investigative teams, providing both vision and leadership over the course of our investigation. They collaborated to ensure efficiency of effort and worked diligently to meet our aggressive deadlines. The lawyers they supervised — Temidayo Aganga-Williams, Marc Harris, Bryan Bonner, Yoni Moskowitz, Robin Peguero, Casey Lucier, Alejandra Apececheca, Josh Roselman, Sean Quinn, Marcus Childress, James Sasso, Jacob Glick, Sandeep Prasanna, Jon Murray, and Brittany Record — approached their important work with tremendous integrity. I was fortunate that my former colleague Kevin Elliker agreed to join our staff, leaving behind his family and a job as a federal prosecutor in Richmond, Virginia. Kevin became an indispensable part of the January 6 committee staff, exceeding his valuable contribution to the Charlottesville report. All of the lawyers on our team consistently identified relevant facts, derived important information from often reluctant witnesses, and summarized our core findings in cogent writing throughout our investigation. They did this work with good humor and a robust team spirit, which lightened our load and provided hours of much-needed comic relief.

A large number of talented staff members performed other functions for the committee and contributed to its work. Staff director David Buckley and chief counsel Kristin Amerling worked closely with the members of the committee, outside agencies, and various other stakeholders over the course of the investigation, providing valuable support to the daily work of the investigative team. Subject-matter experts Jerry Bjelopera, Meghan Conroy, Bill Danvers, Tom Jocelyn, Rebecca Knooihuuizen, Denver Riggleman, Bill Scherer, David Weinberg, and Stephanie Jones added their important voices to our work and helped interpret and explain our findings. Jamie Fleet, Terri McCullough, Hope Goins, Joe Maher, and Steve Devine worked with individual members of the committee and navigated various issues and projects. Professional staff members Katherine Abrams, Richard Bruno, Heather Connelly, Lawrence Eagleburger, Margaret Emamzadeah, Sadallah Farah, Quincy Henderson, Jenna Hopkins, Camisha Johnson, Damon Marx, Jacob Nelson, Elizabeth Obrand, Grant Saunders, and Samantha Stiles all provided invaluable support to the committee and paved the way for our success. Barry Pump, Lisa Bianco, Marcus Clark, Eddie Flaherty, Elyes Ouechtati, Evan Mauldin, and Ray O'Mara joined the staff from other committees and helped us understand the unique features of Congress. Tim Mulvey, Hannah Muldavin, and Jackie Colvett managed the committee's communications and the intense media interest in our work. Finally, Doug Letter and Todd Tatelman of the House General Counsel's Office represented the committee in court and managed our substantial docket of litigation. Their advice and counsel were instrumental as we navigated a challenging array of legal issues over the course of the investigation.

The January 6 committee staff came together quickly, from various places and backgrounds. Staff members brought disparate experiences and unique perspectives to our important work. The diversity of the staff was intentional and reinforced my view that teams are made stronger by the inclusion of individuals with differing life and professional experiences and perspectives. I appreciated working in an environment in which people could disagree, sometimes strongly, and engage in constructive discussion about emerging issues. The robust discussions we had during our Monday-morning staff meetings and informally around desks and tables made our work more informed, balanced, and credible. We provided candid advice to our clients — the members of the committee — throughout the investigation, promoting facts that we could corroborate and rejecting those that we could not. The result was a credible report that I am confident will stand the test of time.

Of course, the success of the January 6 committee was ultimately made real by the personal commitment of the nine members of Congress who raised their hands to serve. Speaker Pelosi chose wisely when she designated the committee members, each of whom added value to our process. Chairman Bennie Thompson was the ideal leader of the committee. I watched him skillfully navigate the strong personalities of the other eight members, work quietly with each to ensure that their perspectives were considered, and resolve disputes without ever requiring any individual member to "lose" or be overruled. Chairman Thompson supported my work as chief investigative counsel at various points during the investigation, stepping in to ensure the integrity of our process and reaffirm the values he articulated at the outset. His quiet confidence and leadership ability were instrumental to the committee's success.

Vice Chair Liz Cheney was the member most engaged with the daily work of the investigation, personally participating in the development of facts and articulating the committee's core findings in a coherent and persuasive narrative. Her credibility with many of the committee's most important witnesses was indispensable to our ability to obtain crucial information. Representatives Zoe Lofgren, Adam Schiff, and Jamie Raskin are seasoned, formidable lawyers who asked important questions over the course of our interviews and internal discussions. Representatives Pete Aguilar, Adam Kinzinger, Stephanie Murphy, and Elaine Luria similarly contributed valuable thoughts and insights that helped translate our work and make it more persuasive. In contrast with most congressional committees, the members of the January 6 committee personally participated in both our fact gathering and the public presentation of our findings, joining interviews and meticulously scripting every word of our hearings and final report.

Since the committee's work concluded in the first few days of 2023, I've had many opportunities to talk about the facts surrounding the attack on the Capitol and their broader implications for democracy. MSNBC anchor Nicolle Wallace was the person who first invited me to discuss the committee's work when I appeared with her on *Deadline: White House* in January 2023. She has asked me to return to her program dozens of times in the months since to discuss the ongoing threats to democracy revealed by our investigation. Nicolle asks insightful questions and goes deeper into the stories that dominate each day's news. Talking with her is always meaningful, and she encouraged me to write this book. Her superstar team of Lisa Ferri, Querry Robinson, and Marci Santiago are unceasingly professional and make it easy for me to add my voice to these important discussions. Other journalists at MSNBC, CNN, ABC News, NPR, and various newspapers have periodically given me chances to provide my perspective on the attack on the Capitol and larger threats to democracy. I have honed many of the specific thoughts outlined in this book over the course of these appearances, for which I am grateful.

My partners at Willkie Farr & Gallagher have supported my desire to speak out about these issues, on television and in this book. I joined the firm after my work on the committee ended and have been engaged in the private practice of law for the past couple of years. Mike Gottlieb and David Mortlock in our DC office were the partners most directly involved in recruiting me to the firm and facilitating my integration. They saw and continue to see the potential to use the experience outlined in this book for clients who face crises and need seasoned counsel to navigate the way forward. The firm also hired my January 6 colleague Soumya Dayananda, who continues to be my partner as we build a robust investigations practice. Soumya has been my friend and confidante since our committee service ended and will always be a friend on whom I rely for both good judgment and levity.

Soon after the onset of the pandemic, I was in desperate need of human interaction. To counteract the isolation we were all forced to endure, a group of friends in Charlottesville started getting together in person on Friday evenings. The early gatherings were conducted while we all sat six feet apart, outdoors regardless of weather. They evolved with the pandemic and became regular happy hours at the end of busy weeks. These Friday meetings became a forum for robust discussion of everything from families to world affairs. They have continued after the pandemic and survived several life changes for me and others in the group. Andy Block, Jim Ryan, Bill Antholis, Wistar Morris, Jack Bocock, Leon Szeptycki, Joe Hoskins, and Tom Perriello are the unofficial members of this group and regular attendees at our happy hours. During the January 6 committee's investigation, I often rushed back from Washington for these Friday-evening gatherings. Discussions with this group of close friends helped shape the perspectives outlined in the pages of this book. They not only helped me endure the pandemic but have made me smarter and enriched my life in innumerable ways as well.

Most important of all has been my family, without whose love and support I could not have written this book or done any of the things described in its pages. When the prospect of service on the January 6 committee first arose, I told my wife, Lori Shinseki, that it would involve high-pressure work that would be regularly criticized, require my daily presence two hours away in Washington, and entail a substantial pay cut. "Of course. No-brainer. You have to do that," was her response. Her supportive approach to my work on the committee was consistent with the numerous times she has supported my professional choices and pursuits. Lori has always said yes to my many ideas despite the personal sacrifice they require of her. She has allowed me to pursue this work and so many other endeavors over the course of our life together, despite the demands on time, financial sacrifice, and scrutiny that it brings to our family. My kids — Joe, Jack, and Maggie — have similarly supported me over the course of my public service. I've missed too many games, performances, and other important events in their lives due to my work on these investigations and other professional pursuits. Nonetheless, they have encouraged and celebrated me at every step and given me countless moments of pure joy throughout their lives. I am proud of the people they are becoming and very optimistic about their ability to fix the mess our generation is leaving for them. They are up to the task, I am certain.

NOTES

Introduction

1. Nelson Mandela, "We should forgive but not forget," *Guardian*, July 2, 1999, reprinted from *Civilization Magazine*, https://www.theguardian.com/world/1999/jul/03/guardianreview.books7.
2. George Santayana, *Reason in Common Sense* (London: Archibald Constable, 1910), accessed online: https://books.google.com/books?hl=en&lr=&id=BOU3AQAAMAAJ&oi=fnd&pg=PA1&ots=Naxo_HgwZm&sig=h8CCdKgJtJpqT63f3O_FsP3Xl2g#v=onepage&q&f=false.
3. Winston Churchill, speech to the House of Commons, 1948, as quoted by the International Churchill Society, accessed online: https://winstonchurchill.org/resources/in-the-media/churchill-in-the-news/folger-library-churchills-shakespeare/.

Chapter One

1. https://www.monticello.org/sallyhemings/.
2. As quoted in *Staunton (VA) News Leader*, https://www.newsleader.com/story/news/local/2017/07/07/kkk-marchers-say-they-armed-saturday-charlottesville-virginia-rally/460019001/?fbclid=IwAR3SO5vM1OGM3b8V7eacnaJu6iCQHkIIoh6xb1S5XRq8IjXW4E5ZDlbKub4.
3. Heaphy Report.
4. Heaphy Report, page 59.
5. Heaphy Report, page 63.
6. Heaphy Report, page 62.
7. Permit as enclosed in exhibits to the Kessler complaint, page 19, accessed online: https://www.acluva.org/sites/default/files/field_documents/kessler_complaint-and-exhibits.pdf. Additional resources: https://www.acluva.org/en/cases/kessler-v-charlottesville; https://casetext.com/case/kessler-v-city-of-charlottesville/.
8. https://www.cvilletomorrow.org/independent-review-announced/.
9. Heaphy Report, page 51.
10. As quoted in Heaphy Report, page 34.

11. Heaphy Report, pages 6, 130.
12. https://web.archive.org/web/20170810090710/; https://charlottesville.org/
    Home/Components/News/News/8406/635.
13. See *Gregory v. City of Chicago*, 394 U.S. 111 (1969) (Black concurring)
    (arresting demonstrators as a result of unruly behavior of bystanders
    constitutes a "heckler's veto" in violation of the First Amendment).
14. Heaphy Report, page 98.
15. Heaphy Report, page 150.
16. Heaphy Report, page 133.
17. https://www.washingtonpost.com/local/vanguard-america-a-white-supre
    macist-group-denies-charlottesville-attacker-was-a-member/2017/08/15
    /2ec897c6-810e-11e7-8072-73e1718c524d_story.html; https://www.splcenter
    .org/hatewatch/2017/08/12/alleged-charlottesville-driver-who-killed-one
    -rallied-alt-right-vanguard-america-group.
18. https://www.justice.gov/opa/pr/ohio-man-sentenced-life-prison-federal
    -hate-crimes-related-august-2017-car-attack-rally.
19. Heaphy Report, page 135.
20. The one exception to the wholesale criticism of the city government
    contained in the report was the efficient, timely performance of emergency
    responders. Ambulances responded to the scene of the Heyer murder within
    minutes, and skilled health care workers were able to triage and extricate
    twenty injured people and transport them to hospitals within thirty minutes
    of the vehicular assault. Their success reflects the thorough training,
    interagency coordination, common terminology, and standard approach to
    emergency management that was missing in the law enforcement response.

Chapter Two

1. https://amp.cnn.com/cnn/2021/05/14/politics/january-6-commission
   -agreement/index.html.
2. https://www.house.gov/committees/committees-no-longer-standing.
3. Since the select committee concluded its work, the Cannon Caucus Room
   has been named for former Speaker Nancy Pelosi. It is now called the
   Pelosi Caucus Room.
4. Final January 6 report, page 49.
5. Final January 6 report, page 378.
6. Final January 6 report, page 197.
7. Final January 6 report, page 42.
8. Order Re Privilege of Documents Dated January 4–7, 2021, at 36, 40, 44,
   Eastman v. Thompson et al., 594 F. Supp. 3d 1156 (C.D. Cal. Mar. 28, 2022)

(No. 8:22-cv-99-DOC-DFM) ("Based on the evidence, the Court finds that it is more likely than not that President Trump and Eastman dishonestly conspired to obstruct the Joint Session of Congress on January 6, 2021").

9. President Trump's full tweet read: "Peter Navarro releases 36-page report alleging election fraud 'more than sufficient' to swing victory to Trump https://t.co/D8KrMHnFdK. A great report by Peter. Statistically impossible to have lost the 2020 Election. Big protest in D.C. on January 6th. Be there, will be wild!" President Donald J. Trump: Tweets of December 19, 2020, The American Presidency Project, available at https://www.presidency.ucsb.edu/documents/tweets-december-19-2020.

10. Officer Edwards testified before the select committee that she received a concussion when she was struck with a bicycle rack at the Peace Circle. Despite her injury, she moved with the crowd to the West Front of the Capitol, where she defended the building from further intrusion. She was then struck with pepper spray, which exacerbated her injuries. She moved inside the building and continued to attempt to repel rioters. Her testimony is indicative of the bravery exhibited by many uniformed officers who protected the Capitol on January 6. Without their persistent efforts to protect the building and its occupants, the damages caused by the rioters would have been worse.

11. Final January 6 report, pages 595–96.

Chapter Three

1. Ayres Testimony at Select Committee Hearing, July 12, 2022, accessed online: https://www.npr.org/2022/07/12/1111123258/jan-6-committee -hearing-transcript.

2. Ayres Transcribed Interview, June 17, 2022, page 7, accessed online: https://www.govinfo.gov/content/pkg/GPO-J6-TRANSCRIPT-CTRL0000916061/pdf/GPO-J6-TRANSCRIPT-CTRL0000916061.pdf.

3. Ayres Transcribed Interview, June 22, 2022, page 8.

4. The Use of Social Media by United States Extremists, 2018, https://www.start.umd.edu/pubs/START_PIRUS_UseOfSocialMediaByUSExtremists_ResearchBrief_July2018.pdf, as quoted in *Homegrown: Timothy McVeigh and the Rise of Right-Wing Extremism* by Jeffrey Toobin, page 59.

5. https://www.washingtonpost.com/opinions/2019/08/04/there-are-no-lone -wolves/.

6. *Making #Charlottesville: Media from Civil Rights to Unite the Right*, pages 30–31.

7. https://unicornriot.ninja/2017/charlottesville-violence-planned-discord -servers-unicorn-riot-reports/.

8. https://revealnews.org/article/in-chat-rooms-unite-the-right-organizers -planned-to-obscure-their-racism/.

9. https://www.justice.gov/usao-wdva/pr/three-members-california -based-white-supremacist-group-sentenced-riots-charges-related.

10. Independent Review report, page 152.

11. Independent Review report, page 153.

12. https://trumpwhitehouse.archives.gov/briefings-statements/remarks -president-trump-election/.

13. Ayres Transcribed Interview, June 17, 2022, page 7.

14. Ayres Transcribed Interview, June 17, 2022, page 9.

15. Ayres Transcribed Interview, June 17, 2022, page 8.

16. Ayres Transcribed Interview, June 22, 2022, page 27.

17. President Trump's full tweet read: "Peter Navarro releases 36-page report alleging election fraud 'more than sufficient' to swing victory to Trump https://t.co/D8KrMHnFdK. A great report by Peter. Statistically impossible to have lost the 2020 Election. Big protest in D.C. on January 6th. Be there, will be wild!" President Donald J. Trump: Tweets of December 19, 2020, The American Presidency Project, https://www.presidency.ucsb.edu/ documents/tweets-december-19-2020.

18. Final January 6 report, page 499.

19. Final January 6 report, page 520.

20. Final January 6 report, page 514.

21. Final January 6 report, page 522.

22. Final January 6 report, page 524.

23. Final January 6 report, page 525.

24. Final January 6 report, section 6.10 and appendix 1.

25. https://www.nytimes.com/2023/05/25/us/what-is-seditious-conspiracy -insurrection-treason.html; https://www.nytimes.com/2023/06/01/us/ politics/oath-keepers-jan-6-seditious-conspiracy-sentences.html; https:// www.nytimes.com/2023/05/04/us/politics/jan-6-proud-boys-sedition.html.

26. https://www.justice.gov/opa/pr/court-sentences-two-oath-keepers-leaders -seditious-conspiracy-and-other-charges-related-us#:~:text=Today's%20 sentencing%20affirms%20the%20rule,and%20three%20days%20of%20 deliberations.

27. https://www.splcenter.org/fighting-hate/extremist-files/group/oath -keepers.

28. Rhodes et al. indictment, available for download at https://www.justice. gov/usao-dc/defendants/rhodes-elmer-stewart-iii; https://www.justice.gov/ opa/pr/court-sentences-two-oath-keepers-leaders-seditious-conspiracy -and-other-charges-related-us#:~:text=Today's%20sentencing%20 affirms%20the%20rule,and%20three%20days%20of%20deliberations.

29. https://www.justice.gov/usao-dc/case-multi-defendant/file/1510966/ download.

30. https://www.washingtonpost.com/dc-md-va/2023/09/05/proud-boys
-sentencing-enrique-tarrio-jan-6-seditious-conspiracy/.

31. https://www.justice.gov/opa/pr/proud-boys-leader-sentenced-22-years
-prison-seditious-conspiracy-and-other-charges-related#:~:text=On%
20May%204%2C%202023%2C%20a,6%2C%202021.

32. Ayres Transcribed Interview, June 17, 2022, page 13.

33. Ayres Transcribed Interview, June 17, 2022, page 31.

34. https://www.justice.gov/usao-dc/case-multi-defendant/file/1511636/
download.

35. https://apnews.com/article/capitol-siege-prisons-congress-government
-and-politics-e92224f875d2003ab4f29of0c4e06ead.

36. Ayres Transcribed interview, June 17, 2022, page 38.

37. https://winstonchurchill.org/resources/in-the-media/churchill-in-the
-news/folger-library-churchills-shakespeare/.

38. All Eric Barber content is from his transcribed deposition, accessed online:
https://january6th-benniethompson.house.gov/sites/democrats.january6th
.house.gov/files/20220316_Eric%20Gene%20Barber.pdf.

39. All Herendeen content is from his transcribed interview, https://www.gov
info.gov/content/pkg/GPO-J6-TRANSCRIPT-CTRL0000055540/pdf/
GPO-J6-TRANSCRIPT-CTRL0000055540.pdf.

40. Jeff Sharlet, *The Undertow: Scenes from a Slow Civil War* (W. W. Norton &
Company, 2023), page 150.

41. https://www.pewresearch.org/journalism/fact-sheet/social-media-and
-news-fact-sheet/.

42. https://www.oyez.org/cases/1963/39.

43. https://www.law.cornell.edu/wex/libel.

44. See, e.g., *Curtis Publishing Co. v. Butts* (1967) (public figures must also
prove actual malice to recover for libel or defamation).

45. https://casetext.com/case/us-dominion-inc-v-fox-news-network-llc-1.

46. https://thehill.com/homenews/media/3903299-one-fifth-of-fox-news
-viewers-trust-network-less-after-dominion-lawsuit-revelations/; https://
variety.com/vip/survey-views-of-fox-news-skewed-by-awareness-of
-defamation-claim-1235555757/.

47. Congressional Research Service, "Section 230: An Overview," January 4,
2024, page 1.

48. 47 US Code §230 (a) (3–4).

49. https://about.fb.com/news/2021/01/how-does-news-feed-predict-what-you
-want-to-see/.

50. https://www.nytimes.com/2021/10/22/technology/facebook-election-misin
formation.html.

51. As quoted in the *New York Times*, https://www.nytimes.com/2021/10/22/
technology/facebook-election-misinformation.html.

52. https://www.cbsnews.com/news/facebook-whistleblower-frances-haugen
-misinformation-public-60-minutes-2021-10-03/.
53. Herendeen, page 7.
54. https://www.propublica.org/article/white-hate-group-campaign-of
-menace-rise-above-movement.
55. https://www.techtransparencyproject.org/articles/white-supremacist
-groups-are-thriving-on-facebook.
56. https://www.theguardian.com/world/2018/jul/25/charlottesville-white
-supremacists-big-tech-failure-remove.
57. https://www.techtransparencyproject.org/articles/white-supremacist
-groups-are-thriving-on-facebook.
58. https://www.techtransparencyproject.org/articles/white-supremacist
-groups-are-thriving-on-facebook.
59. Final January 6 report, chapter 6, footnote 97.
60. Facebook Help Center, "About Our Policies," available at https://www
.facebook.com/help/1735443093393986#.
61. https://www.bbc.com/news/technology-57088382; https://www.theverge
.com/2019/2/25/18229714/cognizant-facebook-content-moderator-inter
views-trauma-working-conditions-arizona; https://www.forbes.com/sites/
rebeccabellan/2020/03/20/facebook-shifts-content-moderation-to-full-
time-employees-fearing-mental-health-crisis/?sh=7510078376b1; https://
restofworld.org/2020/facebook-international-content-moderators/.
62. https://restofworld.org/2020/facebook-international-content-moderators/.
63. C. Zakrzewski, C. Lima-Strong, and D. Harwell, "What the January 6
Probe Found Out About Social Media but Didn't Report," *Washington Post*,
January 17, 2023.
64. Transcribed interview, September 1, 2022, https://www.govinfo.gov/
content/pkg/GPO-J6-TRANSCRIPT-CTRL0000917176/pdf/GPO-J6
-TRANSCRIPT-CTRL0000917176.pdf.
65. https://slate.com/technology/2021/03/section-230-reform-legislative
-tracker.html.
66. https://www.aclu.org/news/free-speech/section-230-is-this-the-end-of-the
-internet-as-we-know-it.
67. https://www.thune.senate.gov/public/index.cfm/2023/7/thune-s-big-tech
-algorithm-transparency-bill-unanimously-approved-by-commerce
-committee#:~:text=The%20Filter%20Bubble%20Transparency%20
Act,result%20of%0a%20secret%20algorithm.
68. https://www.cisa.gov/sites/default/files/publications/tactics-of-disinforma
tion_508.pdf; https://www.nytimes.com/2019/09/26/technology/govern
ment-disinformation-cyber-troops.html.
69. https://www.cna.org/our-media/indepth/2021/04/social-media-bots-and
-section-230.

Chapter Four

1. John F. Heaphy, "The Future of Police Improvement," in A. Cohn (ed.), *The Future of Policing* (Sage Publishers: Beverly Hills, 1978), pages 275–95.
2. https://www.ojp.gov/pdffiles1/nij/248654.pdf.
3. https://www.npr.org/2022/06/10/1104156949/jan-6-committee-hearing -transcript; https://www.govinfo.gov/content/pkg/GPO-J6-TRANSCRIPT -CTRL0000082302/pdf/GPO-J6-TRANSCRIPT-CTRL0000082302.pdf.
4. https://www.npr.org/2022/06/10/1104156949/jan-6-committee-hearing -transcript; https://www.govinfo.gov/content/pkg/GPO-J6-TRANSCRIPT -CTRL0000082302/pdf/GPO-J6-TRANSCRIPT-CTRL0000082302.pdf.
5. Final January 6 report, page 5.
6. Heaphy Report, page 152.
7. Heaphy Report, page 152.
8. https://slate.com/news-and-politics/2019/08/terry-mcauliffe-charlottesville -unite-right-racist-rally-anti-fascist-anniversary.html.
9. Heaphy Report, page 152.
10. Heaphy Report, pages 96–97.
11. Heaphy Report, page 98.
12. Heaphy Report, page 133.
13. https://www.propublica.org/article/white-supremacists-joked-about-using -cars-to-run-over-opponents-before-charlottesville.
14. Heaphy Report, pages 88–89.
15. January 6 report, section 6.10, https://www.govinfo.gov/content/pkg/ GPO-J6-REPORT/html-submitted/index.html#ch5_fn304.
16. January 6 report, pages 645–47.
17. In testimony before the select committee, Chief Sund said, "I do believe that intelligence existed that would have greatly helped the department, you know, our oversight — when I say that, I mean the Capitol Police Board leadership — in making critical decisions that could have made significant differences that day. I do believe that there was probably intelligence that existed that could have helped us, yes." Sund Interview, page 67 (https://www.govinfo.gov/content/pkg/GPO-J6-TRANSCRIPT -CTRL0000071087/pdf/GPO-J6-TRANSCRIPT-CTRL0000071087.pdf). Chief Sund's statement is curious, given the fact that his own department possessed that specific intelligence yet he failed to request that the Capitol Police Board deploy the National Guard.
18. https://www.congress.gov/117/meeting/house/113969/witnesses/HHRG-117 -IJ00-Wstate-FanoneO-20210727.pdf.
19. https://www.justice.gov/usao-dc/24-months-january-6-attack-capitol.
20. https://www.justice.gov/usao-dc/24-months-january-6-attack-capitol.
21. Executive summary of January 6 report, https://www.govinfo.gov/content/ pkg/GPO-J6-REPORT/html-submitted/index.html.

22. https://www.govinfo.gov/content/pkg/GPO-J6-TRANSCRIPT-CTRL000 0071087/pdf/GPO-J6-TRANSCRIPT-CTRL0000071087.pdf.

23. https://www.govinfo.gov/content/pkg/GPO-J6-TRANSCRIPT-CTRL000 0071087/pdf/GPO-J6-TRANSCRIPT-CTRL0000071087.pdf.

24. Select committee transcribed interview with Donell Harvin, pages 62–64, https://www.govinfo.gov/content/pkg/GPO-J6-TRANSCRIPT-CTRL000 0038866/pdf/GPO-J6-TRANSCRIPT-CTRL0000038866.pdf.

25. Select committee transcribed interview with Chad Wolf, https://www.gov info.gov/content/pkg/GPO-J6-TRANSCRIPT-CTRL0000038865/pdf/ GPO-J6-TRANSCRIPT-CTRL0000038865.pdf; select committee tran scribed interview with Ken Cuccinelli, https://www.govinfo.gov/content/ pkg/GPO-J6-TRANSCRIPT-CTRL0000034623/pdf/GPO-J6-TRAN SCRIPT-CTRL0000034623.pdf.

26. Spencer Reynolds and Faiza Patel, A New Vision for Domestic Intelligence: Fixing Overbroad Mandates and Flimsy Safeguards, Brennan Center for Justice, accessed online: https://www.brennancenter.org/media/10908/ download.

27. FBI Domestic Investigations and Operations Guide (DIOG), last updated September 17, 2021, FBI Records: The Vault, US Federal Bureau of Investi-gation, https://vault.fbi.gov/FBI%20Domestic%20Investigations%20 and%20Operations%20Guide%20%28DIOG%29, 1-2.

28. DIOG, 3-3.

29. The issue of FBI 1A restrictions is also discussed in detail in Quinta Jurecic's piece in *Lawfare*, "Why Didn't the FBI Review Social Media Posts Announcing Plans for the Capitol Riot? Lawfare blog, June 29, 2021, https://www.lawfaremedia.org/article/why-didnt-fbi-review-social-media -posts-announcing-plans-capitol-riot.

30. Transcribed interview, https://www.govinfo.gov/content/pkg/GPO-J6 -TRANSCRIPT-CTRL0000916069/pdf/GPO-J6-TRANSCRIPT-CTRL000 0916069.pdf.

31. Transcribed interview, https://www.govinfo.gov/content/pkg/GPO-J6 -TRANSCRIPT-CTRL0000916069/pdf/GPO-J6-TRANSCRIPT-CTRL0000916069.pdf.

32. https://www.intelligence.senate.gov/sites/default/files/94755_II.pdf.

33. https://www.senate.gov/about/powers-procedures/investigations/ church-committee.htm.

34. *United States v. Katz*, 389 U.S. 347 (1967).

35. *United States v. Katz*, 389 U.S. 347 (1967).

36. *United States v. Katz*, 389 U.S. 347 (1967).

37. https://www.washingtonpost.com/dc-md-va/2023/01/10/baked-alaska -sentenced-jan6-capitol-riot/; https://www.justice.gov/usao-dc/defendants/ gionet-anthime-joseph.

38. https://www.adl.org/resources/blog/nicholas-j-fuentes-five-things-know.
39. https://www.cnn.com/2023/02/09/politics/kevin-seefried-confederate-flag
-capitol-riot/index.html; https://www.usatoday.com/story/
news/2021/01/07/capitol-riot-images-confederate-flag-terror/6588104002/.
40. https://www.npr.org/2021/07/27/1021197474/capitol-police-officer-testifies
-to-the-racism-he-faced-during-the-jan-6-riot.
41. https://www.adl.org/resources/backgrounder/proud-boys-0.
42. https://www.govinfo.gov/content/pkg/GPO-J6-TRANSCRIPT-CTRL000
0087481/pdf/GPO-J6-TRANSCRIPT-CTRL0000087481.pdf.
43. https://www.justice.gov/opa/pr/proud-boys-leader-sentenced-22-years
-prison-seditious-conspiracy-and-other-charges-related; https://www
.justice.gov/usao-dc/pr/court-sentences-two-oath-keepers-leaders-18
-years-prison-seditious-conspiracy-and-other#:~:text=Rhodes%2C%20
57%2C%20of%20Granbury%2C,36%20months%20of%20supervised%20
release.
44. https://www.nytimes.com/2022/10/17/us/politics/oath-keepers-weapons
-jan-6.html; https://apnews.com/article/capitol-siege-florida-virginia
-conspiracy-government-and-politics-6ac80882e8cf61af36be6c46252ac24c.
45. https://www.justice.gov/usao-dc/case-multi-defendant/file/1492996/dl;
https://www.washingtonpost.com/dc-md-va/2023/09/05/proud-boys-sen
tencing-enrique-tarrio-jan-6-seditious-conspiracy/.
46. https://www.reuters.com/article/idUSKBN26R1MM.
47. https://www.nytimes.com/2020/06/10/us/politics/national-guard-protests
.html.
48. https://www.washingtonpost.com/national-security/2021/04/15/dc-guard
-helicopter-george-floyd-protest/.
49. https://www.nytimes.com/2021/03/20/us/protests-policing-george-floyd
.html.
50. https://www.govinfo.gov/content/pkg/GPO-J6-TRANSCRIPT-CTRL000
0086314/pdf/GPO-J6-TRANSCRIPT-CTRL0000086314.pdf, pages 74–76.
51. https://www.justice.gov/opa/pr/department-justice-announces-new-depart
ment-wide-implicit-bias-training-personnel.

Chapter Five

1. Heaphy Report, page 69.
2. https://virginialawreview.org/articles/payne-v-city-charlottesville-and
-dillons-rule-rationale-removal/#28.
3. https://1061thecorner.com/news/064460-jason-kessler-proud-boys-take
-to-downtown-mall/.

4. https://www.adl.org/resources/news/richard-spencer-five-things-know.
5. https://www.splcenter.org/fighting-hate/extremist-files/group/identity -evropaamerican-identity-movement.
6. https://www.splcenter.org/fighting-hate/extremist-files/group/league -south.
7. https://www.splcenter.org/fighting-hate/extremist-files/group/traditionalist -worker-party.
8. https://www.adl.org/resources/hate-symbol/vanguard-america.
9. https://www.adl.org/resources/blog/two-years-ago-they-marched-charlott esville-where-are-they-now.
10. https://www.nytimes.com/2017/08/16/us/politics/trump-republicans-race .html.
11. https://www.washingtonpost.com/politics/2020/05/08/very-fine-people -charlottesville-who-were-they-2/.
12. Rhodes's view of the Insurrection Act was incorrect, as the president's invocation of the act would authorize the deployment of active-duty military to quell the threat to public safety, not citizen militias; https:// policy.defense.gov/portals/11/documents/hdasa/references/insurrection _act.pdf.
13. https://www.documentcloud.org/documents/23573448-201223-rhodes -open-letter-to-trump-1008.
14. https://www.justice.gov/opa/pr/jury-convicts-four-leaders-proud-boys -seditious-conspiracy-related-us-capitol-breach.
15. https://www.washingtonpost.com/national-security/william-barr-trump -election-fraud/2020/11/10/ae2d1d5e-239d-11eb-a688-5298ad5d580a_story .html.
16. Final January 6 report, executive summary.
17. https://www.govinfo.gov/content/pkg/GPO-J6-TRANSCRIPT-CTRL000 0062449/pdf/GPO-J6-TRANSCRIPT-CTRL0000062449.pdf, page 185.
18. See final January 6 report, appendix 3: The Big Rip-Off: Follow the Money.
19. https://www.npr.org/2021/02/10/966396848/read-trumps-jan-6-speech-a -key-part-of-impeachment-trial.
20. https://www.govinfo.gov/content/pkg/GPO-J6-TRANSCRIPT-CTRL000 0916061/pdf/GPO-J6-TRANSCRIPT-CTRL0000916061.pdf.
21. https://mediamanipulation.org/sites/default/files/2022-07/j6_motivations_ working_paper.pdf.
22. https://www.salon.com/2021/06/30/white-nationalist-groyper-leader -doubles-down-on-jan-6-capitol-riot-calling-it-awesome/.
23. https://www.reuters.com/article/us-usa-trump-capitol-arrest/baked-alaska -arrested-in-capitol-hill-riot-fbi-idUSKBN29L0RN/.
24. https://www.justice.gov/usao-dc/case-multi-defendant/file/1407951/dl.

25. https://www.nbcnews.com/politics/politics-news/charlottesville-tiki-torch
-carrier-pleads-guilty-jan-6-riot-case-rcna148644.

26. https://arstechnica.com/science/2022/03/anti-vaccine-doctor-behind-covid
-misinfo-pleads-guilty-to-jan-6-riot-charge/.

27. https://mediamanipulation.org/sites/default/files/2022-07/j6_motivations_
working_paper.pdf.

28. https://www.businessinsider.com/read-1776-returns-jan-6-proud-boys
-capitol-attack-dc-2022-6.

29. https://twitter.com/RepMTG/status/1517852261963243521; https://twitter
.com/laurenboebert/status/1346811381878845442.

30. https://www.washingtonpost.com/nation/interactive/2021/far-right
-symbols-capitol-riot/.

31. https://news.gallup.com/poll/388988/political-ideology-steady-conserva
tives-moderates-tie.aspx#:~:text=The%20percentage%20conservative%20
was%2031,%2C%20including%2020%25%20in%202021.

32. https://www.archives.gov/electoral-college/history; https://www.archives
.gov/electoral-college/provisions#A12.

33. https://www.thelancet.com/journals/lancet/article/PIIS0140-6736(20)32545
-9/abstract, as quoted in https://www.theguardian.com/us-news/2021/
feb/10/us-coronavirus-response-donald-trump-health-policy.

Chapter Six

1. https://twitter.com/EricHolder/status/176305718741161176.

2. https://wamu.org/story/14/01/31/crack_the_drug_that_consumed_the
_nations_capital_transcript/.

3. https://www.justice.gov/archive/ndic/pubs07/723/cocaine.htm.

4. https://www.latimes.com/archives/la-xpm-1993-10-23-mn-48867-story
.html; https://www.washingtonpost.com/archive/politics/1993/10/26/
clinton-rejects-call-for-guard-in-dc/9fc8dd6e-0215-4de5-b448-9e04fb8d45
e6/; https://www.nytimes.com/1993/10/26/us/clinton-denies-washington-s
-request-to-use-guard.html.

5. https://www.justice.gov/ag/bio/attorney-general-eric-h-holder-jr#:~:text
=President%20Barack%20Obama%20announced%20his,by%20Vice%2D
President%20Joe%20Biden.

6. Alaska, Arizona, California, Colorado, Idaho, Michigan, and Montana all
have independent commissions that operate with no final control by the
state legislature. https://redistricting.lls.edu/redistricting-101/who-draws
-the-lines/.

7. https://www.census.gov/topics/public-sector/congressional-apportionment /about.html.

8. https://prologue.blogs.archives.gov/2018/06/21/the-gerry-in-gerryman dering/.

9. https://gerrymander.princeton.edu/; https://gerrymander.princeton.edu/ redistricting-report-card.

10. https://news.harvard.edu/gazette/story/2023/07/biggest-problem-with -gerrymandering/.

11. https://www.brennancenter.org/our-work/analysis-opinion/gerrymander ing-competitive-districts-near-extinction.

12. https://apnews.com/article/virginia-election-state-legislature-what-to -watch-f5901d85cec6081d6c04093212908d63.

13. https://www.hagemanforwyoming.com/post/conservative-republican -harriet-hageman-to-announce-challenge.

14. https://thehill.com/blogs/blog-briefing-room/3605032-hageman-cheney -focused-on-trump-obsession-instead-of-wyoming/.

15. https://abcnews.go.com/US/virginia-governor-orders-national-guard- standby-ahead-alt/story?id=49163162.

16. https://redistricting.lls.edu/redistricting-101/who-draws-the-lines/.

17. https://wedrawthelines.ca.gov/about-us/.

18. https://redistricting.lls.edu/redistricting-101/who-draws-the-lines/.

19. https://www.americanbar.org/groups/crsj/publications/human_rights_ magazine_home/economics-of-voting/the-rise-and-fall-of-redistricting -commissions/.

20. https://www.americanbar.org/groups/crsj/publications/human_rights_ magazine_home/economics-of-voting/the-rise-and-fall-of-redistricting -commissions/.

21. https://www.commoncause.org/our-work/constitution-courts-and-demo cracy-issues/for-the-people-act/; https://www.brennancenter.org/our-work /research-reports/breaking-down-freedom-vote-act; https://www.congress .gov/bill/118th-congress/house-bill/11.

22. https://www.rcvresources.org/where-is-rcv-used.

23. https://ballotpedia.org/Top-two_primary.

24. https://fairvote.org/resources/data-on-rcv/#voter-support.

25. http://eamonmcginn.com.s3-website-ap-southeast-2.amazonaws.com/ papers/IRV_in_Minneapolis.pdf.

26. https://startribune.com/minneapolis-hits-record-for-turnout-in-a-muni cipal-election-with-54-of-voters-casting-ballots/600113521/.

27. https://www.cogitatiopress.com/politicsandgovernance/article/view/3914.

28. https://www.cogitatiopress.com/politicsandgovernance/article/view/3914.

29. https://today.usc.edu/top-two-open-primary-elections-less-extreme-law makers-usc-study/.

30. https://schwarzenegger.usc.edu/wp-content/uploads/images/files/Grose_ JPIPE_June_2020_Preprint_Official_Article.pdf; https://vote.minneapo lismn.gov/results-data/election-results/2009/.

31. 424 U.S. 1 (1976).

32. 558 U.S. 310 (2010).

33. 558 U.S. 310, 348 (2010).

34. https://www.brookings.edu/wp-content/uploads/2012/04/20120301_super_ pacs.pdf, page 12.

35. https://www.npr.org/2012/01/20/145500168/superpacs-celebrate-anniver sary-of-citizens-united-case.

36. https://www.washingtonpost.com/politics/democratic-groups-move-to -ramp-up-financial-firepower-for-clinton/2016/02/12/23ca8e00-d1b1-11e5 -abc9-ea152f0b9561_story.html.

37. https://peabodyawards.com/award-profile/the-colbert-report-super-pac -segments/.

38. https://www.opensecrets.org/outside-spending/faq.

39. https://www.opensecrets.org/political-action-committees-pacs/top-recip ients/2022.

40. https://www.clubforgrowth.org/about/what-we-do/.

41. https://www.opensecrets.org/outside-spending/detail?cmte=C00487470& cycle=2022.

42. https://www.opensecrets.org/outside-spending/detail?cmte=C00486845& cycle=2022.

43. https://www.opensecrets.org/outside-spending/by_group/2022?chart=V& disp=O&type=A. The other 5 percent went to "independent" candidates or organizations.

44. https://www.cga.ct.gov/2009/rpt/2009-R-0339.htm.

45. https://www.blueprintsfordemocracy.org/model-public-funding-system.

46. https://cfb.mn.gov/pdf/quicklinks/public_subsidy_program.pdf.

47. https://www.blueprintsfordemocracy.org/model-campaign-finance-restric tions-and-lobbying.

48. https://www.blueprintsfordemocracy.org/model-coordination-regualtions.

49. https://www.blueprintsfordemocracy.org/model-matching-funds-program.

50. https://www.brennancenter.org/our-work/research-reports/donor-diversity -through-public-matching-funds.

51. https://www.seattle.gov/democracyvoucher/about-the-program.

52. See *Elster v. City of Seattle* (cert. denied, March 20, 2020).

53. https://www.brennancenter.org/our-work/research-reports/benefits-public -financing-and-myth-polarized-small-donors.

Chapter Seven

1. https://unicornriot.ninja/2017/data-release-unite-right-planning-chats -demonstrate-violent-intent/.
2. https://www.justice.gov/opa/pr/ohio-man-sentenced-life-prison-federal -hate-crimes-related-august-2017-car-attack-rally.
3. https://casetext.com/case/sines-v-kessler-1.
4. https://www.cnn.com/2021/11/19/us/unite-the-right-trial-charlottesville -rally/index.html.
5. Rhodes, as quoted in final January 6 report.
6. Final January 6 report, executive summary, page 56.
7. Final January 6 report, page 56.
8. https://www.c-span.org/video/?507744-1/trumps-jan-6-rally-speech.
9. Frank Bruni, *The Age of Grievance* (Avid Reader Press/Simon & Schuster, 2024), chapter 2
10. https://www.pewresearch.org/politics/2023/07/12/voter-turnout-2018 -2022/.
11. https://www.census.gov/newsroom/press-releases/2022/2020-presidential -election-voting-report.html.
12. https://www.census.gov/content/dam/Census/library/publications/2022/ demo/p20-585.pdf.
13. https://www.pewresearch.org/short-reads/2023/10/24/americans-are -following-the-news-less-closely-than-they-used-to/#:~:text=In%20 turn%2C%20a%20rising%20share,said%20the%20same%20last%20year.
14. https://www.pewresearch.org/short-reads/2023/10/24/americans-are -following-the-news-less-closely-than-they-used-to/#:~:text=In%20 turn%2C%20a%20rising%20share,said%20the%20same%20last%20year.
15. In 2018, 28 percent of survey respondents had no trust and confidence in media. In 1974, that percentage was only 6 percent. https://news.gallup .com/poll/403166/americans-trust-media-remains-near-record-low.aspx.
16. https://news.gallup.com/poll/642548/church-attendance-declined-religious -groups.aspx#:~:text=A%20table%20showing%20changes%20in,Americans %20have%20shown%20modest%20increases.
17. https://www.pewresearch.org/short-reads/2024/03/12/majorities-of-adults -see-decline-of-union-membership-as-bad-for-the-us-and-working-people /#:~:text=The%20share%20of%20U.S.%20workers,was%20bad%20for%20 the%20country.
18. https://s.wsj.net/public/resources/documents/WSJ_NORC_ToplineMarc _2023.pdf.
19. Social Capital Project, "What We Do Together: The State of Associational Life in America," as quoted in The Space Between, SCP Report No. 8-19 (December 2019), a project of the Joint Economic Committee. https://www

.jec.senate.gov/public/index.cfm/republicans/analysis?id=78A35E07-4C86
-44A2-8480-BE0DB8CB104E.

20. https://www.pewresearch.org/short-reads/2023/10/12/what-does-friendship
-look-like-in-america.

21. https://annehelen.substack.com/p/the-friendship-dip.

22. https://www.vox.com/the-highlight/24119312/how-to-find-a-third-place
-cafe-bar-gym-loneliness-connection.

23. https://www.vox.com/the-highlight/24119312/how-to-find-a-third-place
-cafe-bar-gym-loneliness-connection.

24. https://publicagenda.org/resource/the-political-alienation-barometer/.

25. https://publicagenda.org/wp-content/uploads/Alienation-Barometer
-Report_HR_FINAL.pdf.

26. https://uchicagopolitics.opalstacked.com/uploads/homepage/Disinfo-Press
-PDF.pdf.

27. https://www.pewresearch.org/politics/2023/09/19/americans-dismal-views
-of-the-nations-politics/.

Chapter Eight

1. https://www.c-ville.com/conversation-starter-zyahna-bryant-is-the-newest
-addition-to-americans-who-tell-the-truth-series.

2. Nora Neus, *24 Hours in Charlottesville: An Oral History of the Stand Against
White Supremacy* (Boston: Beacon Press, 2023), page 15.

3. Heaphy Report, page 128.

4. Heaphy Report, page 135.

5. Neus, *24 Hours in Charlottesville*, epigraph.

6. https://www.washingtonpost.com/lifestyle/magazine/her-daughter-died
-while-protesting-in-charlottesville-what-has-life-been-like-since/2018
/08/06/192495e2-83c8-11e8-8f6c-46cb43e3f306_story.html.

7. https://www.cvilletomorrow.org/independent-review-announced/.

8. https://www.rev.com/blog/transcripts/house-jan-6-committee-holds-first
-of-several-public-hearings-on-capitol-riot-6-09-22-transcript.

9. https://www.govinfo.gov/content/pkg/CHRG-117hhrg45472/pdf/CHRG-117
hhrg45472.pdf.

10. https://www.washingtonpost.com/national-security/2022/06/21/ruby-free
man-shaye-moss-jan6-testimony/.

11. https://www.willkie.com/news/2023/12/jury-awards-148-million-in
-damages-to-willkie-clients.

12. https://www.cbsnews.com/philadelphia/news/philadelphia-city
-commissioner-al-schmidt-defends-election-integrity-after-president
-trumps-scathing-tweet/.

13. Final January 6 report, executive summary.
14. https://www.govinfo.gov/content/pkg/GPO-J6-TRANSCRIPT-CTRL000 0928885/pdf/GPO-J6-TRANSCRIPT-CTRL0000928885.pdf, page 214.
15. "One minute after the President's tweet, at 2:25 P.M., the Secret Service determined they could no longer protect the Vice President in his ceremonial office near the Senate Chamber, and evacuated the Vice President and his family to a secure location, missing the violent mob by a mere 40 feet." Final January 6 report, executive summary.
16. https://www.cnn.com/2019/01/10/us/deandre-harris-charlottesville-racial -beating-sentencing/index.html; https://www.fair360.com/charlottesville -attacker-finally-sentenced-to-20-years-for-assault-on-black-man-2/.
17. For example, this case: https://wset.com/news/local/unite-the-right -torch-carrying-marchers-indicted-charlottesville-virginia-rally-richmond -grand-jury-albemarle-county-commonwealth-attorney-april-2023.
18. https://www.washingtonpost.com/local/black-man-beaten-in-charlottes ville-found-not-guilty-of-assaulting-white-supremacist/2018/03/16/ 92160a88-288f-11e8-b79d-f3d931db7f68_story.html.
19. https://apnews.com/general-news-d7e9d3e4bad4483dbd53a4b3fec15250.
20. https://www.nytimes.com/2017/10/16/us/charlottesville-arrests-corey-long .html.
21. https://dailyprogress.com/news/local/corey-long-convicted-of-disorderly -conduct-sentenced-to-20-days/article_a51f9012-6b34-11e8-9d0a-7358221b 4a40.html.
22. https://medium.com/@solidaritycville/charlottesville-demands-joe -platania-drop-the-charges-against-deandre-corey-and-donald-coafcc bfbbfd.
23. https://dailyprogress.com/news/local/prosecutor-responds-to-activists -calls-for-charges-to-be-dropped/article_42d37426-2351-11e8-9115-a734 be6d4824.html.
24. https://www.nbcnews.com/news/crime-courts/james-alex-fields-found -guilty-killing-heather-heyer-during-violent-n945186.
25. https://www.justice.gov/opa/pr/ohio-man-sentenced-life-prison-federal -hate-crimes-related-august-2017-car-attack-rally.
26. https://www.justice.gov/usao-wdva/pr/three-members-california-based- white-supremacist-group-sentenced-riots-charges-related.
27. https://www.law.georgetown.edu/icap/our-work/addressing-political -violence-unlawful-paramilitaries-and-threats-to-democracy/city-of -charlottesville-v-pennsylvania-light-foot-militia/#:~:text=of%20Charlot tesville%20v.-,Pennsylvania%20Light%20Foot%20Militia,by%20 court%2Denforceable%20consent%20decrees.
28. https://www.washingtonpost.com/dc-md-va/2021/11/23/charlottesville -verdict-live-updates/.

29. https://www.justice.gov/usao-dc/capitol-breach-cases.
30. https://www.npr.org/2021/02/09/965472049/the-capitol-siege-the-arrested-and-their-stories.
31. See "Referrals to the U.S. Department of Justice Special Counsel and House Ethics Committee," executive summary.
32. https://d3i6fh83elv35t.cloudfront.net/static/2023/08/CRIMINAL-INDICT MENT-Trump-Fulton-County-GA.pdf.
33. https://www.usatoday.com/story/news/politics/elections/2024/04/24/arizona-michigan-georgia-nevada-fake-electors/73447556007/.
34. https://apnews.com/article/trump-capitol-riot-jan-6-civil-lawsuits-7f80a140e728247ea5ec8db9d4d46eb2.
35. For more information, see: https://apnews.com/article/rudy-giuliani-georgia-election-workers-defamation-case-cde7186493b3a1bd9ab89bc65f0f5b06; https://www.npr.org/2023/07/12/1187318029/fox-news-sued-ray-epps-defamation-jan-6.
36. https://www.cnn.com/2024/05/02/politics/john-eastman-law-license/index.html; https://www.nbcwashington.com/news/politics/rudy-giuliani-recommended-for-disbarment-in-dc/3630618/; https://www.forbes.com/sites/brianbushard/2024/01/19/lawyer-for-sidney-powell-faces-disciplinary-charges-over-trump-election-case/?sh=174ad3732e77; https://stateuniteddemocracy.org/ellis-charges/; https://www.politico.com/news/2024/04/04/jeffrey-clark-ethics-rules-00150631.

Chapter Nine

1. https://ballotpedia.org/California_2024_ballot_propositions.
2. https://ballotpedia.org/California_Proposition_1,_Right_to_Reproductive_Freedom_Amendment_(2022); https://ballotpedia.org/California_Proposition_17,_Voting_Rights_Restoration_for_Persons_on_Parole_Amendment_(2020); https://ballotpedia.org/California_Proposition_1,_Housing_Programs_and_Veterans'_Loans_Bond_(2018); https://ballotpedia.org/California_Proposition_4,_Women's_Suffrage_Amendment_(October_1911).
3. https://sos.oregon.gov/voting/Pages/registration.aspx?lang=en.
4. https://www.ncsl.org/elections-and-campaigns/table-18-states-with-all-mail-elections.
5. https://www.eballot.com/blog/these-states-allow-online-voting-for-their-citizens-is-your-state-one-of-them.
6. https://www.usa.gov/who-can-vote.

7. https://www.sentencingproject.org/reports/locked-out-2022-estimates-of-people-denied-voting-rights/.

8. https://www.sentencingproject.org/reports/locked-out-2022-estimates-of-people-denied-voting-rights/.

9. https://felonvoting.procon.org/state-felon-voting-laws/.

10. https://www.themarshallproject.org/2019/06/11/in-just-two-states-all-prisoners-can-vote-here-s-why-few-do?gad_source=1&gclid=CjoKCQjw97SzBhDaARIsAFHXUWBMsgT7JMgjOk_us2nw1vnygcSsMp2qqwrNnpMkkxiLLQEBkUVTofAaArYEEALw_wcB.

11. https://www.fountainfund.org/.

12. https://web.archive.org/web/20220127164236/https://www.afsc.org/testimonies/decision-making.

13. https://www.mfriends.org/quaker-process/.

14. https://www.mfriends.org/quaker-process/.

15. See, e.g., https://law.lis.virginia.gov/vacode/title8.01/chapter11/section8.01-345/.

16. https://www.uscourts.gov/services-forms/jury-service/juror-selection-process#:~:text=Jury%20service%20is%20a%20way,a%20source%20of%20prospective%20jurors.

17. https://www.nacole.org/nacoles_most_urgent_programmatic_priorities.

18. https://policeoversight.uchicago.edu/agencies.

19. https://abcnews.go.com/US/police-oversight-boards-proliferating-work/story?id=77919091.

20. https://abcnews.go.com/US/police-oversight-boards-proliferating-work/story?id=77919091.

21. https://www.nyc.gov/content/appointments/pages/boards-commissions.

22. https://www.nyc.gov/site/communityboards/about/about-nyc-cbs.page.

23. https://obamawhitehouse.archives.gov/blog/2011/09/22/petition-white-house-we-people.

24. https://www.pewresearch.org/internet/2016/12/28/we-the-people-five-years-of-online-petitions/.

25. https://www.amnesty.org.au/campaigns/write-for-rights/; https://www.amnesty.org.au/campaigns/write-for-rights/; https://www.amnesty.org/en/latest/campaigns/2017/11/15-big-wins-for-write-for-rights/; https://www.amnestyusa.org/press-releases/amnesty-international-launches-annual-letter-writing-campaign-amid-clampdown-on-human-rights/.

26. https://www.nytimes.com/2024/06/17/health/surgeon-general-social-media-warning-label.html?smid=nytcore-ios-share&referringSource=articleShare.

27. https://newslit.org/about/mission/.

28. https://newslit.org/for-everyone/.

29. https://newslit.org/about/mission/#nlp-mission.

30. https://millercenter.org/democracy-dialogues.
31. https://www.thinkagainuva.com/mission.
32. https://www.vanderbilt.edu/dialogue-vanderbilt/; https://www.american
    .edu/spa/civic-dialogue/; https://news.harvard.edu/gazette/story/2024/01/
    harvard-dialogues-creates-forum-for-respectful-debate/; https://news.yale
    .edu/2023/12/07/space-dialogue-yale-series-models-civil-discussion-hard
    -topics.
33. https://www.interfaithamerica.org/mission-vision/.
34. https://www.interfaithamerica.org/sectors/civic-life/.
35. https://americorps.gov/about/faqs.
36. https://americorps.gov/serve/fit-finder; https://americorps.gov/about/
    what-we-do.
37. https://americorps.gov/sites/default/files/document/2023%20SOE%20
    Report_090123_final_508_0.pdf, pages 56–57.
38. https://americorps.gov/members-volunteers/faqs.
39. https://time.com/4824366/year-national-service-americorps-peace-corps/.
40. https://thehill.com/opinion/campaign/4253664-americans-support-manda
    tory-national-service/.
41. https://webarchive.archive.unhcr.org/20230530095423/; https://www.ref
    world.org/docid/3ae6aba944.html.
42. https://www.nysc.gov.ng/serviceyear.html.
43. https://cepr.org/voxeu/columns/conscriptions-comeback-everlasting
    -appeal-age-old-policy#:~:text=Indeed%2C%20research%20has%20
    found%20that,2022).
44. Friedrich Nietzsche, *Die Götzen-Dämmerung* (Twilight of the Idols),
    accessed online: https://www.handprint.com/SC/NIE/GotDamer.html.